Upside-Down Marketing

Yes, the cover is *intentionally* printed upside down. The techniques you'll discover in these pages will turn your whole business philosophy upside down too. Whether you're in sales, customer service, or financial services, you will profit bountifully from upending traditional marketing strategies and replacing them with upside-down marketing.

Upside-Down Marketing

Turning Your Ex-Customers into Your Best Customers

George R. Walther

McGraw-Hill, Inc.

New York   San Francisco   Washington, D.C.   Auckland   Bogotá
Caracas   Lisbon   London   Madrid   Mexico City   Milan
Montreal   New Delhi   San Juan   Singapore
Sydney   Tokyo   Toronto

Library of Congress Cataloging-in-Publication Data

Walther, George R.
   Upside-down marketing : turning your ex-customers into your best
customers / George R. Walther.
      p.   cm.
   Includes index.
   ISBN 0-07-068047-7
   1. Marketing—Management.   2. Sales management.   3. Customer
relations—Management.   I. Title.
HF5415.13.W255   1994
658.8—dc20   93-45916
                                          CIP

1 2 3 4 5 6 7 8 9 0 DOC/DOC 9 0 9 8 7 6 5 4

ISBN 0-07-068047-7

*The sponsoring editor for this book was Betsy Brown, the editing supervisor
was Jane Palmieri, and the production supervisor was Suzanne Babeuf. It was
set in Palatino by McGraw-Hill's Professional Book Group composition unit.*

Printed and bound by R. R. Donnelley & Sons Company.

This book is printed on recycled, acid-free paper containing a
minimum of 50% recycled, de-inked fiber.

This book is dedicated to teachers everywhere. Our professional educators receive far too little recognition, appreciation, and compensation. They sacrifice fair pay yet carry the weighty responsibility of teaching our children. Our society, and especially every parent, owes them a great deal. I encourage you, my reader, to think about the teachers who profoundly influenced your life. I hope you will track them down so you can express your personal thanks. While working on this manuscript, I contacted Madalen Rentz, who was my wonderful eighth-grade teacher back in 1963. I told her about the positive impact that she has had on my life and how her inspiration helped lead me to my profession. She deserved and appreciated the recognition, and I felt wonderful about having thanked her. You and your teachers deserve to feel that way too.

Contents

Preface   xiii

Acknowledgments   xix

Introduction: The Conveyor Belt Analogy   1

The Three Key Goals of Any Organization   2
    Getting Customers on the Belt   2
    Keeping Customers on the Belt   2
    Getting Customers Back on the Belt   3
The Uncommonest Common Sense   3
Just Another Theory?   3
Go to It!   6

Part 1. Getting Customers Back on the Belt   9

1. Changing Shouts to Touts   11

The Surprising Truth about Those Grouchy Complainers   11
    White House Research Started It All   11
Why You Should Actually *Encourage* Complaints   13
    What If Your Customers *Don't* Complain?   13
    What Happens If Your Customers *Do* Complain?   14
    Caution: Don't Aim at Your Foot   15
The Three Ultimate Aims of Complaint Resolution   16
    1. Get Your Customer Back   16

2. Find Out What Went Wrong   16
3. Neutralize Negative Publicity   17
Treat Complainers as Valued Researchers   18
Example: Westin Profits from an Unhappy "Guest
Researcher"   18
What Can You Learn from This Example?   19
Simple Strategies That Turn Complainers into Comrades   19
Example: MedSurg Learns to Face the Music—Sooner   20
What Can You Learn from This Example?   22
Example: Ameritech Publishing Gets Personal   23
What Can You Learn from This Example?   25
Example: Results, Ltd., Focuses on the Long-Term Goal   25
What Can You Learn from This Example?   28
Example: Ingram Puts the "Three Ps" into Practice   29
What Can You Learn from This Example?   30
Example: How Embassy Suites Takes the H-E-A-T   30
What Can You Learn from This Example?   35
The Complaint-Handling Game Plan   36
Preparation Is Vital   36
Listen Up—Actively   37
Begin Creating Rapport   38
Empathize to Understand   39
Build Bridges   40
Ask for Help in Creating Your Plan   41
Secure Your Agreement and Confirm It   44
Follow Through and Gift Wrap the Package   45
What Can You Learn from This Chapter?   46
Action Summary: What You Can Do *Now*   47

2. Pay Up or Kiss Off   **51**

Are Your Customers Deadbeats?   51
The Psychology of Labels   52
Priority 1: Purge Negative Labels   52
Coercion Creates Antagonistic, Vindictive
Ex-Customers   52
What's Your Customer's Lifetime Value?   54
How Much Is Your Customer Worth Today?   55
Example: Retail Chain Gives Customers the Silent
Treatment   56
What Can You Learn from This Example?   57
Reframe Your Views on Valued Assets   58
What Delinquent Customers Are *Really* Saying   58
Example: AAA Resells Lapsed Members   58
What Can You Learn from This Example?   61
Reselling Now Prevents Payment Problems Later   61
The Magic of Positive Reinforcement   62
Invest in Relationships   63

"I Won't Pay" Really Means "I Want Your Attention!"   64
    Example: TCI Cable TV Stops That Truck!   64
        What Can You Learn from This Example?   66
Using a Positive Partnering Approach Pays Off   67
    Example: US WEST Cellular's "Friendly but Firm"
    Approach   67
        What Can You Learn from This Example?   70
Quickstep Partnering with Slow-Pay and No-Pay
Customers   70
    Take Action Early   70
    Your First-Contact Goal   71
What Can You Learn from This Chapter?   72
Action Summary: What You Can Do *Now*   73

3. The Silence Is Killing You   **75**

Most Relationships Wither from Neglect   75
If We're Really Partners, Why Don't We Listen More?   76
Playing Deaf Is Dumb   77
    Example: A Cruise Liner's Crew Plugs Its Ears   77
        What Can You Learn from This Example?   79
Most Silence Is Unintended   79
    Example: Graphic Controls Mines Gold from Tailings   80
        What Can You Learn from This Example?   82
The High Costs of Plugging Your Ears   82
    The Opportunity Cost of Silence   83
    Product Improvements   83
    Process Glitches   84
    Competitive Moves   84
    New Product Development   85
    Missed Complaints   86
Listening Aggressively   87
    Example: Bankers Profit from Aggressive Listening   87
        What Can You Learn from This Example?   90
    Example: AEI Music Network Listens between the
    Lines   91
        What Can You Learn from This Example?   94
The Value of "Exception Reporting"   95
Listening to the Silence   97
What Can You Learn from This Chapter?   97
Action Summary: What You Can Do *Now*   98

Part 2. Keeping Customers on the Belt   **101**

4. Know Thy Customer   **103**

Starting New Relationships Right   103

Example: Washington Mutual Merges with New
  Customers   105
    What Can You Learn from This Example?   108
Friends and Partners Talk, So Why Don't Buyers and
  Sellers?   108
    Example: Thorndike Press Develops Unity with
    Librarians   109
      What Can You Learn from This Example?   109
Find Out What Your Customers Want   109
    The Trouble with Newsletters   110
    Make Personal Contact and Listen between the Lines   110
    Example: CareerTrack Listens for a Triple Win   111
      What Can You Learn from This Example?   112
    Benchmarking Won't Tell You Where to Go   113
    Focus Groups Help Shy Customers Talk to You   113
    You Are the Best Researcher   114
    Put MBCC to Work for You   115
Middlemen Can Isolate Your Customers   116
    Example: Clinipad Finds Out What It Didn't Know It Didn't
    Know   116
      What Can You Learn from This Example?   120
What Can You Learn from This Chapter?   120
Action Summary: What You Can Do *Now*   121

5. The Critical Value of Staying in Touch   125

More Contact Brings Better Ratings   126
    The Halo Effect   126
    A Tip of the Day Keeps Resentment at Bay   127
Contact Continuity Counts   128
    Example: Brock Control Systems Practices What It
    Preaches   128
      What Can You Learn from This Example?   132
    Example: IBM Becomes More Attentive   133
      What Can You Learn from This Example?   135
Customers Welcome More Attention   136
    Err Toward Too Much   136
    If They're Not Complaining, Increase Your Contact   137
Continue Contact, Even When Buying Wanes   137
    Relationship Means More Than Just Exchanging Money   137
    Example: Celestial Seasonings' Great Tea, Plus Something
    from T   138
      What Can You Learn from This Example?   140
Three Business-Based Relationship Builders   140
    1. Upgrade Volume for Your Customers' Benefit   140
    2. Practice Cross-Selling for More Hooks   142
    3. Bond with Referrals   143
What Can You Learn from This Chapter?   146
Action Summary: What You Can Do *Now*   147

6. Strengthening Partnerships by Meeting Needs   149

Don't Ask Unless You're Going to Act   150
  Analyzing Customer Needs Is an Ongoing Imperative   150
  Whose Department Is It?   151
  Example: Airborne Is Big Enough to Deliver, Small Enough
    to Listen   151
    What Can You Learn from This Example?   153
They'll Talk If You'll Listen   153
  Where's Your *Real* Product-Development
    Department?   154
  Example: High-Tech Firms Stay Attuned to Their
    Customers   154
    What Can You Learn from This Example?   156
Think Beyond Your Product   156
  Example: The Lexus *Concept* Includes a Car   157
    What Can You Learn from This Example?   159
A Promise Is a Promise   159
  Example: How Apple Underpromised, Then
    Overdelivered   160
    What Can You Learn from This Example?   162
What Can You Learn from This Chapter?   163
Action Summary: What You Can Do *Now*   164

Part 3. Getting Customers on the Belt   167

7. Al Dente Prospecting and Qualifying   169

Prospect for Relationships, Not Sales   170
The High Cost of Lead Fulfillment   170
Why Companies Seek Leads   171
  The Role of the Media and Advertising Agencies   172
The Importance of Saying "No"   174
  Do You Want Busy-ness or Business?   175
  Who Benefits When You *Disqualify* Prospects?   176
  My Own Qualification System   176
Salvaging Value from "No Sale"   178
  Make Prospects Feel Glad You Won't Pursue Them   178
  Getting Leads from Unqualified Prospects   179
What Can You Learn from this Chapter?   179
Action Summary: What You Can Do *Now*   180

8. Time Is of the Essence   183

Checking Yourself Out   183
  Sleuthing with Phony Department Codes   184
First Impressions Set the Tone   184
  If You Deliver Slowly Now, What About Later?   186

Technology Can Accelerate Your Relationships   187
    How MCI Won My Business   187
    Fax-on-Demand   189
    Voice Mail   190
    Problem Resolution Is Especially Time-Critical   190
What Can You Learn from This Chapter?   191
Action Summary: What You Can Do *Now*   191

9. Selling—Breathing Life into Relationships   193

What Does *Selling* Really Mean?   194
Closing Sales versus Opening Relationships   194
Vitalizing Relationships   195
    Consulting to Discover Needs   195
    Personalizing to Demonstrate Alignment   197
    Recommending What's Good for the Customer   198
What Can You Learn from This Chapter?   199
Action Summary: What You Can Do *Now*   200

Epilogue   201

Index   205
An Invitation from the Author   213

Preface

Everybody in business faces the same three critical challenges:

- Job 3: Pursuing new customers and "closing sales"
- Job 2: Keeping current customers happy so that they buy repeatedly
- Job 1: Winning back ex-customers so that they buy again

Why Is This Book So Upside Down?

Because it's time to upend your thinking about marketing priorities! Those challenging jobs are numbered upside down because that's the order in which you should tackle them: from bottom to top. Unfortunately, almost all marketers are doing exactly the opposite. They relentlessly pursue as much new business as possible. Then they begin to neglect their hard-won new customers, providing only as much customer service as it takes to keep complaints down to a manageable level. Winning back ex-customers is their very last priority. After all, dealing with angry or unhappy customers can be rather unpleasant, and besides, most marketers are too busy chasing after new prospects.

Upside-Down Marketing shows sales and marketing professionals *why and how* to turn their priorities upside down so that they can concentrate on selling more to their present customers *and* to their former customers.

This approach goes far beyond simply advocating good customer service. *Upside-Down Marketing* emphasizes a totally overlooked sales opportunity: winning back and selling to ex-customers. This book shows that there's something even more profitable than rendering excellent customer service: rekindling fizzled buying relationships. This isn't just a sales book. It's a step-by-step guide for delivering superior customer service to current customers, and renewing relationships with customers who have stopped buying.

Upside-Down Marketing "starts at the finish line." It begins with the job that's usually ranked at the bottom of the list, winning back former customers. That's where the biggest untapped profits lie. Relationship scenarios characterized by customers who are complaining and upset, refuse to pay their bills promptly, or give you the silent treatment actually represent the most significant profit opportunities in marketing—*if* you know how to turn them around. In these pages you'll find abundant case studies of organizations like US WEST Cellular, AAA, Embassy Suites, and Ameritech Publishing, all of whom are reaping the benefits of rekindling relationships with customers who had stopped buying from them. You'll also learn the detailed, step-by-step strategies and techniques that will help you breathe new life into dead relationships. You *can* turn your ex-customers into your best customers.

After exploring ways to recapture the most highly leveraged profits, we'll move on to the second-most-profitable job: solidifying, nurturing, and cultivating relationships with your *current* customers, the ones who will respond positively and enthusiastically when you give them more of the right kind of attention. You'll see how CareerTrack Seminars, IBM, Airborne Express, Apple Computer, and Lexus all benefit from strategies that keep their customers so happy and satisfied that they become long-term, repeat customers. Again, step-by-step action plans show you how you can capitalize on similar opportunities with *your* customers.

The last section reveals the best techniques for winning *new* customers by prospecting and qualifying much more effectively, moving quickly to establish a profitable dialogue, and getting relationships started on the right foot. You'll see how Weyerhaeuser, U.S. Bank, and MCI all use effective techniques that you can employ in your company. Right away you'll be able to implement the qualifying techniques that will bring you more business with less busy-ness and help you activate an effective "CPR" approach to open relationships. As

you'll learn in Chapter 9, the three essential steps in launching enduring relationships are to Consult, Personalize, and Recommend.

Who Should Read This Book?

If you're concerned about the long-term health and profitability of
your organization, *you* should. I say "organization," because these
ideas aren't limited to traditional company and customer situations.
They're equally effective at helping build successful long-term relationships with association members, or charity donors.

If you're a marketing director or sales manager, use the many case
studies that follow as seeds to stimulate your own creative thinking.
You can guide your organization to much greater profits by emulating
and improving on the examples you'll read about here.

If you're a salesperson responsible for nurturing buying relationships with individual customers, you'll find many suggestions here
that will help you generate more revenue and more profits with less
work. In fact, that's one of the most remarkable characteristics of
upside-down marketing, it's actually much easier and more satisfying
than traditional selling.

If you're in customer service, you already realize that your interac-
tion with customers has a much greater impact on your company's
long-term profitability than that of the person who closed the first
sale. One of the best things you can do is to get your sales team to read
Upside-Down Marketing. When sales representatives *close the sale*, it's
easy for them to think of the job as being finished. If they think instead
in terms of "opening the relationship" and recognize that the job of
generating profits has just begun, their work will be easier, and they
will be functioning as a team.

If you're involved in financial services, accounts receivable, or collections, my hat is already off to you. Very few financial professionals
would read a book that has "marketing" in the title. In reality, *you* are
selling every time you come into contact with a customer. And many
of the customers you talk with are at a highly sensitive, critical stage in
their relationships with your firm. When they stop paying on time,
the relationship is vulnerable. The way you treat them when an
account is past due will determine whether you alienate them and
incur losses, or rekindle relationships and restore them to a profitable
status.

Throughout the 1980s, the word *synergy* cropped up often in business literature. Simply put, *synergy* refers to working together, to combined action or operation. Synergy is taking effect when the whole is greater than the sum of its parts. Upside-down marketing has its biggest impact when an organization takes advantage of synergy. It's great to have a sales force focus more attention on keeping customers happy. It's terrific to have a customer service department concentrate on preventing defections by dissatisfied customers. And it's definitely wise to have accounts receivable and collections personnel focus on saving wavering customers and getting them back on a solid footing. But maximum profits for any organization result when *all* the members of the customer contact teams, including sales, customer service, and accounts receivable, share the common synergistic aim of getting as many customers as possible to stay with you for as long as possible.

A Few Words about the Format of This Book

As soon as you saw the upside-down cover, you knew something was going to be different about this book's approach.

We'll Start Where They're Falling Off

If you want to prosper and benefit from profitable relationships, the first thing to focus on is the customer relationships that aren't going well. So that's where *Upside-Down Marketing* begins. First, we'll capture the most highly leveraged profits by salvaging dying relationships with customers who are upset and unhappy, who are delinquent with their payments, or whose accounts have lapsed into inactive status.

Real Examples—With Practical Lessons

Throughout *Upside-Down Marketing* you'll read about companies that are starting to benefit from these ideas already. These examples will serve as case studies of what can happen when you employ these techniques. In a very few instances, I've been asked to conceal the identities of the organizations whose programs I'm describing, but they are all real and most include the actual names, dates, and statistics. Every example concludes with a section titled "What Can You Learn from This Example?" in which you'll find the lessons already summarized for you.

Action Is the Goal

Every chapter ends with a section titled, "Action Summary: What You Can Do *Now*," which lists action steps drawn from the chapter you've just read. Again, I want to make it as easy as possible to crystallize the lessons of *Upside-Down Marketing* so that you can put them to work immediately.

How to Get the Most Value from *Upside-Down Marketing*

Start Wherever You're Interested

It's not necessary to begin with Chapter 1. Start wherever you like. Flip around to the sections that interest you most. Because this book emphasizes the importance of capturing profit opportunities in the order of their relative leverage, you'll find that the chapters steadily decrease in size as the opportunities become less leveraged. Your biggest potential payoff comes from customers who are mad at you and have stopped buying, so Chapter 1, "Changing Shouts to Touts," is the longest. The last chapter is the shortest. It deals with the more conventional, less highly leveraged practice of selling to *new* customers.

Use the Action Summaries as a Review

When you finish a chapter, start taking action. Don't go on to the next chapter until you have *done something*. Every chapter summary section is broken down into many small steps that you can take right away.

Pull Your Team Together

As you read *Upside-Down Marketing*, keep thinking about the other people and departments you need to cooperate with in order to capture maximum profit leverage. You can't do it all alone, although you *can* definitely take important steps that will make a big difference.

The best thing to do right now is begin. Read the Introduction, then flip to the chapter you want to start with, and get ready to do something about capturing your most highly leveraged profits by turning your ex-customers into your best customers.

George R. Walther

Acknowledgments

I want to acknowledge the many upside-down marketers who have generously cooperated by sharing their own case studies and detailing their successes in these pages. Very few asked for anonymity, and the specifics of their experiences are a very important part of this book. Their contributions will encourage you and countless other readers to reap the rewards of turning your strategies upside down too.

My speaking clients and audience members have also helped tremendously by embracing these upside-down strategies and proving their effectiveness. Their support and enthusiasm have helped inspire me to get this message out to you in written form.

My professional speaking colleagues in the National Speakers Association have encouraged and guided me throughout the writing and publishing process, and I thank them too.

McGraw-Hill has proven to be an excellent publishing partner, and I thank my editor, Betsy Brown, my publisher, Phil Ruppel, and my enthusiastic and supportive agent, Jeff Herman.

My wife and daughter, Julie and Kelcie, nourish me with their love and patience. It's not easy to live with someone who is obsessed with a manuscript deadline, and I appreciate the balanced, comforting home environment they provide.

Finally, my great thanks go to Carole Olson, my patient, loyal, very hard working personal assistant.

Introduction: The Conveyor Belt Analogy

Throughout *Upside-Down Marketing* we'll be using the analogy of a conveyor belt to signify profitable customer relationships.

Visualize a conveyor belt that's about three feet wide and infinitely long. It starts right in front of you and stretches off into the distance. Most marketers concentrate on getting prospects to step up onto that belt—to buy something, to begin a customer relationship. They prospect, coax, persuade, and often pressure new prospects to take that first big step and make an initial purchase. Closing an initial sale is like getting a customer onto the belt. A marketer's *acquisition cost* is the total investment necessary to convert a lead into a prospect into a customer. Typically, this cost far exceeds the revenue gained from that first transaction.

Once they're on the belt, though, most new customers receive relatively little attention. Why? Because marketers and salespeople are so busy concentrating on the difficult task of coaxing *other* prospective customers to make their first purchases. Landing new accounts and getting 'em on the belt is almost like pursuing prey. It's exciting to close the initial sale and get that first contract signed. By comparison, eliciting future orders from an established customer is rather dull. However—and this is critically important—those mundane repeat orders are far more profitable than the initial transactions. The high acquisition cost has already been expended. Future orders from current customers are increasingly profit-leveraged because those revenues are not offset by continuing high initial sales costs.

All customers fall off the belt at some point, and here's where the biggest opportunities—and the biggest profits—are waiting. Very few organizations pay attention to their customer turnover, or "churn rate," the rate at which customers let their accounts lapse into inactivity. Few sales and marketing professionals pay much attention to ex-customers, those who have stopped buying. Customers whose payments are delinquent, or who write angry complaint letters, or who just quietly slack off in their ordering activity, have either fallen off the belt, or are about to. But *these customers represent the greatest profit opportunities.* Yet at best, these people get too little positive attention, and at worst, they get too much negative attention. Instead of being seen as profit opportunities, they're called deadbeats, complainers, and problem customers.

Think of it this way: The greatest profits in business result from getting customers to stay on the conveyor belt and continue generating long-term revenues. So does it make more sense to hustle like crazy getting new ones onto the belt, or to find out why good customers have fallen away and then concentrate on getting them back?

The Three Key Goals of Any Organization

Simply put, every organization faces three key challenges.

Getting Customers on the Belt

Meeting this first challenge is tough, costly, usually not profitable, and frequently unsuccessful. Still, this is the area that gets the most emphasis in most organizations. The sales representative who lands the big new customer and gets him to step up on the conveyor belt with an opening order or a signed contract gets all the glory, the trip to Cancun, and the fat bonus check.

Keeping Customers on the Belt

This challenge is much more easily met, but it's not exciting. There are no big prizes for the customer service representative or the inside sales specialist who carefully nurtures long-term buying relationships. This goal is vastly more profitable than winning initial sales, but there are few rewards associated with stimulating ongoing orders.

Getting Customers Back on the Belt

Dealing with unhappy customers who have jumped or been pushed off the conveyor belt is rarely even recognized as a company goal. This is odd, because it's the most profitable thing any organization can do. By contacting and being attentive to ex-customers, you stand an excellent chance of generating future orders, of learning about service or product deficiencies you need to correct, and of neutralizing negative publicity in the marketplace. But who does it? Usually, nobody.

The Uncommonest Common Sense

It makes sense to find out what's wrong with the way you serve your customers so that you can correct it. It's eminently logical that businesses should concentrate on generating their most profitable orders—those that come from existing customers. *Upside-Down Marketing* is about putting good old common sense to work and seeking to maximize the profit potential of your organization's relationships with its customers. It's not commonly practiced, yet, and you have the opportunity to lead your field by embracing these simple ideas and implementing them.

Just Another Theory?

Is this more than just a theory? Is *anybody* starting to take an upside-down approach to selling? You bet, and they're reaping great rewards. Some organizations have recently embraced customer service as a profit center rather than a cost center. A few have even built a consistent sales philosophy and delivery system that factors in the correctly ordered priorities of the three big jobs in sales and marketing.

It's usually the smaller, less rigid companies that succumb to common sense and adopt upside-down marketing well before the monolithic behemoths do. While IBM experiments, entrepreneurs go whole hog.

New Pig Corporation is a company built on innovation. They market absorptive barriers that resemble long nylon stockings filled with kitty litter. When a factory worker spills oil or a noxious chemical, he quickly surrounds the spill with one of these "pigs" and later picks it up for disposal, rather than sprinkling sawdust and then calling in the sweeping crew.

If you're a maintenance engineer, and for some reason you fall off the New Pig Company conveyor belt and stop ordering pigs, several things will happen. As soon as your account is flagged as inactive, you'll get a frank and provocative mailing that asks, "Did we screw up?" (The graphic, of course, is a pig's corkscrew tail.) You're asked to phone 1-800-HOT-HOGS right away to explain what caused you to stop buying.

You'll also receive the New Pig catalog with an outer paper wrapper that's similar to a magazine's "This is your last issue" technique. In this case, though, the wrapper is a "Re-pork Card" that asks for your candid feedback about service, prices, product quality, etc. New Pig takes the trouble to find out why you've stopped buying.

And of course, you'll also receive a personal call from your sales representative. Twice a year, New Pig gears up for a "P-Day" campaign. Phone salespeople and customer service agents alike are issued battle fatigues and the walls are adorned with banners heralding the unified, companywide theme: *Win back lost customers at any cost!* Once they reach an inactive customer, the reps take a very sincere, personal approach: "We're bummed out that we lost your business. What can we do to get you back?"

According to Nino Vella, New Pig's president and CEO, nothing the company does is as important or as profitable as attending to customers in danger of falling away. Even if an inactive account is not successfully reactivated, the personal contact is an opportunity to discover new trends in the marketplace. In a recent "P-Day" campaign, the product management team had to face the fact that customers cited pricing as the number one reason they stopped buying. So New Pig reduced its prices across the board to stay competitive. The company was determined not to ignore customer feedback and be left in the dust as its 140 new competitors fought to steal the business by selling similar products at lower prices.

No matter what, New Pig's old customers are always recycled back into the mailing list of prospective new customers. And always, they respond in higher percentages than prospects on all other purchased lists. New Pig's ex-customers are always their best prospects to start buying (again).

I don't mean to imply that none of the big companies are starting to see the wisdom of turning their priorities upside down. In fact, this book is built on the successful examples of widely diverse organizations that are experimenting with upside-down marketing and finding out that it pays off big-time. Even IBM glimpses the wisdom of conveyor-belt marketing. In 1990, they founded an after-market group on a test basis. The pilot program was set up as a telemarketing unit dedicated to contacting customers who had purchased from IBM in the past 10 years, but who had lost contact with their marketing reps and become inactive. In many cases there had been a lot of turnover within IBM, and the customers simply felt ignored and lost in the shuffle. The purpose of the program was proactive: to contact these customers, find out what IBM had to do to reestablish their loyalty, and increase customer satisfaction.

After a brief trial period with a test core of 300 customers, IBM was quickly convinced that the program was a big winner. The results prompted IBM to roll out the program across the United States and then internationally. Contacted customers show a willingness to purchase right away, and their satisfaction levels are raising at an annualized rate of 10 percent. They appreciate being important enough to get IBM's call, and they particularly welcome having the continuity of a single contact person, even though it's a phone representative they're not ever likely to see.

American companies operating overseas are often more on the ball than their stateside counterparts. American Express, for example, phones all European cardholders who cancel their American Express cards to find out why. One phone center in Germany is responsible for reaching 200 cancelers every day. In addition to gaining valuable market feedback about American Express merchants and competitors, the callers successfully reactivate 16 percent of the people who have already mailed in their cancellations. With an average charging lifetime of eight years, that translates to a very profitable long-term revenue stream. Once again, American Express's ex-customers are their best prospects.

Another company that has converted to conveyor-belt marketing with very profitable results is US WEST Cellular. This is one of the many young companies that market cellular phone services. Its service area is concentrated in 14 Western states. US WEST executives reasoned that the most important thing they could do was prevent customers from falling or jumping off their conveyor belt. So, they have taken a close look at why, how, and when their customers have canceled their cellular phone service contracts. The answers have become the basis for their conveyor-belt marketing strategy:

Why? Customers have canceled because their phone service seemed too expensive.

How? They called the customer service department and simply said they wanted out of their contract.

When? They often did it right after getting their very first phone bill.

As a result, rather than focusing exclusively on securing new subscribers, US WEST Cellular has revamped the entire marketing process to ensure that new customers will stay with the company. A new customer's very first outgoing call is electronically intercepted by a US WEST representative who says, "Welcome. We're glad to have you as a new customer. What questions may I answer for you?" Then, just as the first monthly bill is mailed, another rep calls and explains the various activation charges to lessen the "sticker shock" that often causes new customers to cancel their service. Because of several new account activation charges, that first bill is always unusually high, and the rep carefully explains that future bills will be lower. Three times a year, a member of the company's proactive team calls customers to offer helpful suggestions, answer questions, and remind customers that US WEST Cellular appreciates their business. And when someone does ask to cancel, a member of the elite customer loyalty team takes over and does everything possible to keep the customer.

In other words, the major shift in strategic thinking at US WEST Cellular has been to turn sales priorities upside down. Rather than working hard to win new customers at great cost—only to let them slip away and erode the company's profits—the company has turned its focus to current customers. Specifically, it has decided to do everything possible to keep its customers happier, longer, and to win them back when their loyalty wavers.

The results? US WEST Cellular is now a national leader in the cellular phone industry. These conveyor-belt marketing strategies have chopped the company's customer attrition rate in half and dramatically boosted profits. Every employee throughout the company is keenly aware of the current attrition rate, and it's the primary measure of US WEST Cellular's success. There's a single-minded purpose at this company that is very different from that of a typical organization. Instead of "How many new customers did we sign up today?" everybody pays attention to "How many customers did we win back and keep happy today?"

Go to It!

Over the last fifteen years, I've stood before hundreds of audiences as a keynote speaker or seminar presenter and watched as key executives figuratively smacked themselves on the forehead. After hearing the conveyor belt analogy, they think to themselves, "Gee, this makes an awful lot of sense. And, it sounds pretty easy. I'm going to get my teams headed in this more profitable direction and turn our marketing programs upside down." Instead, though, they return to their normal way of doing things, get caught up in their day-to-day routines, and ultimately perpetuate their own traditional marketing strategies. A few, though, take action and follow through. They're the ones who write me wonderful letters about the easy profits their organizations reaped by upending their priorities. They're the ones whose actual examples you'll be reading about in this book. You, too, can put these principles to work—quite easily—in your own organization. I guarantee that you'll be amazed at the results. Go to it!

PART 1

Getting Customers Back on the Belt

When you want to maximize the profitability of your customer relationships, the place to begin is with those customers who are falling—or who have already fallen—off your relationship conveyor belt. The most-highly-leveraged opportunity you face is the prospect of rebuilding relationships with ex-customers, those whose associations with you have ended dramatically after an angry outburst, or gradually fizzled out following a series of small skirmishes, or—more likely— slowly, uneventfully, faded away.

Only by contacting these ex-customers can you find out what drove them away in the first place. Once you know, you can fix any service or product deficiencies that may also be threatening your other, current relationships.

By reaching out to ex-customers, you'll also be able to neutralize the very costly effects of their negative word-of-mouth publicity in the marketplace. Even if you aren't able to correct the scenario that made them stop buying from you in the past, you can demonstrate your sincere concern, and that will go a long way toward eventually restoring your alliances.

The three chapters in this first section deal with customers who are already falling (or jumping!) off your conveyor belt. They may be calling you with angry complaints, or sending nasty letters to the president, or withholding payments on their accounts, or, more likely, just quietly slipping into inactivity. In each case, you'll find specific strategies for dealing with them, as well as ample examples drawn from organizations that are already successful at getting customers back on their conveyor belts.

1
Changing
Shouts to Touts

Most people detest receiving complaint letters and irate calls. Managers cringe when their secretaries say, "I have an angry customer on line two, and he's pretty upset. Do you want to talk with him, or shall I transfer him to someone else?" Most customer service representatives stiffen the moment they sense impending invectives.

The Surprising Truth about Those Grouchy Complainers

But are you ready for this? Your angriest, most upset customer can become your most valuable customer, *if* you handle the complaint appropriately. The outcome is totally dependent on how you and your team view and respond to the *opportunity* that a complainer represents. The most authoritative research proves that complaining, unhappy customers can become a company's most loyal supporters, *if* their feedback is welcomed, acted upon, and treated as valuable marketing input. Rather than sending a pain to your bottom, upset customers can be your surest way to send profits to your bottom line.

White House Research Started It All

In 1979, the White House commissioned a study under the auspices of the United States Office of Consumer Affairs. An independent research organization, Technical Assistance Research Programs (TARP) set out to study how consumers behaved when they had complaints about the way they were handled in business transactions. In a nutshell, here's what the study found out. There are basically two types of people in the world: those who get mad, and those who get even. The ones who get mad cause a ruckus, write nasty letters, call the company they think did them wrong, and basically sound off about how they feel. These people make up as little as 5 percent of all consumers. The big majority of unhappy customers, up to 95 percent, don't complain to the management people who can change things.

Think about what happens when you go out for dinner and you aren't really impressed with the meal. You talk candidly with your dining companion: "My fish was kind of dry, and did you notice the wilted lettuce in the salad? This place really isn't that good. I thought the service was pretty lackadaisical, too. Considering the prices, I'd say it's way overrated." Just then, the waiter approaches and asks, "Is everything satisfactory?" Most of the time, most people nod and say, "Yes, fine." We seldom give completely honest feedback. Maybe we don't want to cause a stir or seem like grouchy complainers hoping for a free meal. It's a little embarrassing to tell the waiter what we *really* thought about the meal.

Perhaps, as you read this scenario, you're thinking to yourself, "Wait a minute. I *do* complain!" Good for you. That's the very best thing you can do. It's just that most people don't. The most usual course of action is that people don't complain; they just don't come back. Yet without feedback, a poorly performing restaurant isn't likely to improve.

There's a new flower shop in my neighborhood called Flawless Flowers. That's a misnomer because the shop has at least one striking flaw. Instead of emitting floral fragrances, it reeks of tobacco smoke. I don't know if it's the owner or an employee who smokes in the shop, but the result is that the store smells exactly the opposite of what I expect when I go shopping for flowers.

Yet for some reason I'm uncomfortable about telling the owner exactly how I feel. It shouldn't concern me if he wants to smoke. I don't want to preach about his health, and I have no business giving him advice about how to run his store. So instead, I just don't go back. There are plenty of flower stores that waft blossom scents rather than burned butts. I go elsewhere. The result, though, is that the owner is deprived of input that could help him become more profitable. Lacking customer feedback, I feel sure that the store will fall short of its potential because nonsmokers who dislike the smell will shop else-where and never tell the proprietor why they left.

Why You Should Actually *Encourage* Complaints

It's simple: complaints lead to profits. Right now, you do have cus-tomers who are less than satisfied with your product and/or service. Let's take that as a given. Many of those unhappy customers have valuable feedback that would be tremendously beneficial to your orga-nization—if you heard it.

What If Your Customers *Don't* Complain?

If only a small minority actually voice their complaints, what about those who don't? Up to 95 percent won't complain directly to someone who can do something to improve the situation, they'll "get even" instead. And they do it by spreading the word. They tell others—often lots of oth-ers—about their negative experience with you. Further TARP research pegged the numbers at 10 to 12 for the average unhappy customer, but noted that a vocal minority, about 13 percent, will make it their business to tell 20 or more others about their negative experience with your firm.

This negative word-of-mouth publicity can be very costly. Market researchers have consistently shown that of all the various types of advertising, the most persuasive form is word-of-mouth anecdotes from someone you know. It doesn't matter how many slick commer-cials and wonderful brochures you see promoting a certain automotive brand, if your neighbor owns one and has complained to you about its poor performance or persistent mechanical problems, you're not likely to buy that type of car.

Keep in mind that this negative publicity often gets out of hand as the unhappy customer distorts the actual facts. People tend to exag-gerate a bit when they tell their friends about how horrible something was. The litany of woes—true or not—grows longer and more horrible with each recitation. There's the down-the-line impact to figure in, too: "Oh, you're considering buying a new Zoomer? Well, my neighbor told me an awful story about the bad luck he's had with his Zoomer. Wait 'til I tell you what happened to him...."

What Happens If Your Customers *Do* Complain?

Fortunately, some of your unhappy customers *will* tell you about their dissatisfaction, rather than spreading the word all around town. When this happens, you are presented with a rich opportunity to profit.

The same pioneering TARP studies, as well as subsequent industry-specific research, examined the continuing purchase behavior and loyalty of customers who complained. The results were surprising. In many problem situations, customers who complained were actually *more* loyal—and if handled right, were *much more loyal*—than those who were dissatisfied, but didn't take the trouble to complain directly. Just the act of complaining *doubles* the likelihood that an unhappy customer will be back to buy from you again in the future. If you do more than listen, and actually *fix* the problem they're concerned about, the likelihood of their buying again *increases by six times.* If you fix it quickly, professionally, and handle their complaint superbly, they are *nine times more likely to buy from you again.*

So it comes down to this simple logic. You have unhappy customers. Most won't let you know why they're unhappy; they'll just go away. But they won't go quietly, they'll talk. And what they'll be saying to many of their friends and associates will hurt your business. If those same unhappy customers *do* complain, though, you're immediately ahead of the game. And if you handle the complaint well, you're *way* ahead of the game.

(Shhhhh! Don't spread this around, but there's a bizarre twist to this complaint behavior research. If you are confident that your system for recovering from complaints will make disappointed, unhappy customers feel very satisfied very quickly, it may be in your best interest to *create* dissatisfaction. If you're an overnight courier service, and always perform superbly, it may make sense to *intentionally* screw up once in a while, and then do an outstanding job of making things right. Instead of delivering the package by 10 a.m., call the shipper and the recipient at 9 a.m., explain that the delivery won't be complete until 10:15 a.m., apologize profusely, and offer to waive the charges. Your customer will really think you're terrific—even more so than if you had just once again routinely delivered on time. Caution: Odds are that you have a few extra unhappy customers already without setting out to create more. Be sure you've done an outstanding job of handling all the *unin*tentional errors before setting out to intentionally create any more.)

So what's the most sensible thing to do about complaints?

- Assume that there are many unhappy customers who aren't telling you about their dissatisfaction. In fact, if the figure for your business approximates the extremes of the TARP study, the 95 percent whose complaints don't reach management are being spoken for by the 5 percent who do get through and speak up.

- View the few who do complain as advocates representing the others. The vocal 5 percent, or 1 in 20, are representing the other 19 who choose instead to engage in sabotage and are out there bad-mouthing you right now. Change your thinking about complainers. Rather than saying to yourself, "Here's another one of those cranky oddballs out there trying to cause trouble," think, "Here's somebody who's willing to speak up on behalf of the 19 others who feel similarly about some deficiency in our firm's product or service. If I listen and act, I can prevent other customers from running into the same unsatisfactory situation, and can probably regain this customer's loyalty."

- Spread the word within your organization. Pass this book around. Hold briefings with department managers. Write articles for the company newsletter.

- Keep reading. The main aim of this book is to show you exactly what to do when complaints reach you so that you'll be able to profit from them.

Caution: Don't Aim at Your Foot

As I interviewed John Goodman, TARP's founder, he added an important caution. Don't make the natural deduction that complaints are so good you should encourage more of them, and then drop the ball when you get them! While the loyalty exhibited by satisfied complainers is extraordinarily high, the loyalty of complainers who aren't satisfied is dreadful. Some organizations have reached the conclusion that complaints are valuable profit opportunities, conveyed that attitude to their customers, and have encouraged them to complain if they're unhappy. Their customers have gladly complied.

That can be an excellent strategy—unless you don't have a smooth, proven, foolproof, follow-through system securely in place. Most companies already have ample opportunities to bungle customer relationships by botching complaint resolutions. Don't shoot yourself in the foot by going gung ho out into the marketplace and encouraging complaints, unless you're *positive* that your team will handle them superbly.

The Three Ultimate Aims of Complaint Resolution

Three very positive outcomes can result from almost any complaint situation. Any one of the three makes it well worth welcoming complaints and setting up a superb system for resolving them. When you can capture all three beneficial results, the argument for encouraging complaints is overwhelming.

1. Get Your Customer Back

As you'll see in many of the examples that follow, it's really not all that difficult to regain the loyalty of unhappy customers. Considering the very high cost of replacing them with new customers, it's well worth doing all you can to get your customers back on the conveyor belt. The strategies and techniques that follow in this chapter show you how to do it.

Most companies that have carefully researched the costs associated with complaint resolution find that it's a fraction of the cost of finding a new customer. Most estimates range from one-fourth to one-tenth. And that doesn't even factor in the destructive costs of suffering from the negative word-of-mouth publicity that results from unresolved complaints. If it costs four to ten times as much to *land* a new customer as it does to *satisfy* an existing one, take the easiest, least costly path!

2. Find Out What Went Wrong

Even if you don't succeed in regaining a customer's loyalty, you can probably find out about the service or product deficiency that caused the dissatisfaction in the first place. Sure, there are some complaints that are totally unfounded, and a very small percentage of your customers may be out to take advantage of you. But not many. The majority of customers who are unhappy with your service or product have good reason to be. They've encountered a bump or rough spot on your customer relationship conveyor belt. They can tell you where it's rough and why it's rough *if* you welcome their feedback.

You must *want to know*, and effectively communicate that sincere desire in order to benefit from unhappy customers' experiences. If you ask in just the right way, they'll tell you what went wrong, even if they're unwilling—at least for the time being—to buy from you again. That gives you the opportunity to get busy and fix things so that other customers you've worked so hard to get on the belt won't fall off when they hit the same rough spot.

3. Neutralize Negative Publicity

Even if you don't get the customer back, and even if you don't learn what went wrong, you still benefit from handling complaints well. By ensuring that customers can reach you easily, tell you about their concerns, get an immediate and sincere apology, and sense your desire to make things better, you can mollify most, and defuse their hostility. At the very least, you can create ex-customers who say:

> We used to do business with them, but we had a really bad experience once. I have to give them credit, though, they really tried to find out what went wrong, and they were very concerned about making sure it didn't happen again. Although we probably won't buy from them again, they seem like a really good company.

In all likelihood, though, that customer *will* be back again in the future, especially if you employ the staying-in-touch strategies you'll find in Part 2, "Keeping Customers on the Belt."

An entrepreneur named Phillip Thackoorie, who attended one of my *Upside-Down Marketing* seminars in Oxnard, California, approached me after the program to ask for advice. His enterprise is named Auto Locator and he scouts car auctions and auto wholesalers to locate specific cars for his customers. He specializes in BMW, Jaguar, Lexus, Mercedes, Porsche, and other expensive vehicles. He told me that he had just sold a BMW to a client, and its battery had exploded within a couple of days after the sale was completed. It wasn't Phillip's fault in any way but the customer was very upset because it cost him $300 to get it repaired. I said:

> Phillip, the kind of people you deal with stick together and talk to each other. I think you'd be investing wisely to pay the $300, even though it wasn't your fault.

One month later, I called Phillip to see if he was putting upside-down marketing to work. He said:

> Yes, I did give that customer a $300 check. He went into shock, gave me a big smile, and then started telling everybody he could think of

that I solve problems quickly and painlessly. He has already referred several well-heeled clients to me, and that $300 is paying off big. In fact, right after I gave him the check, he asked me to sell another vehicle that he hadn't been able to get rid of, and I immediately picked up $2000. I have four other sales pending now that came directly from that one customer with the exploded battery. Keep in mind that my average sale runs between $30,000 and $40,000, so that $300 refund is paying off rather well! This is what marketing should be all about, and upside-down marketing is working out brilliantly. Big dealers don't realize what they're missing.

Treat Complainers as Valued Researchers

One of the best ways to change your complaints from bane to bounty is to think of your unhappy customers as market researchers. It's as if you've hired them to discover and report on the areas where you need to make improvements. Granted, they're not always right, and some are poorly qualified for the job. Few will see things just as you do. But they will see things as *customers* see them, and that, after all, is the only truly relevant view.

If you hired an expensive, highly respected research firm to try and anticipate what your customers' concerns would be and paid them many thousands of dollars to tell you how you need to improve, you'd treat their recommendations very seriously. You certainly wouldn't brush them aside and dismiss their findings as the result of a bad mood, or a grudge.

But "researcher" is actually the role that a dissatisfied customer is playing for you. Customers are uniquely qualified to tell you how things appear from a customer's viewpoint. No research firm could do as good a job of seeing things through those eyes.

Example

Westin Profits from an Unhappy "Guest Researcher"

Matthew Hart, operations manager for Westin's flagship resort at Kaanapali Beach, Maui, recalls an incident that started out ugly, and ended up being very profitable. A *Fortune* 500 company's senior executive and her husband selected the Hawaiian resort for their vacation and, starting on the very first day of their holiday, began noting and listing a variety of service deficiencies.

They called the front desk to complain and were promptly connected with the operations manager. In the hotel business, this is not some midlevel complaint handler, this is the CEO of that particular property. Rather than shuffling the complaint off to an underling or listening condescendingly himself, Mr. Hart offered to meet personally with the guests and review their complaints. They presented a long and carefully itemized list. Most of their complaints were valid. Realizing that there was no single action he could take to solve all of the problems, Hart promised to get to work on them, and said:

> Your views are valid and important, and I want you to enjoy your stay here. If I have to meet with you every afternoon to hear how things are going, that's exactly what I'll do.

And he did. Each afternoon at 5 o'clock, the couple debriefed him on their service observations for that day. Matthew Hart gained valuable ideas on how to improve services at the resort, and many of the changes prompted by the couple's complaints are in effect today. More important, the complaining couple recognized that Westin's management was responsive and valued their opinions. They have returned to the same Westin for their vacation every year since. And, they've sent many friends, touting the Westin Maui as the finest resort in the world, managed by the best team in the business. The same guest has also influenced her company to schedule numerous meetings and incentive trips to the hotel she had originally criticized so bitterly.

What Can You Learn from This Example? The very first contact with the complaining guests is what set the tone for the long-term relationship described here. Your initial reaction to any upset customer determines whether the experience will yield valuable information or deteriorate into an uncomfortable confrontation.

Instead of rebuffing his dissatisfied guests, Matthew Hart welcomed their complaints and won their valuable long-term loyalty while also learning how to improve the Westin's service. You can do exactly the same thing by affecting a fundamental shift in attitude for yourself and your team. An upset complainer is best viewed as a market researcher who's giving you a report about some service deficiencies that you need to correct.

Simple Strategies That Turn Complainers into Comrades

The best way to teach is often by example. In the several encounters that follow, notice how businesspeople like yourself have used their instincts and common sense to turn around some very challenging situations. (Later in this chapter, you'll see how to move beyond simply relying on good instincts and use a step-by-step plan you can share with your colleagues.)

MedSurg Learns to Face the Music— Sooner

Sometimes you can lose a $100,000 customer over a half-cent error. Just ask Anita Haddad of MedSurg Industries. The omission of a small sponge from her customer's order of surgical supplies almost lost her a $100,000 account. But, there's a happy ending to the story, and some simple but valuable lessons you can put to work.

What could be so important about a little half-cent sponge? Well, if you're lying on a hospital's operating table having undergone an appendectomy, and the doctors have just sewn you back up, they're going to be very concerned if the operating room nurse counts up the sponges used during your operation and finds that one is missing. Where could it be? Right. Inside you! The surgical team is going to open you up again to find that missing sponge, rather than risk an infection that could threaten your life—not to mention a multimillion dollar malpractice suit against the hospital. Surgical teams get very upset when the sponge count isn't absolutely accurate.

MedSurg Industries assembles and sells custom surgical trays to streamline a hospital's operating room procedures. When you're wheeled in for that appendectomy, the O.R. nurse reaches for an appendectomy tray that contains all the necessary items for the procedure. Each has been carefully sterilized, arranged, and sealed. If the tray is supposed to contain 10 sponges but there are actually only 9 included, MedSurg is going to be in trouble. That's an extremely rare occurrence, thanks to MedSurg's relentless dedication to quality control. Still, once in a great while, somebody can make a little mistake.

In the health-care industry, the quality performance standard that customers expect is nothing less than perfection. MedSurg missed perfection at one of Anita Haddad's most important accounts by including 9 sponges rather than 10 in one of the thousands of surgical trays it supplies. Although the error was inadvertently made by the sponge manufacturer, MedSurg was responsible to the customer for 10 sponges. There was no disaster to a patient; the O.R. nurses had been alert and vigilant. They caught the discrepancy. But they weren't happy about it. And they let Anita know how they felt.

Like any sales professional, Anita hated hearing that her customer was upset. In fact, at first she tried to stick her head in the sand and just hoped that the problem would go away. After all, she had other professional and personal priorities to deal with. Her South Florida home had been totally devastated by Hurricane Andrew just a few weeks earlier and her professional life had begun to suffer. Anita had plenty of reasons for ignoring the problem of the hospital's missing half-cent sponge.

But the problem didn't quietly go away. Anita's customer felt ignored, and that just made things worse.

Anger tends to inflate and escalate if it's not dealt with promptly. Maybe you've noticed this in your personal relationships, too. What happens when you and your spouse or friend have a slight disagreement? You may both shy away from the subject, hoping you'll each forget about it. Does that work? Almost never. Neglect usually causes small problems to fester.

The hospital O.R. nurse was rankled. Because she and her team felt that Anita had not given them direct attention on the matter of the missing sponge, MedSurg's president, Michael Sahady, received a phone call notifying him that the hospital was canceling its contract for four different types of high-volume custom surgical tray kits.

That got his attention.

And Michael Sahady got Anita Haddad's attention, too. When he called her to ask what was going on with her customer's valuable account, she made an immediate, crucial decision. She decided to face the music. Although she had plenty of plausible excuses, she "fessed up" and admitted the truth: she had been ignoring the problem, hoping it would just go away.

In the end, Anita's open, candid admission is what saved her account—and her job. And it's also what led to the happy ending.

The president of MedSurg got on a plane, headed for the Miami hospital, joined up with Anita, and went to visit the operating room staff. That festering annoyance had developed into a rage, and the head nurse came right out and yelled at both Michael and Anita. The nurse had felt ignored and mistreated. She felt that the hospital's business wasn't important to MedSurg.

Jointly, the president and the sales rep admitted their mistakes and apologized. More yelling. Another admission and apology. More yelling. (When your anger has festered for a few weeks, it can take a while to let it all out.) Finally, Michael Sahady firmly stated MedSurg's intentions:

> We have made a mistake, we admit it, and we apologize. We have no excuse. You should have gotten immediate attention from Anita, as well as from me. But you didn't, and we can't change that. What we *can* do, and intend to do, is provide you with exactly what you want and deserve. I flew here to admit our mistakes, apologize, and get back on track

with you. Please tell me exactly what we can do to rebuild
our relationship.

Well, it wasn't quite that easy, since the hospital had already put
the business out to bid with five other custom surgical tray
companies, all MedSurg competitors. After calming the hospital's
O.R. staff, Michael and Anita found out that they had formerly been
very happy with the attention MedSurg had given them, and overall,
quality assurance had been superb. It was only the missing sponge
and MedSurg's subsequent inattention to the matter that had been a
problem.

The hospital staff's true needs boiled down to something pretty
simple: they wanted to be dealt with honestly, and they wanted to
feel important. They felt that MedSurg had ignored them, and they
assumed it was because their business wasn't important enough to
the company.

Michael Sahady immediately instructed his packaging department
to personalize this customer's products by imprinting the hospital's
name on the outer wrapper of their custom surgical trays for all
future orders. Anita Haddad made a commitment to visit and/or
call the hospital weekly. MedSurg's vice president also flew in for a
personal visit (including another apology and another offer to make
things right).

The happy ending? MedSurg is back on track with the hospital. In
fact, they're better off than they were before. Not only did they
recapture the contract for the four types of custom trays they had
already been supplying, they also gained the opportunity to bid on
seven more, potentially doubling the value of the account.

What Can You Learn from This Example?   When things go wrong
and your customer receives poor service, the best thing you can do is
immediately admit the error and take corrective action right away.

1. *Always face the music* quickly *and without reservation.* If Anita had
   dealt with her customer's anger right away, it wouldn't have festered. Her president and vice president probably would not have
   had to make personal visits to assuage the unhappy customer.

2. *It's rarely too late to admit a mistake.* The sooner the better. But if you
   know that a customer has been steamed up for some time, call *now,*
   before the situation gets worse.

3. *People (including customers and bosses) will respect you for being honest.*
   They don't want to hear a lot of excuses; they want the unvarnished
   truth, no matter how awful it may be.

Only after acknowledging her shortcomings did Anita Haddad realize how much she was valued and appreciated by her boss. But she couldn't have saved MedSurg's business—-or her job—without telling the truth.

Example
Ameritech Publishing Gets Personal

If you paid to run an ad in the Yellow Pages and later discovered that the publisher had made a big mistake and printed the wrong phone number in your ad, you'd be pretty upset, wouldn't you? Jacob DeVries, president of F&F Tire Service in Janesville, Wisconsin, sure was when it happened to him. Later, when he closed one of his other tire stores featured in a different Yellow Pages directory, Jacob asked Wisconsin Bell for a concession, since he had purchased the ad expecting to have his two featured locations pay for it, not just one.

The Yellow Pages publisher's response was to send Mr. DeVries a copy of his original contract with the "Terms and Conditions" section highlighted, proving that the company was not obligated to make any concession.

Mr. DeVries had a good relationship with his local sales representative, and wrote him a letter to explain how unhappy he was with the actions of the home office. His letter to the sales rep read:

> Yes, they are correct according to the contract, so they will win that battle. So I have decided not to renew any of my Yellow Pages advertising with Wisconsin Bell in the future. I spend over $60,000 annually on Yellow Pages advertising alone. I was asking for a $7000 concession on their part. Now I am going to take that $60,000 to someone who will work with me under special and unusual circumstances. I realize that you're just the sales rep and this is not your fault, but I am so upset with Wisconsin Bell that I wish they had a lot of competition that would force them to value my business more than they obviously do now.

Jacob DeVries kept his word. Year after year, he threw away all mail from the Yellow Pages advertising company, responded to no phone calls, and generally ignored its attempts to get him back as an advertiser. After five years of this silent treatment, Wisconsin Bell had missed out on at least $300,000 in lost advertising.

By this time, Wisconsin Bell had become Ameritech Publishing, and it now had plenty of competition. It had also seen the light about the value of keeping customers happy. Ameritech had also employed Greg Kraemer as a Yellow Pages advertising account executive responsible for the territory that included F&F Tire Service.

As he prepared to canvas his new territory, Greg looked over the history of F&F's account and realized that its lack of Yellow Pages advertising had to be hurting its tire business. True to his word, Mr. DeVries was punishing the publisher for its insensitivity five years earlier, but in the meanwhile, *his* business was suffering, too. Greg decided that he was going to find a way to turn this situation around. So he called and left a message for Mr. DeVries. It wasn't answered, so he called again. And then sent a neatly typed letter. And then called again. And again. Finally, he realized that the conventional business communication techniques weren't going to work. (Although Greg didn't know it, Jacob DeVries hadn't even opened the letters. He was still so mad that he put any envelope with Ameritech's return address straight into the trash, along with any telephone message slips from Ameritech.)

So Greg pulled out a pen and a pad of lined paper and started to write. The next day, Jacob DeVries received a plain envelope containing Greg's neatly penned personal letter. This time, he got through. The letter started right off with Greg introducing himself and mentioning the name of the prior sales representative, with whom Mr. DeVries had enjoyed good rapport. Greg went on to explain that he was familiar with the unfortunate history of F&F Tire's advertising experiences in the Yellow Pages. Greg had done his homework. He included statistics from Michelin Tire Company about the effectiveness of other dealers' Yellow Page advertising, produced a mock ad, and prepared a proposal to help F&F structure an effective Yellow Pages advertising program.

Greg followed up this personal letter with a phone call. For the first time in five years, Mr. DeVries agreed to talk with someone from Ameritech, though he was still unhappy about his treatment five years earlier. So, Greg let him "ventilate" and patiently listened. He knew that he couldn't move ahead into positive territory until this customer released his pent-up negative emotions. As Greg recalls:

> He really laid into me. The original rep had explained that I should expect some animosity, so I was somewhat prepared. I *wanted* him to vent. Once we got beyond the past, I was ready to move forward and show him how much things have changed at Ameritech.

It worked. By the end of that conversation, F&F Tire's owner had purchased $13,402.80 in advertising, and was working toward a positive relationship that could lead toward a resumption of the previously comprehensive advertising program in many directories.

Don't think that just Greg Kraemer and Ameritech came out ahead. Jacob DeVries may have been the biggest beneficiary of all. Because of the publisher's bungled handling of his reasonable request five years earlier, and his resulting anger and resolve to get back at them, F&F Tire Service may have passed up hundreds of thousands of dollars in tire sales because it had no advertising in any of the directories.

What Can You Learn from This Example? There are plenty of lessons to be learned from Greg Kraemer's handling of the angry tire shop owner. First and foremost, Greg focused on how he could benefit the customer, and he concentrated on helping the customer in the future. He knew the history, but didn't dwell on it. He realized that Jacob was still angry, and he even encouraged him to vent his spleen so they could put the past behind them and move ahead.

Most sales reps who inherit a problem account are tempted to avoid any unpleasant contact. Why should they take a load of grief and get themselves shouted at for a mistake somebody else made years ago? Greg, though, decided to face the music, even though he hadn't composed it.

The *way* he approached the customer is important. He analyzed what *wasn't* working, and changed his tactics. Greg is convinced that his handwritten letter is what got his foot through the door that had been slammed shut and locked tight for five years. He decided to get personal, and that personal letter carried with it a subliminal, unwritten message: "This isn't some computer-generated form letter sent by yet another company bureaucrat. I care personally. I've taken the time and trouble to write by hand. I want to communicate with you one to one."

Remember, when your customer is angry—regardless of who was at fault—your customer is losing out because he's not reaping the benefits of your product or service. A sales representative who takes his work seriously, and personally, will do whatever it takes to get through to that customer and make sure that the emotions surrounding past events don't block out current and future benefits. If that means sitting yourself down to draft a handwritten personal note, do it. Remember that the emotions have to come first, but don't wallow in them. Move ahead. Focus on how you can serve your customer with benefits in the future.

Example

Results, Ltd., Focuses on the Long-Term Goal

Tom Hopkins is one of the best known, most acclaimed sales trainers in the world, and his programs are consistently top-rated—if you

can get in. When his sales representatives say, "This program is
likely to sell out," they're not just using some high-pressure tactic to
close more ticket sales. They don't have to, because Tom Hopkins's
events almost always sell out. The primary hitch when scheduling
his seminars is the maximum capacity of a hotel's main ballroom,
because so many thousands of people want to hear his message.
When sales professionals are upset about Tom's seminars, it's not
because of how he performs, it's because they didn't get to see him
perform.

I interviewed Rob Salisbury, Inside Sales Team Manager at Results
in Sales and Marketing, Ltd., based in Scottsdale, Arizona. Results,
Ltd., is one of only two sales seminar promotion companies
authorized to represent Tom Hopkins in the United States. Rob
oversees the operation that handles the western United States
territory as well as the western provinces in Canada. Rob has been
promoting Tom Hopkins full-time since 1984, so he's a veteran of
many seminars. In talking with Rob, I said, "Tom Hopkins may be
revered throughout the sales profession as a master presenter of
extremely effective sales techniques, but aren't there some customers
who are unhappy with Tom's programs?"

Without hesitation, Rob recalled a situation he described as
"blatantly ugly." Back in October 1989, Tom Hopkins scheduled
two full-day seminars in the Los Angeles area, first at the LAX
Airport Hilton, and a week later at the Universal City Hilton. Rob
and his colleagues at Results, Ltd., were selling enrollments for
both programs, and the tickets entitled purchasers to attend
whichever of the events was most convenient for them. On the day
of the LAX Airport Hilton program, 1350 eager sales professionals
showed up.

But, there were only 1100 seats.

Holding down the fort back in his Scottsdale office on seminar
day, unsuspecting Rob got a call at about 11 a.m. from Jan Thurmon,
district sales manager for Sears Mortgage in Los Angeles. With 72
offices across the country, Sears Mortgage was an important new
client for Rob, and Jan had purchased 18 seminar tickets for her top-
producing loan officers. They had arrived a little late for the sold-out
Tom Hopkins seminar and were turned away by fire marshals who
said the ballroom was already filled to capacity.

Rob answered Jan's call and began with his characteristic ebullient
enthusiasm, "Hi, Jan! It's great to hear from you. Your team must be
enjoying Tom's program right now, as we speak!"

Clearly irritated, she responded:

> No, my whole team was sent home. You oversold the event,
> and lots of people were being locked out. The fire marshals
> turned them away. It was a complete nightmare. I had my
> top producers all take a day away from work. They were all
> enthusiastic about seeing Tom Hopkins live, and now

they're not only disappointed, they've also wasted their mornings driving to a seminar that they couldn't attend.

Thinking back on that conversation, Rob recalls, "Let's just say that her voice was cold enough to start forming icicles on my earlobes."

This was the first report Rob had heard about the mess, so he was taken aback. As a quick-thinking sales professional, Rob recovered fast:

You're right, Jan. We were wrong, and this is a mistake on our part. I'm so sorry. Let me arrange to have your whole team attend the event next week in Universal City at no charge. I'm sorry that we've let you down.

But Jan was not to be appeased:

No, Rob, I don't want free tickets. I want my money back. Every dollar. And I certainly won't ever recommend Tom Hopkins seminars after seeing how badly you oversell your events and inconvenience your customers.

She was *very* angry, and there wasn't much Rob could do to calm her down. Without hesitation, he agreed to send a full refund of the $2250 she had paid for the tickets. The next day, by Federal Express, she received the check, along with his note of apology. And she also got 18 new, free guest passes for the Tom Hopkins Universal City program, even though she had said she didn't want them.

The next day, Rob called to apologize again and ensure that she had received her refund and tickets, but by now she was even angrier. She'd heard from all the individual loan officers, and all had complained about how, having rearranged their schedules, they had driven all that way and gone through the parking hassle, only to be turned away and have to reconstruct their wasted day. Again she told Rob that she didn't think much of Tom Hopkins or Results, Ltd., and wouldn't be using the 18 Universal City seminar tickets. Rob did his best to end the call cordially, but she was not about to be mollified.

After the Universal City seminar, a routine ticket audit showed that two of Sears Mortgage's 18 free guest passes had been used, so Rob called those two individuals and learned that the two loan officers had attended because they both lived in the area. Both reported that the seminar was fantastic. Tom had done an extra great job and, from the platform, had apologized to all those who had been inconvenienced at the LAX program. (The Sears Mortgage loan officers weren't the only ones who had been turned away from the LAX event.) Did their enthusiastic reports thaw Jan somewhat? Not a bit, as Rob learned when he called her to follow up.

Rob phoned again in early January 1990, to let Jan know about the
Tom Hopkins event coming to Orange County at the Anaheim Hilton
near Disneyland. She said she had no interest in it, either for herself or
for her immediate team. However (the break Rob needed), she did have
a new manager in Orange County, and Jan was willing to see if that
manager was interested in going to Tom's program. Six of the officers
did end up attending the Orange County event, and they loved it.

A few months later, the Tom Hopkins program was again
scheduled in Los Angeles, and Rob still had not forgotten the
incident with Jan and the loan officers from Sears Mortgage.
Automatically, he sent Jan *another* 18 free guest passes, and phoned
to let her know they were coming. She was surprised to hear from
him, and had finally, one full year after the incident at the LAX
Hilton sellout, sounded just a little bit warmer and more responsive
to Rob's follow-up attention and sincerity in trying to correct the
previous damage. He asked if she had expanded her staff, and when
she told him she had recently hired six new loan officers, he sent
them free guest passes for the next Los Angeles event, too.

Was Rob giving away the store? No, he was investing in a long-
term relationship. In business—and in life—there's nothing so
valuable as an untainted reputation. Still, no mater how relentlessly
you pursue perfection, things sometimes do go wrong.

That's when you pull out all the stops to recover, as Rob was
doing. He had refunded the original $2250, sent 18 free guest passes,
and now was sending 24 more guest passes, this time front-row
seats. Was he overdoing it? No. His and Tom's reputations were on
the line. Rob was doing the fair thing—the right thing—since Jan's
people had been badly inconvenienced. And he was also doing the
smart thing, since she was certainly in a position to bad-mouth Tom
Hopkins's programs to her colleagues in the 72 Sears Mortgage
offices across the United States.

There's a happy ending to Rob Salisbury's tale. After doing
everything possible to satisfy Jan, the people at Sears Mortgage have
become excellent clients for the Hopkins organization. They buy
videos, send loan officers to seminars all over the country, and have
even provided a persuasive reference letter that helps convince other
organizations to send their people to Tom Hopkins's outstanding
seminars.

For Rob and Results, Ltd., those 42 guest passes and $2250 have
returned over $60,000 in revenues—already.

What Can You Learn from This Example?   The moral of this
story is simple. When you let a customer down, it gives you an opportunity to do everything possible to set things right, even if you can't
exactly undo the original unsatisfactory situation. Whether it's apologizing profusely, sending a refund, shipping free replacements, or
doing all three, think of the expense as an investment you're making

in the relationship, and in your reputation. Since a favorable long-term reputation is of infinite value, whatever investment you must make to maintain it amounts to only a pittance when you consider the lost future opportunities it may cost you if you don't set things right.

Example

Ingram Puts the "Three Ps" into Practice

Beth Alvin, a field sales representative for Ingram, North America's largest book distribution company, is a pro at upside-down marketing. In fact, when I interviewed her, she told me that she hadn't gained a single new account in the last eight months. She focuses totally on strengthening existing customer relationships, and renewing those that start to slip away.

Beth offered the story of her experience with a small Idaho bookstore as one good example of how she uses perseverance, personality, and professionalism to win back customers who have strayed from the fold. The owner of this particular bookstore had designated one of Ingram's nearby distribution centers as his primary shipping point because it meant that he would pay lower freight costs for his orders. By meeting a minimum order size, he would actually pay no shipping charges at all in some cases.

Soon after indicating his warehouse preference, Ingram's computer identified his account as one which should be switched to a different warehouse for his primary point of distribution. Although a form letter had been sent to the store owner explaining this change, he was apparently too busy to read it, and was thus taken by surprise when the change actually happened. He had electronically transmitted an order for 100 books in order to qualify for free shipping, and was surprised to find that they had been shipped from Denver, rather than from the warehouse he had specified. He was hit with a sizable shipping bill, when he was expecting none.

He was so upset over the freight charges and the feeling that he had been jerked around by Ingram's shipping policies that he had a heated conversation with a customer service representative and also spoke directly with Beth, his sales rep. He was so angry that he hung up on her after threatening that he would never do business with Ingram again. There were plenty of other book distributors, including Book People, Baker & Taylor, and Pacific Pipeline, that could adequately meet his needs, and he intended to follow through on his promise to take all his business away from Ingram.

Undaunted, Beth made it her personal mission to win him back. Her first step was to compose and mail a handwritten note of apology. She didn't point out that he had failed to read Ingram's official notice. Her goal was not to show that he had been at fault.

Her aim was to accept responsibility, and she did it in a personal way. It wasn't just, "We here at Ingram accept responsibility." Instead, Beth offered her personal commitment to do everything she could to satisfy him.

Beth identifies the fact that she wrote her note out by hand as an important element of this example. There is so much impersonal, computer-generated business correspondence these days that the odd handwritten note really stands out and gets attention. After mailing her note, Beth made personal phone contact and was careful to call exactly when she said she would. She also identifies this professional punctuality as an important step in regaining her customer's trust.

In the end, this ex-customer became a strong ally for Ingram. In fact, the bookstore owner purchased a complete reference system called *Ingram Books in Print Plus* on CD-ROM, which means that he receives a weekly diskette listing every title that's still in print, plus information on exactly what Ingram has in stock. Now, instead of dividing his business among many other distributors and being furious with Ingram, he has consolidated his business with Ingram as his primary supplier. During the first year after Beth set out to regain his trust, his Ingram orders grew by 28 percent.

What Can You Learn from This Example?   Ingram's Beth Alvin benefited from the "Three Ps" of winning back lost customers:

1. *Be persistent.* Don't let a customer who slams down his phone turn you away. Decide that it's going to be your personal mission to win him back.

2. *Be professional.* Regaining trust is a long, slow process. Your customer is paying very careful attention to many small indicators of your trustworthiness. If you say you're going to phone at 10:30 a.m., phone at 10:30 a.m.

3. *Be personal.* Most customers feel alienated when they're treated as if they're dealing with a large, cold bureaucracy that doesn't pay personal attention to them. Let your customer know, as Beth did, that you accept responsibility and will personally follow through. Her technique of mailing a personal handwritten note rather than some generic computerized form letter can make all the difference.

Example

How Embassy Suites Takes the
H-E-A-T

I had just checked into my clean, spacious accommodations at Embassy Suites in Piscataway, New Jersey, where I was to spend the

night before presenting a customer service seminar for the staff of
Johnson & Johnson Hospital Services. As it turned out, my brush
with a single bad service example that evening provided one of the
best customer service lessons I could have learned. It also showed
me what a fine organization Embassy Suites is.

I decided to go for a jog after getting settled in my room, and
planned to have dinner right afterward. To give room service plenty
of time, I called to place my order at 6 p.m. and requested delivery of
my meal at 7:30 p.m., to coincide with the start of an in-room movie I
wanted to watch. A hotel staff member I'll call Steven took my
simple order for a chicken sandwich, seafood chowder, and Diet
Pepsi. After enjoying my short jog, I returned to the suite, and at 7:25
p.m. called room service. I wanted to let Steven know that I had
returned and remind him that I was ready to eat. He seemed to be on
top of things and thanked me for calling.

By 7:35 p.m., the movie had begun, and although the meal was
only five minutes late, my stomach was already starting to growl
and I was beginning to feel irritable. I realized that five minutes was
no big deal, but, after all, I had taken the extra step of ordering an
hour and a half in advance to give Steven plenty of time and had
even placed the reminder call. Couldn't he do a better job of
planning? I felt myself becoming "parental" and silently scolding
him for being poorly organized.

At 7:45 p.m., Steven called. "Uh, what did you say you wanted to
drink with your dinner?" Although I tersely repeated, "Diet Pepsi," I
really felt like blurting out:

> You fool! I gave you my order nearly two hours ago. If you
> weren't sure what I wanted, why didn't you ask when I
> called again at 7:25? Do you mean to tell me that you
> haven't even begun getting my meal ready yet?

At 7:55 p.m., the innocent server knocked on my door, and I was
not at all welcoming as he entered, tray in hand. Although the delay
hadn't been his fault, I treated him coldly, as if he had been
personally responsible for the poor planning in the kitchen. By now, I
was annoyed *and* hungry, and my perception had changed. I was
looking for negative details to reinforce and justify my negative
opinion of the hotel's room service operation. Sure enough, I found
plenty of what I was looking for. I noticed that the waiter's shirt cuffs
were frayed and dirty, and his pants were wrinkled and stained. He
made no eye contact, and offered no apology for being late.

As he slinked out of my room, I lifted the cover from my chicken
sandwich and found a limp, soggy, warm clump of lettuce beside the
sodden roll. Once again, I felt justified in my low opinion of the
hotel's bad service. And, to make things a little worse, there was no
soup spoon on the tray. Further proof! I sampled the flavorless,
runny, wimpy chowder with my teaspoon and again condemned the

bad room service. By now, though, my judgments had broadened. I didn't just feel negative about my meal, but also felt that way about the whole hotel, and by extension, about the entire Embassy Suites chain.

After grumbling to myself for half an hour, I decided to call the manager on duty. The operator quickly connected me, and a staff member named Jack introduced himself and began by asking, "What may I do for you?"

I wasn't after a free meal, and I really wasn't even angry anymore. I just wanted to voice my displeasure. I didn't want to seem like a grouchy, unpleasant, hard-to-please guest, so I started by calmly explaining, "Jack, I'm not really upset, and I'm not looking for a free meal or anything else. I just want to tell you about a service situation that you need to correct." With the notes I had jotted on my bedside notepad in hand, I recounted point by point exactly what had happened, expecting to hear him try and come up with some lame excuse to counter my dissatisfaction.

Instead, Jack's first words were:

> I agree with you, Mr. Walther. You are right. I understand why you feel disappointed. You deserve a much better experience, and I apologize for letting you down. That's not the way things should be when you order room service at Embassy Suites.

What? No lame excuses? Next, he told me exactly what action he would take:

> The first thing tomorrow morning, I'll meet with my food and beverage director, find out who was responsible for the delay and the bad meal, and take steps to correct the situation.

And then, his coup de grace:

> Even though you're not asking for a free meal, I will credit you for your dinner, and I'd like to invite you to order room service again tomorrow evening—as my guest, of course—so you can see how it should have been done.

Hmmm. I was finding it very difficult to continue feeling annoyed. After I thanked Jack for his offer, he closed with: "I apologize again, and I thank you for letting me know about this situation."

This was a textbook example of how to handle a customer's complaint. First, he listened with full attention. Next, he empathized and agreed with me, completely dissipating any confrontational feelings I had. He took personal responsibility for apologizing. He told me what action he was going to take. And then, he iced the cake by offering me more restitution than I wanted or really even deserved. And finally, he wrapped the whole episode up by thanking me for complaining.

I was so impressed with his handling of my complaint, that I asked Jack if he would meet me in the lobby so I could interview him for *Upside-Down Marketing.* During our conversation, I learned that Jack's response to my situation hadn't been purely a result of his personal instincts. He was a graduate of Embassy Suites' mandatory employee training program, called "The Embassy Suites Way." He showed me the binder that accompanies several video modules, and drew my attention to the section entitled "Extraordinary Service Opportunities." It's significant that the program isn't titled, "How to Handle Problem Guests," or "Guidelines for Dealing with Angry Customers." Starting right with the title, it's clear that Embassy Suites personnel (everyone takes the course, from housemen to maids to general managers) are trained to view complaints as "extraordinary opportunities to serve." (Steven, the young man who had bungled my meal, could use a brushup!)

As Jack explained, "Anybody can provide a clean room. Our goal with "The Embassy Suites Way" is to create 100 percent customer satisfaction. We can continually improve our business through the customer loyalty that's created when we turn a complainer into a satisfied customer." Jack Deschene is no neophyte in the hotel business. His hospitality résumé includes seven years in the hotel business, starting as a night auditor. (That's the guy who holds down the fort in the wee hours, checking over the day's paperwork, preparing guests' bills for early morning checkouts, and dealing with the oddball situations that crop up during the night.)

He told me about some of his most unusual "Extraordinary Service Opportunities." There was the very agitated guest who checked in late one night and seemed very edgy. Jack asked what was wrong, and the business traveler explained that he had forgotten his necktie, had an early morning meeting, and had no time to buy a new tie before the important appointment. Jack loosened his own tie, gave it to the guest, and capitalized on an extraordinary opportunity.

Or, there was the night that an exceptionally heavy woman checked into her room and called Jack half an hour later to indignantly complain that the toilet's ceramic base was broken. Although he had personally inspected and approved the suite earlier that day and surmised that her weight must have been responsible for the destruction, Jack graciously and apologetically escorted her to another room, and thus ensured her continued customer loyalty.

Jack loaned me Embassy Suites' "Extraordinary Service Opportunities" training manual, and as I looked it over in my room that evening, I saw that Jack's attitudes, and those of other Embassy Suites staffers, are the result of a top-down commitment to handle complaints positively. The excellent manual includes a grid dividing guests into four categories. "Patrons" are satisfied customers who tend to keep quietly returning. "Praisers" are also satisfied, but they let others know about it. "Walkers" are dissatisfied guests who avoid causing a stir, but quietly take their business elsewhere and don't return. "Talkers" represent the biggest opportunity group. When they're dissatisfied, they tell the staff on duty, and their friends, and passengers they meet on the plane, and their company travel departments, and business colleagues, and anyone else they can find.

When you run across a "Talker," instructs the manual, it's best to "take the H-E-A-T":

H: *Hear them out.* Listen to the guest. Let him vent.

E: *Empathize.* Understand that the guest feels bad and wants attention. Just like me after my unsatisfactory room service experience, "Talkers" are unsatisfied guests who usually have good reason to feel let down. When you take the heat, it's important to go beyond just listening and offering understanding, empathetic feedback. "I can understand why you feel upset, and I don't blame you. You're right."

A: *Act.* This is where many organizations fall short. Embassy Suites has empowered its frontline people to do whatever it takes to resolve situations quickly and favorably. There was no committee, regional manager, or policy directive involved when Jack invited me to be his guest for another room service meal. He took action himself, immediately.

T: *Take responsibility.* Although Jack had played no direct personal role in preparing or serving my late, inferior meal, he acted as if he *had* been in charge. He acknowledged his personal responsibility, and apologized. He might easily have said, "I don't work in the kitchen, but I'll see if I can find out who was on duty and have them get back to you." But instead, Jack took responsibility himself, as if the reputation of Embassy Suites was resting in his hands. (It was.)

And, by the way, my dinner the next evening was excellent. It was promptly delivered, tasty, and attractively presented. Jack had made sure that the room service staff knew that I had been served a disappointing meal the night before, and advised them to be sure I wasn't let down a second time.

My experience at Embassy Suites may seem like one small, isolated, unimportant incident. But it was actually very important, because it gave the hotel chain an opportunity to show its commitment to extraordinary service, and it taught me plenty of lessons. (It also converted me from a "Talker" into a "Praiser.")

What Can You Learn from This Example? You can use your own routine daily service encounters, like mine at Embassy Suites, as great opportunities to take your own pulse. Notice how you feel when you're the customer and things go wrong. Draw from those personal experiences and shape a response strategy you can take back and use in your own organization.

Notice which approaches are effective in satisfying *you*, when you're a customer who is disappointed in another organization's service. Chances are that you can take the same steps to satisfy your own customers if they encounter disappointing service when dealing with your organization.

In your daily life as a customer, view service shortfalls as opportunities to notice how you feel when a vendor lets you down, and then observe how its representatives handle your complaint. Whether you're disappointed about a slow room service delivery, a rude retail clerk, or mishandled travel arrangements, you may notice that:

- Once you're disappointed about one aspect of a company's service, your negative evaluations tend to multiply. Once the meal is late, you also tend to notice that the server is slightly unkempt, the food a little cool, and the soup bland—that the elevators are slow, and the lobby is dirty, and so on.

- Before speaking up, you probably work up an elaborate, detailed justification for your negative opinion in your own mind. You want to be right, so you ensure justification by building your case. As you do so, your disappointment solidifies so that it becomes increasingly difficult for the other guy to dissuade you.

- You're probably also quite willing to forgive if the person you complain to handles the situation coolly and takes the heat.

How should you respond when a customer complains? It's hard to improve on Embassy Suites' simple four step formula:

H: *Hear them out.*

E: *Empathize.*

A: *Act.*

T: *Take responsibility.*

The Complaint-Handling Game Plan

Although some of the complaint handlers you've just met followed their instincts and just did what seemed right at the time, the most reliable course of action is to work from a careful plan.

Preparation Is Vital

As with nearly any endeavor, the most important preparation begins in your head. Adopting the attitude that complaints are good, beneficial, and profitable will help you get the rest of your preparation moving in the right direction. This line of thinking probably won't just automatically pop into your head, and that's why it's important to practice handling such encounters in role-playing situations and internal training sessions.

This is a good time for a quick review of transactional analysis, covered thoroughly in my book *Phone Power* (Berkley, 1986) and plenty of other books. The upset customer voicing a complaint with a nasty letter or irate call is probably acting out one of two behavior states: *parent,* or *child.*

When in their *parent* roles, people tend to harshly judge others. ("You stupid idiots, you can't seem to do anything right around there. You've screwed up my orders before, too. What's the matter with you people?")

In their child roles, people vent their emotions without regard for the impact they'll have on the listener or reader, or any other consequences, for that matter. ("I can't take any more of this! You #$*&^!!@!! people are driving me crazy! I've had enough of this %%$@#&**! You can take your &^`@$^$#@ policy manual and *^^%#@*&.") Both the parent and child behaviors can be very effective at breaking down communications and shifting the attention from facts to emotions. But they're not at all effective at solving problems.

It is critically important to maintain an adult role when the complainer is shouting and screaming in the parent or child role.

Surprisingly, your body language plays an important part in helping you maintain an *adult* role. Whether your complainer can literally see you or not, your nonverbal message will come across in your voice and in your attitude as revealed by your word choice and tone of voice.

Maintain an alert, open, attentive body posture. If the complainer is sitting right there in your office, don't slump down and look bored. You also shouldn't lean forward in a confrontational posture. (Don't do it if you're on the phone, either.) And even if you're writing out a response, the body posture you adopt can influence your frame of mind. Keep your back straight, uncross your arms and legs, and look interested. Even if the complainer isn't watching your body, your body is influencing your own thought processes, and also affects your tone of voice.

Your actual word choice, of course, is also critical in the communication process. By all means, read my book *Power Talking* (Berkley, 1991) and be sure to avoid conflict-causing words by substituting phrases that lead to cooperation and understanding. Instead of saying "I *disagree*," which the complainer will hear as, "You're wrong!" say "I *understand*," and genuinely aim to see the other person's point of view.

Rather than focusing attention on what you *can't* do, explore what you *can* do. Instead of saying, "I'm afraid we *can't* get the replacement out until the end of the week," say, "What I *can* do is get the replacement out to you by the end of the week."

Concentrate on what you *want to achieve,* rather than talking about what you *want to avoid.* You'll create a positive, cooperative atmosphere by saying, "I want to help straighten this situation out so we can continue servicing your office equipment and providing the reliable repairs you expect and deserve." Taking the opposite approach drives the complainer away: "I'd hate to see you cancel your service contract with us; we don't want to lose your business."

And, be sure that your language shows the complainer that you regard handling this complaint as something you want to do, rather than as a burden. "I'd *like* to go pull your file so I have the complete background details, and then I'll *be happy* to call you back this afternoon," sounds far more positive than "I'll *have* to go pull your file, and then I'll *have* to call you back with the details this afternoon."

Be prepared to use calming, cooperative language when the time is right. But it's not time to talk, yet. Your next step is to listen.

Listen Up—Actively

Listening is far from a passive process. Most people think that they're listening if they aren't talking and the other person is. Wrong! Listening is an active process that requires your full attention and concentration. You've already adjusted your body posture to reflect your open frame of mind. Now you need to follow through and act on it.

Listening effectively requires that you clear away all other distractions. If the complainer is there with you, face-to-face, get a pad of paper ready to take notes and ensure that others around you don't interrupt. On the phone, do the same thing. Block out distractions. Turn away from your other work and disallow eye contact with colleagues by closing your office door or facing away from them. Concentrate on your complainer. Remember, this is the most profitable type of call you could be getting. Make the most of it.

Aside from listening quietly and taking notes, one of the most important active steps you can take is to encourage the complainer to tell you more. Suppose you're calling to respond to a written complaint. Rather than starting right off with a justification for what occurred or outlining your game plan for a solution, ask the writer to tell you more:

> I've carefully read your letter and have a good basic understanding of what happened. You've raised some very valid and important points, and I'm quite concerned. To start with, though, I'd like to know a little more about what happened so I can be sure I fully understand and then work toward the best solution. Please, tell me more about what happened.

Whether you're talking to a complainer by phone, or face-to-face, the same principle applies: Let the complainer get it all off his or her chest. There's a kind of cathartic release that takes place when you ask the other person to tell you more. If you don't, you may be sure that the pent-up emotions, disappointment, resentment, and even anger will still be there beneath the surface. Get them out in the open; relieve the pressure.

Begin Creating Rapport

There's a natural inclination for the complainer to think that you and your company are the enemy. In order to justify and reinforce his feelings, the complainer has neatly divided the situation into "me" and "them."

In this scenario, "me" wears the white hat, has parted with hard-earned money, is the "poor customer," and, in the extreme, always feels jerked around by those big, unfeeling, screwed-up, money-hungry companies. Or, in a business-to-business situation, "me" may feel that suppliers consistently mess things up, causing delays, shortages, headaches, and a lot of other trouble.

You, and the organization you represent, are often viewed as the opponent. So once the complainer's anger has been vented, an important step is to break down those imagined barriers that the complainer thinks divide you.

Empathize to Understand

Webster's Encyclopedic Unabridged Dictionary defines empathy as "the intellectual identification with or vicarious experiencing of the feelings, thoughts, or attitudes of another." That's not saying the other person is right, or even saying, "Oh, I feel so sorry for you." It's taking the time to understand and identify with the complainer. Feelings come first. The person who is complaining may feel that he or she has been wronged, or burdened, or hard done by, or inconvenienced, or cheated, or dealt with unfairly, or taken for granted, or who knows what else. You've got to find out before you can move forward and deal with the facts.

Many complaint handlers tend to mentally refute the complainer's charges, rather than seeking to understand them. We can't effectively proceed with resolution, until we *understand*.

My wife and I once attended an excellent marriage-enhancement seminar based on the work of Harville Hendrix, Ph.D., author of *Getting the Love You Want* (Harper Perennial, 1988). One of the key communication exercises is called "The Couple's Dialogue," though it might as well have been named "The Customer Dialogue" and presented as part of a customer service seminar. The idea is that true, clear communication between marriage partners (or business partners, or you and a complainer) is very, very difficult. We tend to muddle things up by silently preparing our responses as the other person is talking, rather than listening.

The exercise goes like this. One partner—in this case, the complainer—talks. The other doesn't interrupt or respond at all. He just listens, actively. That sounds easy, but it's the toughest part of the exercise.

The next step is to mirror what the other person has said. The listener now responds, "I understand that you feel," and repeats back his understanding of what the sender—partner or customer—has just said. The wrap-up is the question, "Did I correctly understand what you said and felt?"

Now, I realize that this sounds very simple and basic. But, try it. I remember going round after round in the seminar. My wife, Julie, said:

> I don't like the way you take out the garbage. I feel like you do it only halfway. You leave some of the containers unemptied, and the most

important one of all, under the kitchen sink, is usually still full when the garbage truck comes.

My immediate reaction was to interrupt, "Hey, what's the problem? I get it all done, don't I?" The seminar leader pointedly reminded me that my role was simply to listen, and we tried it again. Biting my tongue, I took it all in, and proceeded to repeat back what I thought I had heard. "Did I correctly understand what you said and felt?" Well, no, I hadn't gotten it quite right. So we did it again, and again, and again. The conclusion I drew from the exercise is that it's a wonder my wife and I had been able to communicate at all. I'm convinced that even people who share their lives with each other have a very hard time communicating accurately and understanding each other's feelings. So what does that say for strangers? It's extremely unlikely that you'll thoroughly understand a complainer if you just listen casually. Listen actively, and verify your understanding.

As in a marriage, businesspeople are in relationships with their customers, and sometimes those relationships are marked by conflict and misunderstanding. When that occurs and complaints are expressed, it's critical that we understand the facts as believed by the complainer, as well as what the complainer is feeling.

When the complainer is sounding off, resist the natural tendency to jump to conclusions, judge, rebut, and anticipate what's coming next. Listen actively and empathize. The same terminology that works so well in "The Couple's Dialogue" can work with customers. After you've heard him out, repeat your understanding and say, "Did I correctly understand what you said and felt?"

At this point in the resolution process, seek only to understand and empathize. Your initial aim is to have the other person say, "Yes, that's what I said and that's how I feel."

Build Bridges

Since the complainer probably started off viewing you as the guy in the black hat, and you've now taken the time to patiently and actively listen, and have reached the point where you empathize with and understand what he or she thinks and feels, we're ready to move ahead. We need to build a bridge between the customer and ourselves. Customers imagine that we hold disparate goals, when the truth is that we want the same thing. What's good for the complainer is to have the situation favorably resolved so that he or she can feel good about continuing the relationship. What's good for the company is a satisfied customer who will buy again, help it provide better services and products to other customers, and spread positive word-of-mouth publicity in the marketplace. Those are really the same goals.

So, say so:

> Mr. Scoggin, you have every right to expect excellent service. I understand how you feel, and I'm sorry that we have let you down. What I'm after is really the same thing as what you're after. You want service that's so good you'll want to continue doing business with us. And we want to keep you as a satisfied customer. So, since we both want the same thing, let's work together and come up with a solution that will get us what we both want.

Notice the apology. I've found, as a consumer, that I'm rarely apologized to, and quite often I conclude the complaint process wishing that someone had just said, "I'm sorry." In fact, that's quite often all it would take for me to feel much better when I'm doing the complaining. It seems that complaint handlers are either unconscious of the complainer's need for an apology, or they're afraid that saying, "I'm sorry" might constitute an admission of guilt. Remember, the aim is to build a bridge so we can move forward and restore the relationship. If the other person is waiting to hear, "I'm sorry," and feels that an apology is warranted, why not give it? That's the easiest, most direct way to move forward, which is, after all, the ultimate aim of the complaint-handling process.

Ask for Help in Creating Your Plan

Preparing, listening, and responding for rapport are necessary steps in complaint handling, and they lead to the crux of the matter, which is to come up with a solution that will be fair and equitable, make your customer happy, and get him or her back on your conveyor belt.

If this is a teamwork venture, and you want the same thing that your complainer wants, why not act that way? Remember, you're in this *together*. He or she has probably already given a lot of thought to the situation, and may also have a pretty good idea of what will make him happy. Rather than trying to come up with an acceptable solution all by yourself, ask your partner what he or she wants.

> Mr. Scoggin, my aim is to please you. You may already have a good solution in mind, so please tell me what you'd like me to do. How can I regain your satisfaction and patch up our relationship?

I hear you now:

> What! Ask the customer what he wants? George, are you nuts? They're all going to ask for refunds, even if the problem wasn't even our fault. You want my frontline staff to ask complaining customers what they want, and then give it to them?

Yes, that's what I'm suggesting. There are three things I'd like you to keep in mind:

1. *The long-term relationship is what counts.* Giving a refund to satisfy a customer is an investment in that relationship. If that's what it would take to keep the customer happy and generate future purchases, it's almost certain to be far less costly than setting out to find a new customer to coax onto your conveyor belt to compensate for the business you'll lose by alienating the customer you already have.

2. *Employees usually make excellent decisions when you empower them to do so.* One of the great management discoveries of the late 1980s was that multiple levels of management don't enhance decision-making processes. Instead, they slow the process way down, and result in worse decisions. Empowering employees means giving them the authority to do what's best, without first checking with a supervisor for permission. Employees who interact with customers all day long are in the best position to know what decisions will yield the most positive relationships with customers. Many of my clients who've experimented with employee empowerment feared that their people might give away the store. Far from it. Employees who are given the trust and authority to make their own decisions regarding the best way to resolve customer complaints tend to reach very fair resolutions. (You may be sick of Nordstrom stories, but their "Employee Handbook" is worth quoting. It's 73 words all told, the most important of which are: "Nordstrom Rules: Rule No. 1: Use your good judgment in all situations. There will be no additional rules.")

3. It's very costly *not* to give customers what they say they want. Without getting bogged down in extensive mathematical calculations, just follow this simple example. Say a customer calls to tell you that the $100 item she received from you was defective. When you ask what she wants to do about it, she responds that she simply wants you to send a replacement. There are two courses of action you can follow at this point: either you send the replacement right away, along with your apology, or you decide to investigate, just in case the customer is attempting to misrepresent the facts and take advantage of you.

Let's say that at least 80 percent of your customers' claims are legitimate. Although 20 percent is really stretching it, let's very liberally estimate that one out of five of your customers is trying to cheat you. So, how much will it cost to investigate? By the time the employee handling the call checks with other departments, makes a few more calls, writes a letter or two, fills out a couple of forms, and interrupts his normal flow of work (as well as causing interruptions to the people in the other departments he had to check with), the administrative cost is sure to be high. Let's very conservatively guess at $35, though the figure is more likely to be $50 to $100.

Here's what all that means. If you investigate the next 10 such claims, your minimum cost of investigation is going to be at least $350. (Remember, it's really more likely to approach $1000.) Sure enough, you may catch the 20 percent who are trying to cheat you. At a cost of $350, you will have saved $200!

But we're not done yet. The eight customers whose claims were legitimate all along have now had their resolutions delayed during the investigations, so they are going to be less satisfied than if you had sent the replacement right away and shown your trust in the partnership you want with your customers. Over the long haul, the resulting annoyance is likely to be far more costly to you than was the initial cost of investigation.

The bottom line is clear. It's far too costly to investigate routine customer claims that are likely to be legitimate. The most economically sensible course of action is to trust your customers, empower your employees, and invest in customer relationships. Unless the circumstances are very suspicious or quite bizarre, it's best to settle customers' claims immediately and graciously.

One of my clients is a very large global computer company with a highly profitable direct marketing division that sells computer accessories and supplies via catalog and telemarketing programs. They don't want me to tell you this company's name, but I do want you to know about a fascinating discovery made there. The company conducted a financial analysis like the one you've just read, and sure enough, they concluded that when a customer calls about a damaged or defective shipment, the very best course of action is to send out a replacement immediately without doing any investigating. But here's their interesting twist. They don't want their customers to return the damaged or defective items. The cost to have someone in the receiving area open the package, figure out what it is, track down the original details of the customer's order and return authorization, then refurbish and repackage the item and restock it for subsequent sale, would be almost as great as the cost of investigating the claim in the first place. If you buy a $100 laser printer cartridge from this company, then open it and discover that the toner has spilled, or that the instruction sheet is missing, or that it's the wrong cartridge for your specific printer, they'll immediately send you a replacement without charge, and ask you *not* to return the one you've already received.

Of course, they don't say:

> We've conducted a through analysis and discovered that it's just too costly for us to process your return, so please save us some money and throw it away, or give it to a charity, or do whatever you want with it. But, by all means, please don't burden us with the expense of taking it back.

What they *do* say is:

> I'm sorry that the cartridge you ordered isn't in perfect condition. I'll have a replacement sent to you right away. I know your time is very valuable, so it won't be necessary for you to go to the inconvenience of packing up the defective one and shipping it back. Your business is important to us, we trust you, and we value our relationship with you.

Secure Your Agreement and Confirm It

Communicating clearly in the very best of circumstances is chancy. When a complainer is upset and emotions have been running on the warm side, it's quite likely that mutual understanding will be well below 100 percent. This is the time to take extra steps and make sure that you and the complainer both have a clear understanding of the agreed solution and what's going to happen next. Take the time to restate exactly what you're going to do, and seek the customer's agreement that the plan will satisfy him.

> Mr. Scoggin, I want to be sure that I have a clear understanding of what's going to happen next. We've agreed that I will send you a new cartridge for your printer, model XYZ. That'll go out tomorrow via Federal Express at no charge to you. You won't need to send back the bad one. And we'll look forward to helping you with your future orders. Will that take care of things for you?

If there's any misunderstanding at all, this is the time to clear it up. Bear in mind John Goodman's caution: If you receive a complaint and you goof while handling it, you're worse off than if you had never handled the complaint in the first place. Your long-term relationship is at stake, so take the extra steps necessary to be sure it's handled right.

Follow Through and Gift Wrap the Package

Having invested the time, trouble, and money to resolve the complaint, why not leverage that investment by taking one extra step to secure an even higher level of satisfaction? I think of it as gift wrapping the package and adorning it with a pretty bow. The most effective, least costly way to do that is with a phone call. After completing your agreed course of action, take the time to make a quick follow-up call. That's the icing on the cake that can create fanatically loyal customers.

I fly United Airlines a great deal as I travel to and from speaking engagements around the world. While preparing the manuscript for *Upside-Down Marketing,* I got a firsthand demonstration of how this extra step *could* have worked. Returning from a speech in Nashville, my luggage was misconnected when I changed planes in Chicago. I arrived home in Seattle, but my bags didn't make it. I stood in line at the baggage service desk, showed the man my claim checks, and waited while he punched the numbers into his computer. Sure enough, the bags had already been located in Chicago, and were scheduled to come in on the morning flight. They arrived, and a courier delivered the bags to my home, as promised. So far, so good.

Unfortunately, though, the spine of my garment bag had been broken. This is not repairable damage, and I could no longer use the bag. I wrote to United's headquarters in Chicago, described what had happened, pointed out that I'm a loyal United customer who flies a great deal, and sent the receipt for my replacement garment bag. I've found that buying the best luggage I can get really pays off in the long run, so I had gone ahead and purchased another Tumi brand, top-of-the-line model just like the one that was broken. The cost was $427.

I got back a nice letter apologizing and telling me that I should take the damaged bag to my local Seattle baggage desk to file my claim, as they would have jurisdiction in the matter. I did so the next week, and the clerk at the airport wrote out the details, took the bag, and said he'd have my answer in a day or two. I flew off for my next speech carrying the replacement garment bag I had purchased, and stopped back at the counter in Seattle the next day when I returned. The same clerk was there, and he informed me that a check had already been sent. Sure enough, two days later I received an envelope with a check for $427 and a little card that read:

Dear Customer: Enclosed is our settlement check as agreed. We apologize for any inconvenience we have caused and hope to see you back in the "friendly skies" in the near future.

What had United done wrong? Nothing. They trusted me, made the procedure easy, followed through quickly, and didn't waste a lot of their time and resources trying to determine if I was trying to cheat them.

What could United have done even better? Well, several things. First, the person who took my original report could have looked me in the eye and apologized, rather than routinely filling out the report. Also, if he had asked me what I would feel good about, I'd have said that I would be more than pleased if United would pay for half of the replacement bag, since I had already used the now-broken one for about two years, and guessed that it had less than two years of useful life remaining. He could also have acknowledged my "Executive Premier" frequent-flier status and let me know how important my business is to United. And, finally, United could have wrapped their settlement up with a bow. Either the Seattle baggage office or the Chicago headquarters could have made a quick call to be sure that I had received the check, apologized again for the damage and inconvenience, and verified that I was pleased with the settlement. Don't get me wrong, I'm very happy that United paid the entire cost of the new bag. But, they could have paid me half as much and made me even happier if they'd taken just those couple of extra steps.

If you're going to go to the trouble and expense of handling your customers' complaints in a positive manner, leverage your investment and get the biggest return possible by following through and icing the cake.

It's really not very difficult to convert upset customers who are shouting at and about your company into fiercely loyal customers who just as vocally tout your excellent products and services. Very few organizations actively seek complaints, view them as helpful input and an opportunity to convert a shouter into a touter, and provide their staffs—at all levels—with the leadership, inspiration, and training to capture this extraordinary profit opportunity. *You can.*

What Can You Learn from This Chapter?

- Your most upset, unhappy complaining customers can become your most loyal supporters, if their feedback is welcomed, acted upon, and treated as valuable marketing input.

- Most unhappy customers will not directly tell your company about their complaints unless you make it easy for them to do so and make it clear that you welcome their feedback. Instead, they'll tell other customers and potential customers. Their negative publicity can be very costly, and your company will certainly be better off if it lets disgruntled customers know that their feedback is welcome.

- When dealing with complainers, your company should pursue three objectives: (1) win the customer back; (2) find out what went wrong, since whatever the problem is, it's probably alienating other customers, too; and (3) neutralize negative publicity, even if the complaining customer never buys from you again.

- When things start going wrong with a customer relationship, the sooner you face the music and address the issue, the better your chances are for reestablishing a positive alliance.

- If you have made several unsuccessful attempts to resolve a complaint, consider a radical change in approach. If formal correspondence hasn't worked, for example, send a handwritten note.

- Think of the costs involved in resolving a complaint as investments in a new relationship with this customer, as market research, and as positive publicity. Focus on the long-term payoffs from those investments.

- Always be persistent, professional, and personal in seeking resolution.

- It's useful to train staff members to use a simple, easily remembered resolution process such as "Take the HEAT: *H*ear the complaint, *E*mpathize, *A*ct, and *T*ake responsibility."

- An effective complaint-handling game plan includes eight steps: prepare, listen actively, build rapport, empathize, build a bridge, ask for help, secure and confirm the agreement, and follow through.

Action Summary
What You Can Do *Now*

This book will only be helpful, and these strategies will only prove profitable, if you take decisive action now. This section provides a checklist of steps you can take immediately. They're presented in the same order as the contents of this chapter, so it will be easy to refer back for more complete details.

- Ask a friend or colleague to call or write to your company and file a complaint. There's no better way to find out how complainers are *really* being treated. If your voice won't be recognized, do it yourself. Make some unreasonable complaints, too. Get out of line, be gruff and abusive. See how you're handled, and how easily your people are rattled.

- Begin a "Mystery Complainer" program and publicize the results. Get your CEO to take a personal interest in changing the way your company handles unhappy customers. Publish the results in your internal company newsletter. Provide kudos and prizes for people who do an outstanding job of resolving complaint calls.

- Draft a flowchart showing exactly what happens to complaints under your current setup. Look for bottlenecks that make it difficult for unhappy customers to complain. Watch out for any snags that slow down the resolution process.

- Estimate your own cost of replacing lost customers with new ones. Other companies consistently find that it's four to ten times as costly to win a new customer as it is to save a current one. What's your figure?

- Find out what happens to the suggestions your customers are already offering. If someone calls to complain about items damaged because of poor packaging, is there a feedback system that gets that information to the people who need to know so they can improve the packaging?

- Focus with laser precision on the first moments of complainers' contacts with your company. We've seen over and over that it's the very first response that determines the tone and eventual outcome of the complaint-handling process.

- Do everything you can to shorten the time required to resolve complaints. Empower frontline employees to settle matters themselves. Eliminate procedures that delay your customers' satisfaction.

- Calculate the long-term value of your customer relationships. Estimate it by multiplying the average annual revenue per customer, multiplying that by the average relationship duration in years, and then have your financial people calculate the net present value of the expected future revenue stream.

- Use the net present value of the long-term relationship as your benchmark in determining whether or not it's worth doing your utmost to save customers who are falling off your conveyor belt.

- Be flexible and personal with your firm's resolution procedures. If an employee thinks it would be best to write out a personal note rather than send a computer-generated form letter, by all means encourage it!

- Seek to increase your customers' net present value by increasing the average annual revenues of your existing relationships and reducing the churn or customer turnover rate to extend the average relationship duration.

- Encourage your team members to use "the three Ps" of complaint resolutions: be persistent, professional, and personal.

- Start noting details of your own personal encounters with organizations to whom you complain yourself. Notice what techniques they use that impress you positively and negatively.

- Start a column in your company newsletter dedicated to employees who are treated well when they complain to other companies. Offer incentives for your employees to share their examples and draw lessons from them. Consider a "complaint-of-the-month" award and have employees write up their entries via E-mail, or establish a voice mailbox for oral entries.

- Prepare and distribute a complaint-handling game plan that guides your colleagues and employees step by step toward favorable outcomes whenever they encounter unhappy customers.

- Estimate your own investigation cost and find out if it's really cost-effective to start an internal investigation every time a customer claims that your product or service was defective. Remember to figure in the cost of alienating good customers who will eventually be vindicated by an investigation anyway.

- Distribute a list of forbidden phrases that alienate customers. Pick up a copy of *Power Talking* and eliminate relationship-harming phrases like "It's company policy," "I'll have to get back to you," "I disagree," "I can't," and so on.

- Begin taking little extra steps, such as postresolution phone calls, to gift wrap the package and gain maximum profit leverage from your complaint-handling processes.

- Above all, establish and constantly reinforce the awareness that complaints are *good, profitable,* and *welcome* in your organization.

2
Pay Up or Kiss Off

Financial services departments are usually charged with the task of coercing slow-paying customers into settling their past-due accounts. Often their tactics are shortsighted and the collectors pursue the single goal of getting paid—even if it means losing customers and generating negative word-of-mouth publicity. The predominant attitude seems to be, "Pay up, buddy, or kiss off. We'll close your account, sic our lawyers on you, and ruin your credit." This kind of thinking has to be changed if you want to nurture long-term customer relationships and maximize profits. While important, getting paid should be only the *second* objective of any accounts receivable strategy. The first should be to maintain long and profitable relationships that include the timely payment of all bills.

Are Your Customers Deadbeats?

The predominant terminology in the typical accounts receivable or collections department is very derogatory: "deadbeats," "losers," "thieves," "tough cases," "cheats." True enough, there *are* some dishonest customers out there, and they may have no reservations about lying when asked why they haven't sent in their payments. (My all-time favorite was the Michigan man who insisted that he couldn't make his car payments because he was *dead*. I was monitoring the call and heard him indignantly insist that there was no longer any point in phoning, because he was no longer among the living. He had even personally signed a letter attesting to his own demise.)

The Psychology of Labels

The trouble with those negative labels is that they are literally prejudicial in practice. Many, many times I've heard collections personnel talking among themselves before making calls: "Yeah, I've got to call some more of these deadbeats and hammer 'em. Which flakes do you have to call tonight?" And then they begin dialing away. With an outlook like that, it's impossible to take a positive approach toward valuable customers who may have legitimate concerns, may have simply overlooked a bill, or may have been out of town when their reminder notices arrived.

Priority 1: Purge Negative Labels

The very first change any organization must make if it's going to forge long and profitable relationships with customers who have been paying slowly is to purge those labels. They poison any individual collector's thinking, and they interfere with the organization's collective efforts to employ upside-down marketing, enlightened thinking, or flexible policy making in the receivables area.

Get rid of those labels! From the highest levels of financial management down to the newest collections representative, all prejudicial language that interferes with partnership thinking should be immediately abandoned. The aim of any organization should be to make relationships last longer—to form enduring partnerships with customers. When a customer falls behind on payments, it's time to rekindle and nurture the relationship, not threaten it.

For starters, why not post a large sign showing the international symbol of the red circle with a diagonal line crossing out the word *Deadbeat* as a way of getting the point across to your collections personnel? This will be a good visual way to start changing their thinking.

Coercion Creates Antagonistic, Vindictive *Ex*-Customers

Customers generally hold very low opinions of collections personnel. They may have seen television journalists report on the sleazy high-pressure tactics that collectors sometimes employ, and many customers have experienced less-than-ethical treatment themselves. People who get called by collectors are often down on their luck anyway, and the harassing calls just make their lives more miserable. The higher the pressure used, the more alienated such customers feel. They often seek their revenge by bad-mouthing the companies to whom they owe money.

Consider the case of delinquent car payments. Suppose you buy a new Ford and have it financed through your Ford dealership. Chances are that the account will be handled through Ford's financial subsidiary in Michigan. If you fall behind on your payments, you're going to get a series of mailed reminders that emphasize, with escalating intensity, the need to get caught up fast. You'll also get phone calls, many of them made automatically. Finance organizations have embraced the extremely efficient telecommunications technology available today, and many employ predictive dialers that constantly dial, dial, dial and play one recorded message after another, reminding you of the need to make your past-due payment right away.

Eventually a real, live person will talk with you and try to get to the bottom of things. It may be very difficult for that individual to maintain an open mind and project a positive partnership attitude if he or she works all day long surrounded by a lot of cynical people who believe they've heard every lie in the book. The collector is likely to build up an extremely negative attitude, and convey it when he or she talks with customers.

But what if you just can't pay? Even if you have a very helpful collector who is trying to work things out with you, circumstances beyond your control may make it impossible for you to fulfill your obligations at this time. In the auto financing business, the ultimate end result is that your vehicle may be repossessed. So one morning, you walk out the front door to drive to work, and your car is gone. You knew the situation was serious and you had probably been plainly warned that this might happen. But still, it's a shock.

Just then, your neighbor walks out to the driveway, also on her way to work. She says, "Good morning, Tim. Hey, where's your car?"

Now, you tell me, what are you going to say?

> The good people at Ford had to repossess it, because I've been financially irresponsible. I lied to them quite a few times, and I'm afraid I failed to honor my obligations. They did their best, and it's been a fine car, so I can't blame them. I went flaky on them, so they really had no choice. Too bad I caused Ford so much trouble.

Of course not! You're going to say:

Oh, I finally told those jerks at Ford to just tow it away. What a hunk of junk. I've had nothing but trouble with that car, and the Ford people are even worse than the cars they make. I've complained over and over, but they never have gotten it to run right. I'm glad it's gone, and I'll sure never get another Ford. I wouldn't recommend one to my worst enemy. Can I catch a ride downtown with you?

Now, I don't intend to single Ford out and cast them in a negative light. On the contrary, Ford has been particularly conscious of the lifetime value of positive customer relationships. I've also been pleased to present many speeches and training sessions for Ford personnel around the country, always focusing on positive collection techniques based on the idea of upside-down marketing.

The trouble with the heavy-handed collections approach is that it's only rarely successful at getting payments but fairly good at creating hostile, vindictive ex-customers who won't buy from the company ever again, even when their financial situations improve.

What's Your Customer's Lifetime Value?

The starting point for converting "hammer-the-deadbeats" thinking into a sound relationship management strategy is to promote an appreciation of the lifetime value concept.

An excellent example stems from my work with Ford Motor Credit. When financial analysts there computed the lifetime value of a satisfied customer, they took into consideration a complex formula that included many factors:

- A happy customer is likely to buy multiple cars in the course of a lifetime and will demonstrate brand loyalty if treated well during repeated contacts with the company.
- Each purchase will include a profit component; years into the future, the prices of cars will increase, as will the gross profit component of each transaction.
- As that one happy customer continues to buy Ford products, he or she will also influence the purchase decisions of friends, neighbors, and perhaps even a company fleet manager.

The financial calculations are rather complex, and the net result is quite surprising. The expected future flow of profit dollars from a happy Ford customer is discounted to yield a net present value figure. That is, what amount of money would Ford have to put in the bank today, at prevailing interest rates, to generate that same flow of future profits? Their answer: $178,000! In other words, a happy Ford customer is really an asset worth $178,000 to the company *if* he or she is sufficiently happy with Ford to keep buying Ford products and recommending them to others.

Ford also came to realize that for customers who finance their cars through Ford Motor Credit, their monthly payments and associated phone calls comprise their primary ongoing contact with Ford. A typical car buyer has his or her initial contact with the local dealer, who isn't really a Ford company employee. Once the sale is made, the dealer's salesperson takes a powder quickly as he or she resumes the hot pursuit of other new car buyers. (Few car salespeople practice upside-down marketing yet.) The car buyer's next contact is with the servicing organization. A car owner typically stops having a car serviced at authorized dealers once the warranty ends. He or she goes to a local garage or a car repair chain. The connection with Ford is lost—*except for one thing:* those continuing monthly car payments. They constitute the customer's sole ongoing personal contact with Ford. Even though Ford Motor Credit is actually a separate subsidiary company, the customer's perception is not differentiated. The representative who calls to track down a late car payment *is* Ford as far as that customer is concerned.

How Much Is Your Customer Worth Today?

Whether you own a grocery store, manage a diaper service, sell subscriptions for a newspaper, or represent a manufacturer of industrial goods, the calculation process is the same, and the results will be surprising. Each customer relationship has the potential of being worth a great deal of money—if it's handled right.

It's well worth going through the process of calculating your own lifetime value figure. How much business can you expect from a happy customer over the course of a year? If you keep the customer happy, how long can you hang on to the relationship? Remember to add in the multiplier effect, too. A delighted customer will, over the course of the relationship, refer others to you and speak positively about the experience of being your customer. That in itself is worth a great deal. In the end, what you're looking at is a stream of revenue flowing to you as a result of the relationship.

Discounting to net present value means figuring out how much money you'd have to have sitting in the bank today to yield that same flow of cash. The net present value of *your* customer relationships is likely to be surprisingly large. Isn't it worth treating that intangible asset as if it were an ingot of pure gold on your conveyor belt?

Example

Retail Chain Gives Customers the Silent Treatment

When you've spent seven years in the collections department for a major department store chain, you've heard just about every imaginable excuse from customers who are behind on their charge card payments. ("I won't pay for the mattress because I left it in the hallway and it just disappeared! My neighbor was waiting for the truck to move it, but she had to run an errand and suddenly the darn thing vanished.")

Yet after all the stories, Lindamarie Duarte, collections supervisor for a chain of upscale department stores headquartered in Los Angeles, has concluded that very few customers are dishonest, lying cheats. The vast majority are honest people who sincerely want to maintain their accounts in good standing. Some face daunting financial difficulties, and a high percentage have customer service concerns.

I asked Lindamarie what she trains her collectors to say when they want to uncover the truth about why an account is delinquent. She answered:

> It's not what we say, it's what we *don't* say. The best possible way to find out what's causing a delinquency is to state why you're calling, and then shut up!

When you think about it, this approach makes a lot of sense. If you want to know what's going on with your customers, you have to give them a chance to tell you. Lindamarie's collectors begin each call by saying, "I'm calling about the delinquent balance on your account" (pause). And then they wait—and listen—for the initial response. They don't just notice the facts, they also listen for sincerity and willingness to pay.

Ask Lindamarie to tell you about some of her unusual experiences, and she'll start right in: "There was the couple with the eight-thousand-dollar chandelier they wouldn't pay for because they decided they didn't like it (after two years)! And then there was the lady who ordered a custom-dyed lavender lambskin jacket and then wouldn't pay after she realized she didn't like the way it looked on her."

All of Lindamarie's stories have a common theme. Presented with circumstances that could easily have terminated the customer's relationship with the store, she and her team patiently *listened.* I don't mean that they let customers walk all over them; they're quite adept at dealing with the few customers who do lie and break their promises. Most, though, can be helped along so that they can restore their accounts to good standing and keep using their charge cards. After all, a charge card customer does have a significant lifetime value based on the department store's average annual customer charges of nearly $3000, and *that's* the figure Lindamarie has in mind when talking with a customer who's behind on payments. It's not the amount of this individual monthly payment that really matters, it's the value of the relationship.

For example, one business customer was completely unresponsive to repeated mailings about his past-due balance. When Lindamarie phoned, she found that his business telephone number had been disconnected. Dunning letters were returned by the U.S. Postal Service with no forwarding address. Sounds like a dead customer, right? As a matter of fact, as his hospital records later confirmed, the customer had been in critical care on a life-support system for 45 days! Thanks to Lindamarie's gentle, sensitive handling of his situation—and her patient listening—he remains an active customer today.

Another customer had a string of personal setbacks over the course of a year, and his department store charge account suffered. He did, too. First a divorce, then a layoff, then an extended illness, and so on. Yet in the end, he brought his account current and sent a letter *thanking* the collector. As he put it, "You listened and made me feel like a person instead of a problem." As he stumbled from one disaster to another, he was hounded by numerous creditors: harassing calls, computer notices, lawyers' threats, nasty letters. Yet many of the *other* creditors never got paid. The reason he paid his department store bill was because of the collector's attitude. After finally getting his payments all caught up, the customer wrote to the manager saying,

> No matter what happened, I made sure I paid her first. She was professional, yet she had a very friendly attitude and she listened. I felt that I wanted to keep my commitments to her.

What Can You Learn from This Example? When facing what may appear to be a bad account, characterized by delinquent payments and a past-due balance, withhold judgment. Rather than setting out to browbeat the customer, *listen.* Hear between the lines and cultivate an intuitive sense that can tell you whether the debtor is lying or is sincere and willing to pay but facing a situation that is making things difficult. Call with the aim of understanding and helping. Motivate the customer to *want* to pay you. If this person is having trouble with your account, he or she is probably delinquent with others, too. Think of the customer's tall stacks of unpaid bills, and the shorter stack of available dollars. That person is going to have to decide who gets paid and who doesn't. You want to be on the top of the stack that gets paid, and the best way to do that is to maintain positive personal contact.

Reframe Your Views
on Valued Assets

The single most important message to get across to collections and accounts receivable personnel is that they aren't interacting with "bad" people who are "guilty" of past-due payments. They're caring for extremely valuable, tangible assets. It's as if the person they're writing to and phoning is really a precious jewel teetering on the edge of the conveyor belt. Treated right, that valuable asset will stay on the belt. Rough treatment *might* get this month's payment, perhaps even the balance in full, but it will also knock the asset off the belt.

What Delinquent Customers
Are *Really* Saying

Visualize your customer opening your invoice. In front of him or her are two stacks of bills. One stack is for immediate payment. The other stack is for bills that will be delayed or not paid at all. If your customer opens your invoice and thinks, "This makes sense; it's what I expected; I'm getting good value; I like dealing with them," your bill gets stacked with those that will be paid.

If your bill isn't paid, it may mean that your customer holds that invoice for a moment and says, "This doesn't make sense; it's not what I expected; I'm not getting good value from these people; I don't like dealing with them." If you're not getting paid, your customers may be sending you a message. They could be saying, "I'm confused and/or disappointed and/or not getting enough value for my money." Your customer may need to be resold.

Example

AAA Resells Lapsed Members

If you're like almost 34 million Americans, you're a member of the AAA. And chances are, one of these years you'll forget to send in your $38 annual renewal fee, or perhaps decide to cancel your membership. If you do, you're going to get a call from Tom Maloney, sales executive at AAA Mid-Atlantic, or from one of his 2000 colleagues in AAA offices throughout the United States. Tom's job—and his personal goal—is to resell you on the benefits of your auto club membership so that you'll renew.

Each evening, after his regular day job in the Newark, Delaware, AAA office, Tom heads home with a sheaf of unrenewed membership records. He begins calling at exactly 6:20 p.m.

> You see, I've found that if I call any earlier, they're having dinner with their families, or they've just gotten in the door from work. I only get the names after three months, which means the member has already received several mailed reminders. Most of the people I call are very busy. Once in a very great while, somebody has actually just overlooked the mail. I love it when that happens, but it's rare. Almost everybody I call has already decided not to renew for one reason or another.

It's very clear to Tom that the number one reason people don't renew is that they aren't taking full advantage of what their membership offers them. They've been paying membership dues year after year, but haven't fully realized the benefits. Tom's job as he sees it is to resell members and show them how to start taking full advantage of the benefits they've been paying for all along.

Most members think of AAA as emergency road service only. In fact, 24-hour-a-day, 365-days-a-year emergency road service—while an important and valuable membership benefit—is a very small part of what your membership buys you. You get the annually updated maps, AAA's exclusive Triptik route planners, fee-free travelers checks, new-car buying advisory service, charge card protection, mechanic referral services, hotel discounts, tour and travel planning books, and bail bond protection, not to mention travel agency services and a full line of insurance programs. Still, most people immediately think only of that tow truck with the AAA emblem coming to rescue them from some dark roadside.

Call after call, Tom begins:

> I was looking at my computer sheets here, and I noticed that we haven't received your renewal yet, and what I'd like to do is help you keep your membership in force for this coming year. I can renew you now, by phone, because you're still within the grace period, so you won't need to pay the ten-dollar initiation fee. You'll be ahead of the game, too, because I'll make the effective date today, even though your membership ran out three months ago, so you'll be good for another full year starting today.

"Well," Tom estimates, "about a quarter of the people I call hang up on me and definitely don't want to renew. But the other 75 percent are my challenges. It's a game, and I like it." And he's good at it.

People often say, "Well, I just bought a brand new car, and it's under warranty, so I don't think I'll need any towing." Perfect! Tom responds right away with:

> Towing is just the very last resort. We're here to help you with a locksmith if you lock your keys inside, gas if you run out, or a jump start if you leave the lights on at the mall. And you'll always want to have updated, accurate, current maps in your new car, and that's all included in your membership.

When I asked Tom about his toughest situations, he said, "Sometimes I reach an elderly lady who doesn't drive anymore, her husband has died, and she has no car." That sounded to me like a pretty good reason for her to drop her membership. But not to Tom:

> Lots of people think that the membership goes with the car, but it doesn't. It's the person who's the member. And that means that—especially when you're older and don't drive any longer—you carry all the benefits right with you, regardless of who is driving you around or whose car you're in. So, say your son or a friend is taking you shopping. You can always use the card if their car breaks down or they run out of gas or lock their keys inside. What better way to be a gracious guest than to help out the people who are being kind to you by giving you a lift?

Tom's key challenge is to be creative in finding a way to have members take better advantage of AAA:

> Lots of times I talk with a real estate agent who's decided to cancel her AAA membership. I ask the agent, "Hey, wouldn't it help your business if you gave out a 'Welcome to Your New Neighborhood' packet every time you sold someone a house? You could pick up a set of local maps, the tour book covering their area, and even a set of AAA's local restaurant discount coupons." Real estate agents usually don't realize that an AAA membership can actually help in their business.

Sometimes, he comes across members who are angry when he calls. They didn't renew for good reason: they're still furious about some negative experience in the past. "What! You have the nerve to call me after I waited two hours in the rain for the AAA tow truck last winter? I finally gave up and had a friend come help me." Tom immediately apologizes and makes it clear that AAA wants to hear about it when members feel let down. With nearly 34 million members and 17.9 million service calls a year (49,000 per day!), it's no wonder that the logistics aren't always absolutely perfect.

When a member starts talking about a negative experience, Tom offers his own personal telephone number and says:

> If anything like that ever happens again, I want you to call me directly so I can take care of it. If we let you down, I want to hear about it so I can fix things.

One thing I realized after my interview with Tom is that he's sold on AAA himself. In fact, he said: "I wouldn't let my own mother be without it. I want *everyone* to be a member. Even if they never take a trip, the majority of car breakdowns occur within three miles of home."

Tom is very successful at saving customer relationships for several reasons:

- He believes in what he's doing; his goal is to resell past members, and he's able to do it well because he's sold on AAA himself.

- He wants to hear about problems so he can get to work and solve them. His genuine concern comes across.

- He recognizes that members have to benefit from membership before they'll renew it. And Tom recognizes that his job is to creatively help members take advantage of AAA.

What Can You Learn from This Example? It's likely that your customers are receiving less than they're paying for. Not because you're withholding something from them, but because they don't realize and take advantage of the many ways you can help them. Use every possible opportunity to educate and reeducate your customers about what they're already paying for so that they'll regularly reaffirm the value they're receiving. One of the best times to reeducate is when you're asking for money. When customers aren't paying on time or aren't paying at all, it's a strong indication that they may no longer be sold on the value you're providing.

Reselling Now Prevents Payment Problems Later

I've been an American Express cardholder for years, and I carry their Platinum card. It's much more expensive than any other credit card, and a couple of times a year, especially at renewal time, I question whether I really need a $300-a-year card when there are plenty of good free ones. AMEX seems to anticipate my doubts and at just about that same time of year sends me a little brochure listing all the exclusive benefits available only to me as a Platinum cardholder. With every bill I get a newsletter that always includes a couple of appreciation letters from cardholders who have been so delighted with their Platinum service that they take the time to write. It seems as though they're always being rescued by helicopter from some posh Swiss ski resort after calling Platinum Travelers Emergency Service. Or they want a special necklace their spouse saw in a little shop in Laos, but they can't remember the name of the store, and the Platinum concierge tracks it down for them. American Express is constantly reselling me on the value of my membership. (I guess I'll keep it for another year.)

One of the best ways to avoid payment delinquencies is to make sure that your customers are constantly resold on the value of your products and services. That way, when it comes time to pay, they won't put your invoice in the pile of others they're not sure are really worth paying. *Reeducating is reselling.* You want your customers to know what they're able to get from you and are probably already paying for.

What are you doing to resell your customers and remind them to take advantage of what they're already paying for? The ideal time is at—or better yet *before*—payment time.

The Magic of Positive Reinforcement

Why is it that we always have time to pay attention to customers whose behavior is not acceptable, but rarely take time to reward the customers who are doing what they should?

Most collectors go to great lengths to negotiate, cajole, and pressure their past-due customers to make a monthly payment, and then move on to tackle the next customer. The next month, the slow-paying customer is often back on the call list, delinquent again.

Put yourself in this picture. You fall a couple of months behind in making payments for your health club membership. A collector finally calls and negotiates a payment plan with you. You agree to send $20 this week and $20 for each of the next three weeks until you get caught up. A couple of days after sending this week's payment, the same collector phones you again. Defensively, you mentally prepare to protest: "Hey, I sent the check on Monday. Don't blame me if the mail is a little slow. Back off and quit bugging me." Instead, the collector says:

Mrs. Brown, I'm calling to thank you. You promised to send your twenty-dollar check last Monday and I did receive it. I really appreciate the fact that you kept your promise, and I want you to know that I realize it can be tough to keep your word when you're under financial pressure. You did, and that carries a lot of weight with me. Thank you.

If you got such a call, wouldn't you be likely to send next week's payment on time?

Invest in Relationships

Take the time and allocate the resources you need to contact customers who are maintaining their accounts in good order. When a customer has had some payment problems and then has lived up to his agreement and gotten the account current again, be certain that he or she knows you noticed. This will help prevent the customer's tendency to fall into a slow-pay cycle in which he gets caught up, then falls behind, then gets caught up, and then again falls behind, requiring constant attention from you.

The single most effective strategy for dealing with slow payers is to notice and reward their behavior when they start turning things around and paying on time. Investing the resources necessary to contact a customer who is living up to his agreement pays off. It's not only the fair and right thing to do, it's also the most resource-efficient course of action. Making a "Thanks for keeping your promise" call this month means you probably won't have to make a "You're late and broke your promise again" call next month. And you probably won't have to make one the following month either.

If you keep that long-term, positive-relationship goal in mind, you'll see that the positive-reinforcement strategy doesn't just help your customers improve their future payment patterns, but also builds their long-term loyalty.

There's one more important impact to consider. What about the effect on the collectors who make the "thank-you" calls? In a well-managed, efficiently equipped call center, a collector will make well over 100 customer calls per day. In busy spurts, an active collector may be talking with 20 customers an hour. If every one of those calls concerns a customer who has failed to honor a commitment, is offering an excuse, or is seeking to renegotiate a broken payment promise, you can imagine that it's going to be depressing and frustrating work. What a relief to be able to call a customer who kept his promise and say, "Thanks!" Your employees and customers also benefit from a ripple effect, as the collector now feels better and treats other customers and colleagues better, too.

"I Won't Pay" Really Means "I Want Your Attention!"

Quite often customers vocally refuse to pay what you believe they owe you. A typical response to such stonewalling is to threaten recourse. However, if treated with respect and patience, many such customers can turn out to be long-term valuable assets. But you must take the time to listen. Their blustering threats may be the result of other frustrations, and if you get into a showdown because you know you're in the right, you may end up losing, even if you get paid. The long-term relationship is what counts.

Example

TCI Cable TV Stops That Truck!

Far too often the people responsible for collecting delinquent accounts have little empathy for their customers and no appreciation of the long-term value of their customers' relationships. They get hardened from dealing with deadbeats and forget about the payoffs that result from fostering positive relationships with *good* customers. When a customer is slow or late in paying, an accounts receivable clerk's first reaction may be to "send out the truck." (In auto financing, it's "send out the tow truck." In your business, it may be "Put them on credit hold," or "Pull their card," or "Stop all shipments.")

It's surprising where your needed education may come from when you're shepherding accounts worth $50,000 per month. For Mike Kelly, now with the giant cable TV operator TCI West, one of his most telling lessons came in a parking lot in front of the Group W Cable offices in Columbia, Missouri. As plant manager for the cable television operation there, Mike was arriving for work one day when he was verbally accosted by a quite irate woman. For 20 minutes she yelled and screamed and swore at him, leaving no doubt that she had a very negative opinion of Group W and the cable television industry in general. Her TV wasn't working, and she wasn't about to pay her cable bill! Finally, she began to run out of steam and said to Mike, "Well, don't *you* have anything to say?"

Mike patiently responded, "Yes, but I don't want to interrupt you, please go on." And she did. She said she had been sent to the cable company's office by her husband, who was furious that he couldn't watch the baseball game he'd hoped to enjoy after a tiring weekend with too many relatives as house guests. Like most cable TV customers, they had occasionally experienced poor reception resulting from a temporary cable break or from a moisture buildup in one of the cable system's junction boxes. But this time, her husband was irate because he couldn't get any picture at all.

When the woman finally calmed down, Mike offered to drive to her home and investigate the trouble himself. After meeting (and getting an earful from) her equally upset husband, Mike turned on the TV. Nothing. It was immediately clear to him that there was no power getting to the set—whether the cable was working or not. Although Mike suspected this wasn't a cable problem, he continued to help by asking the critical question: "When did the TV last work, and what has changed since then?" Well, the set had worked fine until all those relatives came to visit, when the furniture had been rearranged to convert the family TV room into a guest room for the visiting grandparents. Sure enough, the TV had been moved back into position and plugged back in after the guests left. But without anyone noticing, it had been plugged into a switched outlet, and the wall switch that controlled it was turned off. Presto! Mike turned on the wall switch, and the TV began blaring the baseball game, complete with a crisp picture and clear sound.

The cable customers were embarrassed about having put Mike to all that trouble just to correct their own dumb mistake. They were appreciative, too. Now, you might think that Mike went way overboard and did far too much, considering the circumstances. Way back in the parking lot, Mike could tell from the woman's description of her situation that this probably was not a cable problem. Anyway, the account was only worth about $15 per month, and Mike had much more important responsibilities as the plant manager for the whole city's operation.

Although the couple sent Mike a letter of apology and appreciation, Group W's big payoff came months later. When Group W increased its programming from 26 to 42 channels, they had to seek approval from the local Public Utilities Commission Cable Council to increase basic subscriber rates accordingly. This always involves a public hearing, including statements and input from customers, who are rarely supportive. When any public utility seeks a rate increase, there's usually a long line of vocal citizens sounding off about how they're already overcharged and poorly served. But this hearing was different. The woman Mike had first encountered as she hollered and cursed in the parking lot was the first citizen who lined up to offer her comments.

She spoke sincerely and passionately about how wonderful Group W's cable service was. She recounted the parking lot incident and offered her own experience as an example of how service-oriented the company was. She had not been asked to appear and speak. She was there because she was grateful to have had Mike's attention when she needed it.

Her little speech was persuasive enough to help convince the cable council that Group W deserved its rate increase, and the request was granted. The revenue increase for Group W amounted to hundreds of thousands of dollars annually for that one community. Take 14,000 customers, increase their monthly bills by $1.50 monthly, and pretty soon you're talking about $252,000 a year.

It may seem that the treatment of a single cable TV customer is relatively unimportant. But what if that one customer's account were worth $50,000 per month, rather than $15 or $20? Since the cable TV industry has largely become deregulated, they've gotten into the telephone business, and cable TV companies now compete directly with the local phone companies that have languished for decades in monopolistic environments. A single commercial customer who uses its local cable TV company to provide a DS3 circuit for telephone and video communications can easily be worth more than $250,000 in revenues annually. Even a retail store that has background music piped in via a coaxial cable like the one that comes to your home may be paying a monthly charge of $600.

Mike explains that one of his main challenges in his current position at TCI, the world's largest cable TV company, is wiping out the "send-out-the-truck" mentality. As at most companies, hardened bill collectors tend to lack patience and act harshly when customers miss payments. In some companies' collections departments, the battle cry is "Close their account," or "Hold all future shipments," or "Have their car repossessed," or "Foreclose the mortgage." In the cable TV industry, it's often "Send out the truck," meaning, "Dispatch a service truck to disconnect the customer's TV cable and retrieve the converter box." But what about that clothing store that has a $6000 music system installed by the cable TV company? When a payment is late, should the company rip out the equipment and forfeit the monthly $600 payments? Should it cut off a commercial customer's phone system and lose $50,000 per month? Of course not.

What Can You Learn from This Example?   Whether you're han-dling a $15 a month cable TV account or a $50,000 commercial commu-nications account, dealing with the company's smallest customer or its largest, the long-term value of the customer relationship is what counts. When a customer says he or she won't pay your bill, it's all too easy—and too common—to slip into a confrontation. The normal ten-dency to judge quickly and act harshly when a customer is slow or late with payments can be very costly, because it necessitates the greater expense of replacing that revenue stream with a new customer, who may or may not be any better. It's worth taking extra steps to salvage a long-standing relationship, even when it means driving out to a cable subscriber's home when you're pretty sure the problem is not your company's fault.

Using a Positive Partnering Approach Pays Off

It seems that most companies view customers who are behind on their payments as adversaries rather than partners. Remember, these are the people who pay our salaries and can make our organizations profitable. In fact, the profit contributions of accounts receivable departments are more highly leveraged than others, including sales. Once the product has been sold or the service rendered, the primary cost components have already been expended. You've gone to the trouble of prospecting, selling, closing, fulfilling, and billing. Now, the accounts receivable department can either lose all of those expenditures by letting the account be written off, or secure payment and reinforce the relationship so there will be many more future transactions.

Example

US WEST Cellular's "Friendly but Firm" Approach

Use a term like "bad account" with Scott Tweedy, major accounts supervisor at US WEST Cellular, and he'll stop you in midsentence.

> We don't have "bad accounts" here. We just have some customers who need friendly but firm attention.

His team's success stories are legion. One custom home builder, for example, had 27 separate cellular phones in various vehicles but fell on hard times when the construction market in his area dried up. The account was in serious trouble and was on the verge of being written off and turned over to a collection agency. In such cases, the payoff is usually about 30 cents on the dollar after collection costs are accounted for. Today, though, that same company has 42 active phones and hasn't been late on a single payment for over six months.

Scott identifies one key to successful collections as the underlying fundamental belief that most customers are sincere and honest. Many are simply confused about something and others have some problem unrelated to the bill that needs attention. The second key is US WEST Cellular's constant reinforcement of this positive attitude. The collectors sit in front of their computer keyboards all day with their hands resting on little cushioned wrist pads. Each pad carries four messages silk-screened into the surface:

1. Say, "I'm calling to confirm."

2. Show empathy.

3. Fact-find.

4. Be friendly but firm.

Collectors always begin their calls with the phrase, "I'm calling to confirm that you've sent your payment of $xx.xx to cover this month's cellular phone bill." Scott puts it this way:

> If your friend borrows twenty dollars from you at lunch on Monday, and by Friday still hasn't mentioned it, you start to feel uncomfortable. It's awkward to say, "Hey, uh, Toby, what about the twenty bucks?" So you put it off for a few days. Meanwhile, you're feeling uneasy, and your friend's recollection is fading. You need an icebreaker to bring the subject up. Well, imagine sitting in front of a computer all day, calling about 150 people who owe your company money. You *really* need an icebreaker. We find that the "Calling to confirm" phrase works well because it's non-judgmental, and it starts the call off on a positive note. After all, we want to begin by assuming that they have honored their obligations, and the payment is just delayed in the mail or held up in their accounting department.

The "show empathy" motto is important too. After all, the people who owe you money are just people, often facing the same types of situations you face. If Scott calls someone who says, "Well, no, I haven't sent in my payment because my car broke down and the repairs have been pretty expensive. I'm a little short this month," he's *not* going to respond, "Well, tough luck, buddy. You still have to pay your bill!" Through constant reinforcement, the habit of empathizing almost becomes second nature: "Well, I can understand your situation. I've had expensive car repairs myself, and I know it can throw your budget out of whack in a hurry."

Of course, the collector isn't going to leave it at that. ("Be friendly, *but firm*"):

> "How much short are you of the balance in full?" or, "Shall we put this on a credit card?" or, "Can you borrow the money?" or, "Let's make an agreement on a payment plan that will protect your credit with us."

In other words, the collector will always move ahead to show that US WEST Cellular takes past due bills seriously but wants to work with their customers. Scott told me:

> As collectors with a commitment to customer service, loy-alty, and retention, we know that the cellular billing is not the most important bill to the customer. We have to "get in

line" behind other creditors. Our behavior while in this line has a big impact on customer loyalty and in my opinion is as important as the decision to purchase our service at the moment of the sale. Does it make sense to have a cellular phone if you don't first make your house payment, car payment, and feed your family? Obviously not! It's our job at this point to resell the value of our service and help the customer find ways to get the bill paid.

We once suggested to a customer that he borrow from his life insurance policy to pay the bill. He did, and we kept his service on. He was able to continue communications and got an important call from a client the next day that resulted in a commission worth several thousand dollars from a real estate sale. The customer called us back to thank us for helping him find this solution since he was able to pay back his insurance loan and got a referral from the real estate sale that he felt was also a hot lead. He said he owed it all to us. Meanwhile his bill was growing, and his ability to pay it has improved significantly!

"Fact-find" reminds the collector to do a little investigating and find out what's behind the failure to pay in a timely manner. It's quite common for customers to hold their bill hostage. They want some attention, and not paying the bill is a good way to get it.

Scott recalls a customer who stated that he wasn't going to pay the bill because the service was so lousy. Immediately, the phone representative set about finding the facts. The customer explained that there was so much static during calls that he could hardly communicate at all. So the rep probed to find out where this was happening. Cellular phone companies keep detailed maps showing problem areas so that they can examine the coverage there and consider the installation of additional cell sites. In this customer's case, the area where he was having trouble was a location where everyone else's phones worked fine. In the end, the collector surmised that the cause of the trouble was the phone itself and arranged for the customer to take it in to a repair center for a free tune-up. Sure enough, it turned out that the phone's built-in antenna was defective. The customer had certainly been enduring poor-quality service, but through no fault of US WEST Cellular. Since one of the collector's fundamental aims was to fact-find, the customer's service was improved, and he's now getting top-quality service and happily paying his bills each month.

A collection call from US WEST Cellular is nothing like the typical threatening, heavy-handed dunning call many other companies place. Scott stresses the need to begin and end every call on a positive note. When the negotiation is concluded and an agreement has been reached, every collector asks one more question: "What else can I do for you today?" It's surprising how often the customer does have another concern that would have gone unexpressed. It may be an area of confusion: "Actually, now that you ask, I don't understand this six-dollar charge on page two of the bill. I've noticed it before, too. What's that for?" Once it's explained, the customer is usually much more cooperative and forthcoming with future payments.

Every call ends with the same friendly close: "Thank you very much. We really appreciate your business." Every collector knows that his livelihood depends on keeping customers satisfied (and paying!) over the long haul. Once again, lifetime value comes into play. US WEST Cellular doesn't want to reveal its specifics, but you can bet they're even higher than the industry average of a 30-month life span, with average monthly billings of $70, or a customer value of about $2100.

What Can You Learn from This Example?   Making collections calls is tough work that can be emotionally draining. Anyone who does it for a living needs constant reinforcement in order to maintain a positive attitude. US WEST's wrist pad reminder is an excellent example of how you can be creative in driving a positive message home over and over again. Odds are that your collectors are using computer terminals or PCs in their work. Consider having periodic reminders flash on the screen to keep them focused on the long-term goal of keeping customer relationships alive and profitable. Come up with your own nonjudgmental icebreaker to start the call in a positive direction. Empathize with customers so you'll understand what their situation is and be able to help with creative solutions. Find out the facts behind the slow payments. Be friendly but firm.

Quickstep Partnering with Slow-Pay and No-Pay Customers

As each example has shown, the best way to handle any customer who's behind on his payments is to treat him as a valuable asset whose continued profitable patronage is your overriding goal. Each collector who comes into contact should treat the customer with friendly respect and should be focused on discovering the facts necessary to understand the problem, so that your company can help solve it and *keep the customer*.

Take Action Early

Move quickly! Problems escalate when action is delayed. At the earliest sign that a payment is delayed, make personal contact. A confirming telephone call is best, because it can easily move into a fact-finding call if necessary. Most people and companies get into financial difficulty gradually. Get in line as early as you possibly can. You'll do more than establish an important legal precedent. You'll also begin building a personal relationship based on mutually kept agreements. Later, when things may get much worse for the debtor, you want to be getting special attention from him. You don't want to be lumped in with all the others who eventually start making contact late in the game after several mailed reminders have been ignored.

Your First-Contact Goal

In addition to getting paid, you're out to achieve a subtle goal during the first call. You want this customer to know that although other companies may be lax in their tracking of customers' accounts, you are not. Make sure that your customer knows that you are personally involved and that you notice what's going on with his account. In that first contact, begin with the "confirming" approach. Then move into fact-finding if the payment has not already been sent. Overall, you want the customer to know that you'll be paying careful attention.

It all comes down to that customer's stack of bills. You want the customer to put yours on top of the stack for payment as soon as possible, every time. The goal of the first contact is to get your bill separated out from the others so that it gets special, prompt attention.

And then of course, you want a commitment to act. As the call proceeds, aim for a specific agreement about what you'll both do next. After negotiating the payment plan, get the customer to repeat back, in his own words, what his understanding of your agreement is. Again, you want this customer to know that other creditors may be sloppy about their agreements, but you're going to be very conscientious about securing and monitoring them. Once you've agreed on the commitment, end the call on a positive note, as they do at US WEST Cellular, so that the customer knows you value the relationship and want it to continue.

It's especially important in the early stages of a negotiation to follow up and reinforce the agreement. Put it in writing and fax or mail a copy immediately. If the customer has promised to mail a check on the fifteenth, call on the fourteenth to remind him. And then, when you receive the check, call to reward and reinforce the behavior. If the relationship is going to go sour and require other means of collection, you want to know as early as possible. On the other hand, what you really want to do is contact, negotiate, remind, and reinforce at the first sign of difficulty, before the relationship deteriorates seriously.

The way your organization handles customers who are behind on their payments makes a dramatic difference to your bottom line. If you choose an attentive, prompt, respectful, friendly but firm approach, you can get them back on your conveyor belt and enjoy the benefits and profits of a long-term relationship.

What Can You Learn from This Chapter?

- Getting paid is the second most important objective of an effective accounts receivable strategy. Maintaining long and profitable relationships is the first.

- It's essential to purge prejudicial labels such as "deadbeat" or "flaky customer" because they perpetuate negative thinking among collectors.

- Heavy-handed collections approaches are only rarely successful at getting payments, but fairly good at creating hostile, vindictive customers.

- Calculating a customer's "lifetime value" usually yields a surprisingly large figure and dramatizes the value of retaining good, positive relationships with customers.

- Listening between the lines is one of an effective collector's most valuable skills.

- Many customers who pay late or not at all are trying to tell your company that they need to be resold on the value of your product and/or service.

- Collectors themselves must be sold on your product or service before they can effectively resell delinquent customers.

- Most organizations completely overlook the least costly, most profitable collection tactic: positive reinforcement for those customers who honor their agreements.

- It's best to begin collection calls with a positive confirmation statement such as, "I'm calling to confirm that you have sent in this month's payment."

- Personal empathy goes a long way toward creating rapport between the collector and the customer.

- The collector's initial role is to be a fact finder and determine why the payments in question haven't come in as agreed. It's necessary to really understand the factors that contribute to the situation before setting out to create a solution.

- It's important to be friendly, and it's no less important to be firm. An approach that balances both considerations works best.

- For best results, take positive action quickly at the very first sign that a customer may be slacking off in making timely payments.

Action Summary
What You Can Do *Now*

- Purge negative terms from your accounts receivable vocabulary. Eliminate judgmental words like *deadbeat,* starting with the top level of management, and going right down to every single collector.

- Post prominent visual displays reminding your team of the derogatory words that are inappropriate.

- Consider an incentive contest that rewards representatives as they progress in their effort to eliminate negative terms from their vocabulary.

- Calculate the lifetime value for your customers and discount it to a net present value figure. This value is important in settling complaints, and it's just as important in determining what your collection strategies will be.

- Treat customers in a way that will make them *want* to make payments to you as soon as they're able to. Develop a respectful, cooperative attitude, and let it show.

- Foster conveyor-belt thinking among collectors so that they view the person they're writing to or phoning as a tangible asset teetering on the edge of your conveyor belt. How they handle the situation determines whether the customer will fall off or not.

- Make sure that your collections staff are sold on your product or service themselves. They can't resell it if *they* aren't sold on it themselves. Give them products to use at home; provide them with the same services your customers get.

- Provide your collectors with creative sales training so that they'll be well equipped to handle objections and ask for the order when customers need to be resold.

- Institute a program to resell your customers every time you send them a request for payment. Remind them of the benefits they're receiving when they pay you.

- Implement a positive-reinforcement calling policy so that your collectors can have the pleasure of calling with appreciation and good news at least some of the time.

- Reevaluate your payoff for turning accounts over to a collection agency. Is it really worth it? What about the public relations costs? What's a better way to rekindle the relationship and recoup your investment?

- Look for a way to constantly remind collectors about the positive attitude you want them to project. Could you provide silk-screened wrist pads like the ones used at US WEST Cellular?

- Provide your collectors with suggested icebreaker openings to use with delinquent customers.

- Suggest that representatives ask a question offering customers additional help before ending the call. Wrap up with an expression of appreciation.

- Accelerate the timing of the first contact. Eliminate any procedures that delay personal contact. Review your monitoring systems to be certain that they alert you to possible difficulties at the very earliest sign.

3
The Silence
Is Killing You

It's easy to spot some customers who are falling off your conveyor belt. You feel the brunt of their vocal complaints, or you notice that they've stopped paying their bills. It's much more difficult to detect the far more common behavior of customers whose loyalty is slipping. They just quietly fade away. But their absence has an impact: their departures hurt your profitability.

By far the greatest number of customers who stop doing business with any company do so without a fuss. They don't refuse to pay or write a nasty letter to the president or call up and curse at a customer service representative. They simply stop buying.

It's a shame that most business organizations aren't set up to even notice when this happens. Everyone is so busy chasing new customers and dealing with the vocal complainers and slow-paying deadbeats, that customers who quietly stop buying just slip through the cracks.

Most Relationships Wither from Neglect

In the late 1980s, a study surfaced that purported to explain why customers stop buying. It listed the following statistics:

- 1 percent die
- 3 percent move away

- 5 percent develop relationships with other suppliers
- 9 percent have competitive reasons
- 14 percent feel product dissatisfaction
- *68 percent sense sellers' indifferent attitudes*

Although I've heard many speakers refer to these figures, they all say they've just "seen the study somewhere," but don't know the real source. Yet each and every one of them has accepted the figures as legitimate. I eventually tracked down the original study and found that the source was actually the Wisconsin Restaurant Association. Not exactly a research organization of global importance or gold-standard statistical validity. Still, the figures sound about right for any business. Why quibble with the exact statistics? The key conclusion strikes many of us as valid: *Most customers leave our conveyor belts because we don't show them how important they are.*

This is a good time to point out one of the most important, consistent conclusions drawn by the direct marketing industry in the last decade: Practically speaking, *there's no upper limit to customers' tolerance for increased attention.* Catalogue mailers find that the more frequently they mail you their catalogues, the more orders you will place. These people are very scientific about their business and are constantly testing. If you're receiving frequent mailings from certain marketers, you may be sure that they're not just pumping out mail because they like to print the stuff. They send it because it works. Now, there probably *is* an upper limit at some point. You don't want to get a *daily* Lillian Vernon catalog, but the reason you get as many as you do is that researchers are constantly tracking the returns and they find that the more they send out, the more people buy.

Or, to put it another way, *most of your customers will probably respond positively to increased levels of attention from your company.* Think about the people who sell things to *you.* Are there any who give you too much attention? Aren't there plenty who you would buy more from, if they were more attentive to your needs?

If We're Really Partners, Why Don't We Listen More?

I don't know the answer to this one. Are marketers lazy, self-centered, too busy chasing after new customers, or just not excited about the prospect of stimulating a customer's eightieth repeat purchase? Maybe it's all of the above. Whatever the reasons, we marketers give our customers far too little attention. They don't necessarily notice the lack of it. There probably aren't legions of customers out there saying, "Well, if ABC, Inc., won't call me or mail to me more often, I'll boycott them!" They just silently slip away. Since we haven't actively encouraged them to feel a strong partnership bond with us, they feel little loyalty. They have ideas, suggestions, referrals, unsatisfied needs, and probably some service complaints that they'd be glad to tell us about if we asked and listened. But we seem to be both deaf and uninterested.

Playing Deaf Is Dumb

Most of the deafness companies display in relationships with their customers is accidental and unintentional. A few companies, however, do seem to shut out customer input intentionally. This is both deaf *and* dumb—and very costly in the long run.

Example

A Cruise Liner's Crew Plugs Its Ears

While writing *Upside-Down Marketing*, I attended a humor seminar sponsored by the National Speakers Association on board a very well-known cruise line. During the weekend Bahamas voyage, passengers were presented time and again with an extreme example of what happens when you don't listen to your customers. The situation wasn't meant to be funny, though it certainly turned out to be laughable.

Soon after boarding the vessel, the cruise director's voice came across the loudspeakers beckoning all passengers to make their way to the ballroom for the orientation lecture. Although this was touted as an educational session meant to help us get the most out of our cruise experience, it was really about the following three suggestions: "Buy our trinkets," "Don't forget to generously tip the crew," and "Give us high ratings on your cruise evaluation cards."

Throughout the cruise, passengers were frequently reminded of this advice. The instructions about the evaluation cards particularly caught my interest. The cruise director, in his "Welcome Aboard" lecture to all the passengers, said, "Don't let any negative experiences you may have affect the ratings you give the crew." Now, does that make sense to you? Passengers looked at each other quizzically, wondering if they'd heard him right. Just to clarify any possible confusion, the cruise staff left a little instruction card in every cabin on the next-to-last day of the cruise. Again, the same odd instructions: "Don't let any negative experience affect your ratings."

On the afternoon before we returned to Miami, we were all summoned again to the main ballroom for an "important lecture" about the disembarkation procedures. This, too, turned out to be a final pitch to buy T-shirts and coasters, as well as a reminder that the evaluation forms were very important. The cruise director went on at great length about how hard the crew had worked and how many of them had families who depended on their meager wages (*Tip the poor crew generously!*). He also offered a strange little discourse on semantics. He explained that the cruise industry uses a terminology different from that used by other businesses. *Good*, he pointed out, really means *fair* in the cruise business, so you should actually check *good* even if your cruise experience was only *fair*. (I know you think I'm making this up, but there were hundreds of witnesses!)

At the final dinner, the waiter at each table came around to say "Thank you" while conspicuously picking up the little gratuity envelopes that had been placed in our cabins the evening before and delivering one last lecture about not letting a bad meal or service experience affect our ratings.

The most remarkable thing was that passengers at tables throughout the dining room heard virtually the same exhortation. Since I was cruising with a large group of friends and colleagues, we compared our experiences. It's clear that this was no coincidence. Somebody had coached all the waiters and told them exactly what to say at their tables after the last dinner. Somebody had obviously taught them the script:

> The word *good* has a very different meaning in the cruise business. It means only average. So, if you want to indicate that your experience was a good one, you should mark *excellent* to make the meaning clear. Now, we try our best to serve food that will please everybody, but if you have had a couple of meals you didn't like, please don't let that affect your rating. You can write that separately at the bottom of the form. If you don't feel that you can mark *excellent*, it's best to just leave the rating section blank and write in your comment at the bottom.

I was amazed at how blatant all these comments had been, and thought the senior management of the cruise line company should know that many of their passengers had been offended by or had openly laughed at the crew's instructions. I went to the purser's office and asked for the company president's mailing address. His response was, "For what reason?" I answered that I wanted to send a letter to management. The purser asked, "A positive or negative letter?"

This I really couldn't believe. I said that it was none of his business, and that I was merely asking for the address. He stepped away and disappeared into a back room, and two or three minutes later, someone else came out to take his place, informing me that, "No negative letters should be sent to the president," since a different department handled complaints, and the president shouldn't be bothered. I thought, "Yeah, I'll bet the department is in that little round trash can right under your desk."

I must confess that I never did follow through and write to the president. I found myself living out the TARP statistics we reviewed back in Chapter 1. I'm part of the 95 percent who don't successfully reach the people who should hear their complaints. But I *have* told this story to many people, and I'm sure it hasn't helped the cruise company's sales. (For legal reasons, I've omitted the company's name, but I have sent a copy of this book to its president.)

What Can You Learn from This Example? Top management in any organization must stay in touch with its customers in order to know how they feel about the company's performance. But contrary to popular belief, a survey is *not* always a surefire way to find out what your customers really think. In fact, surveys can, if handled poorly enough, ensure that management *never* finds out what the customers really think. The management of the cruise ship made certain that the management of the company heard only inflated, positive reports. When confronted with the possibility that one of the passengers (me!) might actually reach the home office with a different story, every possible hurdle was erected, right down to refusing to divulge the mailing address.

I've talked with several other cruise takers about my experience, and they report having had similar experiences with the same very popular cruise company. We've concluded that their employees must be treated horribly. It's likely that their future employment prospects are dependent on those ratings. They're probably all frightened that they'll lose their jobs and not be able to get other ones.

Management may have had good intentions in linking employment security and other rewards to customer feedback, but the current system doesn't work. If *you* have such a system linking employee advancement to customer ratings, be certain that it's really helping to open communications between you and your customers, rather than shutting them down.

Most Silence Is Unintended

By far the most common reason for customer silence is that we're just too busy to focus on our current relationships. And ironically, what dominates most organizations' attention is the endless, relentless pursuit of new customers. It's easy to get so caught up in the quest that we fail to properly nurture existing relationships with our current customers. In fact, we sometimes ignore them until they no longer buy, and in doing so, we shove them off our conveyor belts as if it's their fault that the relationship has faded away.

Example

Graphic Controls Mines Gold from Tailings

The customer category name said it all: *To be purged.* But Jim Dombrowski, Graphic Controls' newly promoted information products division manager of U.S. telesales had other ideas. It just didn't strike Jim as logical that the numerous accounts that were classified as inactive and about to be purged from the company's database really could be totally worthless. Like a miner looking at a heap of tailings from a once-profitable mine, Jim thought, "I'll bet there's still some gold in there."

There's great value in using a fresh perspective to question established—but not necessarily logical—business practices. Jim's boss, Vice President and General Manager Bob Evans, had long questioned the company's practice of designating inactive customers as *zero-dollar accounts.* As Jim moved over from Graphic Controls' Medical Products Division and assumed his new role working under Bob's wing, he, too, began to raise questions about the quarterly to-be-purged report. The latest version he was presented with flagged over 3000 customers whom the company's mainframe computer database software had identified as *nonpertinent.* They were just about to be zapped—totally deleted from the database.

Jim was just plain curious, and he had a hunch. "If these customers *used* to buy from us, couldn't some of them buy again if we gave them a little attention?"

Jim sought Bob Evans's approval for a test program to undertake a reactivation campaign. Although the company had about 64,000 active accounts, Jim's interest was aroused by something about the inactive ones: their potential. His boss also thought it was worth trying.

Instead of guessing why these accounts had become inactive, Jim set out to contact each of them by phone and find out exactly what had caused the decline and cessation in their purchasing activity.

Tracking historical sales reports, he found that the to-be-purged accounts had collectively generated $485,000 in revenue in 1990 but that in 1991, their collective activity amounted to zero dollars. In the first nine months of 1992, these former customers had still made no purchases at all. So, in November of 1992, Jim's small team of six telesales reps started calling. For the next three months, they kept careful track of the results.

While some of the contacts had gone out of business or for some other reason were no longer prospects, the number one explanation, representing by far the majority of inactive customers was "lack of attention from Graphic Controls." Lots of the smaller customers had gotten no attention at all after placing initial orders, but that hadn't stopped their businesses from growing. Now many had become much more sizable prospective customers.

The bottom line was that 378 of the 3414 accounts that were contacted during the test—11 percent—had placed orders by year end! These purchases amounted to more than $87,000; 20 percent of the accounts were eventually reactivated, and the conservatively projected annual business from these customers could amount to $350,000. Not a bad return for a solid hunch. Had Jim and Bob not decided to experiment and take personal initiative to intervene, the computer would have simply deleted these zero-dollar ex-customers.

True enough, 15 to 20 percent of the former customers had gone out of business or changed their businesses in such a way that they were no longer potential customers. But the telemarketers quite frequently encountered reactions like, "We wondered what had happened to you guys," and "We didn't know you manufactured those types of supplies."

One small engineering firm, for example, had purchased just $200 worth of Graphic Controls' colored pens for their one relatively primitive small plotter back in 1990 and nothing since. By now though, unbeknown to Graphic Controls, business was booming for the engineers. Just prior to the reactivation call, the firm had purchased three top-of-the-line electrostatic machines for blueprint reproductions. These machines have voracious appetites for the exact type of consumable supplies that Graphic Controls markets. This customer had no idea that Graphic Controls could help them with their supplies for the new machines. That one account alone generated $2500 in just one year.

An Ohio tool and die manufacturer had stopped buying because Graphic Controls' credit department had cut the company off. It owed $600 and wanted to change its payment terms. Instead of listening and adjusting, Graphic Controls had automatically turned the account over to three successive collection agencies during the following two years. Shown a little personal attention and corporate flexibility, the customer was happy to begin buying again. The first year's sales were $1300. A more important reward than the sales, though, was that, in listening to its customers, Graphic Controls had learned that it needed more flexibility and sensitivity in its credit department.

One of the telesales reps, Nadine Robbins, recounted a typical example. A small Kansas City religious publisher had originally purchased about $100 worth of fax paper but nothing since. The account was categorized as zero-dollar. But when Nadine called, she talked with the new purchasing agent and immediately took an order for laser printer cartridges. Annual revenue for the account is now projected at $5200 per year.

Another rep, Dan Geary, called a Massachusetts company that had placed just one small order for plotter pens before being classed as zero-dollar. After asking a few questions, Dan found that they had recently acquired a $50,000 laser plotter. The firm now buys $2800 to $3000 in laser supplies from Graphic Controls annually.

The examples went on and on. All had one theme in common. If you take an order from someone and then give the customer zero follow-up attention, the computer will eventually classify the account as zero-dollar and set about purging it. However, if you make direct personal contact, ask good questions, and listen, you can often reactivate a potentially valuable account.

Aside from the pure economic boon this reactivation campaign generated, Jim Dombrowski was surprised at how happy the customers and telesales reps alike felt about the calls. Rarely were the customers annoyed about being contacted; most were genuinely pleased and welcomed the attention. The telesales reps felt particularly good about making the calls.

What Can You Learn from This Example?   Questioning "the way we've always done it" can be highly profitable. In fact, after seeing the success of this test, Graphic Controls adopted "Make the Change" as the theme for its next annual sales meeting. When you have a hunch that your organization is missing opportunities, follow up on it as Jim did. If you don't, illogical practices are likely to continue.

Contacting inactive accounts is beneficial to your customers as well as to your company. The engineering firm with the electrostatic printers, for example, was delighted to hear that Graphic Controls could help it with the new hard-to-find supply items. Rather than feeling reluctant or annoyed, other customers were enthusiastic about ordering again.

In the past, few companies kept an accurate current accounting of their customers' activity. With the advent of customer-tracking software, it has become easy and more common to track activity and note who your most valuable customers are. A few companies have even taken the next step and identified their inactive accounts. But very, very few have done anything to give them appropriate attention instead of simply purging them from the system.

The High Costs of Plugging Your Ears

The costs associated with insulating your organization from your customers, intentionally or not, are many, and the practice may threaten your firm's economic survival if permitted to continue.

The Opportunity Cost of Silence

One of the most valuable concepts I learned in business school was that of opportunity costs. Although a course of action you or your organization choose may cost nothing in terms of hard dollars, your cost in terms of *opportunities lost* may be staggering. This concept refers to the revenues and profits that you forgo by *not* exploiting potential opportunities. When you're out of touch with your customers, you're missing out on opportunities, and those costs may be huge.

Product Improvements

One of the most common benefits of providing maximum exposure to and dialogue with your customers is the opportunity to improve your products, based on customers' input. More and more, I'm noticing that the most progressive marketers take every opportunity to solicit input. In many cases, the product is really a service. For example, I'm an avid Price Costco shopper. I love those huge warehouses full of 36-roll packs of toilet paper and 24-container boxes of yogurt. I even have much of my business printing handled there. On one recent visit, I was informed that the order forms I wanted to have duplicated would take seven working days. That's usually fast enough, but in this case, I was in a hurry. I said, "I'll bet that if you offered an express service, plenty of customers would be willing to pay a 10 percent or 20 percent premium to get their jobs back faster when they're in a hurry." Instead of shrugging his shoulders and apologizing, the Price Costco employee handed me a form preaddressed to the store manager and jotted down a summary of my thoughts so he could present them orally at the next staff meeting.

The fact is, few customers will take the time to write out their suggestions, so I recommend that Price Costco, and your company, improve this dialogue process by making it even easier for customers to submit their improvement suggestions. Why not institute a 24-hour suggestion line, using a simple answering machine or voice mail system, to make it easy for your customers to report their ideas as they think of them?

One of the nation's top ten insurance companies, The Principal Financial Group, heard its customers complaining that their life insurance settlements would be useless to them after they died. Some were diagnosed with terminal illnesses and they wanted to make that last trip to Hawaii *now*, while they still could, as well as arrange for expensive medical treatment during their remaining weeks or months of life.

The Principal listened and improved its life insurance policies, offering an "accelerated death benefit." With appropriate medical documentation, The Principal's policyholders can now receive a high percentage of their death benefit within just a few days.

Group health plans are an important part of The Principal's business, too. Customers told the company that private doctors seemed more happy to treat patients whose insurance companies paid claims quickly, so The Principal revamped its payment processes to increase speed and accuracy, resulting in happier physicians and group policy clients who are very happy to be The Principal's customers.

Process Glitches

This same accessibility technique will work to smooth processes as well as improve products. I'm always amazed at the hurdles and roadblocks businesses throw up that make it more difficult for customers to buy from them. Again, most customers won't take the time to tell you about the improvements you need to make; they'll simply buy elsewhere.

Rather than passively waiting for ideas, why not demonstrate your partnership with customers by calling them? Ask how you can improve the way you serve them. The *way* you ask can be as important as the *fact* that you ask. I recommend that you banish any question that can be answered with a simple "Yes" or "No." You're not going to turn up many useful ideas if you phone customers and say:

> I'm calling to see if you have any ideas for how we could improve our service to you. Is there anything you've noticed since becoming our customer that you think we should change?

It's much more effective to ask the question in a way that *presumes* there are areas in which you could improve:

> I'm calling you today to find out how we can do a better job of serving you. You've been doing business with us for a couple of months now, and you've probably found that there are a few areas in which we could improve. I'd be really grateful for your input, as my colleagues and I always want to do our very best to serve you well. What's the first thing that comes to mind when you think about areas we need to work on a little harder?

Competitive Moves

Your customers are probably being courted by your competitors right now. If you've done a good enough job of partnering and encouraging an open dialogue with them, they're in the perfect position to alert you to competitive inroads and offerings. Airborne Express, for example, keeps tabs on Federal Express and UPS through its customers. When they call to arrange for shipments, customers often mention new services offered by Airborne's competitors and say, "Hey, why don't you guys have something like that?" But Airborne doesn't just sit back and wait for these competitive intelligence calls; they also proactively contact their customers through a telesales group that's trained to find out which competitive offerings are most appealing to customers so that Airborne's marketing managers can plot their competitive responses and stay out in front.

New Product Development

In the early 1990s, Time-Life launched a video series entitled *Trials of Life*. Television commercials promoting the series included very dramatic footage of a shark attack that practically made you jump back from your set and start experiencing *Jaws* flashbacks. More than a million people purchased the series, and soon after doing so, they got a call from a Time-Life Libraries telemarketing representative asking them about their reactions to the videos. The vast majority loved them, and bought follow-up videos in the series, but a significant percentage were disappointed. Dan Meyerson, president of Time-Life Libraries told me:

> It was amazing how many people related to that shark attack and wanted more graphic scenes. The *Trials of Life* series includes loads of fantastic nature footage, but that's not what some of these people wanted. They didn't care about how birds communicate by using sophisticated chirping patterns. They were looking for more action. So we used that feedback and immediately went into production on a whole new series, called *Predators*. Now, this is definitely *not* family viewing material. If you want to see raw, no-holds-barred animal survival in the wild, this is it. Within six months of its launch, *Predators* was already accounting for 20 percent of our telemarketing sales!

Dan's telemarketers *want to know* how their customers react to the programs they buy. They don't view customers' dissatisfaction as complaining; it's simply valuable product feedback that helps tell Time-Life marketers what customers want in the future. And because the company is definitely seeking long-term repeat-purchase customer relationships, there's never a question about refunding a customer's money if a program doesn't meet his or her expectations.

Time-Life Libraries is hugely successful because it delivers exactly what customers want. When entertainment buyers show their love of 1950s and 1960s music by buying hundreds of thousands of CDs, Time-Life notices, asks them what else they'd enjoy, and creates new products accordingly. The company listens to its customers, and it pays.

Missed Complaints

Right now, you may well have customers who are unhappy with your products and/or services. If they don't complain to you, they'll take their business somewhere else instead and may even speak negatively about your organization to others. But if they *do* complain directly to you, you're way ahead of the game. You can probably keep that customer *and* neutralize any possible negative publicity. And just as important, you can learn about whatever deficiency caused the dissatisfaction and fix it.

In Chapter 2, you read about US WEST Cellular's use of friendly but firm collection techniques. They've also done a marvelous job of encouraging complaints. Cellular coverage can be spotty, and the company depends on its customers to help direct technical attention to problem areas where improved coverage is needed. Their service guarantee stresses their immediate, 100 percent money-back commitment that you will be happy with the quality of your cellular call. If you're not, they *encourage* you to call customer service and request credit. You don't need to fill out any forms, write any letters, or even talk to anybody. Just punch in *-6-1-1 on your cellular phone, and you'll hear a series of prompts asking you to key in the number of minutes you want credit for. After the system automatically confirms that your account has been credited and tells you the amount of your credit, it also asks you to respond to a series of questions: "When you experienced the poor-quality call, what was the nearest street intersection or landmark?" "What type of phone are you using?" "What kind of problem did you have?" US WEST Cellular wants to hear customers' complaints, so it makes it extremely easy for customers to register them. After all, that's the only way its representatives can find out where they should improve their coverage.

US WEST doesn't just sit back and wait for your complaints, though. It also nurtures relationships by periodically calling its customers to find out about their service concerns. A team of specialists is dedicated to making proactive contact with customers, and the program has been extremely successful. The representatives have an opportunity to uncover unasked questions, educate customers about how they can get more value from their phone service, and probe for service concerns or complaints.

Don't miss out on your opportunity to establish an active dialogue with your customers. Encourage them to tell you their complaints, their ideas for improvements, and their suggestions for new products.

Listening Aggressively

Sometimes customers need to be helped along in sharing their ideas with you so that you *can* listen to them. I think of this as *aggressive listening*. It makes a lot of sense to contact your customers so you'll have something to listen to, instead of just being satisfied with silence.

Example

Bankers Profit from Aggressive
Listening

During his years as a senior marketing executive at a leading regional bank, John Bartholomew proved without question that upside-down marketing works. Now he's gone on to found his own Seattle-based firm, TeleMark Financial Group, to help others put upside-down marketing principles into practice in their own organizations.

John's use of upside-down marketing at the bank was designed to impact several stages of customers' relationships with the bank from end to beginning. For starters, bank management realized that customers who closed their accounts and left the institution were cutting deeply into profits. So John's outbound telemarketing sales team was charged with the responsibility of calling customers who had recently closed their accounts. Their aim was to coax customers back into the fold. But while the reps were usually able to find out why the customers had closed their accounts in the first place, they weren't very successful at getting them reopened.

The reason was plain. They were calling when it was too late. By the time the bank realized that customers had left, they had already been warmly welcomed by another bank and weren't about to change their minds again. They'd left the first bank for good reason, and were usually willing to explain their reasons when the phone representative called to ask.

When the reps probed to find out why these customers had left the bank, they turned up some helpful information, none of which came as much of a surprise. Most of the time customers complained about incidents involving bad service or noncompetitive pricing, such as high fees for returned checks. Sometimes they offered suggestions for improvement that the bank was then able to implement. For example, ex-customers frequently noted that they felt they had been treated impersonally and would have preferred a "personal banker" relationship. When the bank's management considered this feedback, they realized that they had set arbitrary criteria for assigning personal bankers. For example, if your account had a balance of $10,000, you were assigned a personal banker whether you wanted one or not. This wasn't the best approach. Some customers had very large loans as well as substantial deposits at another bank, but because they had small savings balances, they weren't considered eligible for a personal banker assignment. The feedback from John's calling program showed that these customers could be induced to move more of their funds to John's bank if they were offered a personal banker relationship. Accordingly, the bank began expanding the criteria for assigning personal bankers to include the customer's potential business and his own request for more attention.

The most important finding of the calls, though, was that to wait until a customer closed his account was to wait too long. To have any success at saving accounts, the bank would have to reach dissatisfied customers sooner. The next logical step was to identify the factors that usually led up to or predicted a customer's intention to leave so that managers could figure out whom to call *before* they closed their accounts.

When accounts are closed at any bank, they're categorized as either *voluntary* or *involuntary* closures. The first category refers to customers who decided to leave on their own, and the second is for customers who are being kicked out, usually because of a persistent overdraft situation. John's team found that a large percentage of the involuntary closures had actually started off being voluntary. For a variety of reasons, the customers had "mentally ended their banking relationship," as John puts it, and taken their business elsewhere. Although they hadn't completely closed their old accounts at the first bank, they had opened new ones elsewhere and let the balance dwindle at the first bank, often resulting in a string of bounced checks and/or service charges.

Since involuntary closures were often the result of these voluntary decisions, the bank decided to concentrate on determining what kind of customer was at risk of voluntarily closing an account. The most easily identified factor was an account in overdraft status. The bank's policy was to automatically close accounts with a negative balance 21 days after they went sour. Rather than simply accepting the traditional assumption that these were bad customers and automatically proceeding with the closures, John's team set out to call all overdraft customers at the 14-day point so that they could find out what was going on.

Quite often the team of telephone sales officers found that they had contacted good, loyal customers who were completely surprised when they were told about their overdraft status. For one reason or another, they hadn't noticed or acted on the bank's mailed notices informing them of the overdraft situation. Some had just returned from extended vacations; others had simply overlooked their mail. Some were elderly and didn't understand what the notices meant. Most of the customers John's team phoned were genuinely grateful for the call and acted quickly to set things straight.

(You can imagine how such customers had reacted in the past when the bank closed their accounts without bothering to talk with them first. When long-standing customers—people who had, in some cases, gone 30 years without so much as bouncing a single check—found that their bank had suddenly slammed the door on them, they were understandably upset. No wonder they had taken their business elsewhere and felt negative and hostile toward their former bank!)

One important lesson was that the best results came about when the phone representatives called their overdraft customers and started out with the attitude that the bank wanted to help, rather than to warn or punish, them. Often, after they had reviewed the customers' account usage and discussed the reasons for the overdrafts, it was clear that the customers had been sold the wrong type of account in the first place. Some people are more comfortable handling their personal financial affairs primarily on a cash basis and are better off with a savings account linked to an ATM card for cash withdrawals rather than using a conventional checking account. Others, who just don't know how to balance their checking accounts properly, appreciate getting simple, clear instructions about how to do so. Once they understand how best to do it, there are no more overdrafts.

Pleased with his team's successes, John expanded the scope of its activities and began placing "Welcome aboard" calls to the bank's newest customers. His intent was to solidify the relationships and answer questions that had cropped up after customers had actually started using the new accounts. The callers checked to make sure that customers had received their imprinted checks, verified that they were correct, and probed for unexpressed questions about the bank's services. Some 10 percent to 12 percent of the new customers they contacted did have questions. Had their questions gone unasked and unanswered, those customers would not have been able to fully utilize and benefit from the bank's services. Oddly, many of these customers initially seemed reluctant to ask their questions, perhaps fearing that they might seem stupid. They were much more willing to discuss their confusion with a phone rep than with branch personnel. Quite often, customers hadn't asked the branch personnel when opening their accounts because the questions only came up after they had been using the new bank's services for a couple of weeks.

One simple question yielded a huge payoff for the bank. When the phone representatives reviewed their bank records and noticed that a new customer hadn't signed up for a credit card along with his or her account, they offered to complete the customer's application over the phone. The card wasn't positioned as new credit, but rather was described as an additional feature of the checking account that would offer overdraft protection Nearly 30 percent of the people who didn't already have a card agreed to apply for one. That generation of new card applications *alone* more than justified the cost of the entire calling program. And of course the credit card accounts also contributed to longer and more profitable relationships between the bank and its new customers.

During acquisitions and mergers, John's team set out to call all new customers who had been involuntarily brought into the bank from an acquired institution. Sure enough, about 10 percent did have questions or concerns that their thick "Welcome Aboard" mail packages had not answered. John's representatives were able to retain 4 percent who indicated that they intended to leave the new bank and open accounts elsewhere. With an average annual profit contribution of $200 to $300 per account household, it was well worth calling 100 acquired customers in order to retain four of them. Those 100 contacts could save four relationships worth about $1000 in annual profits to the bank. You might think that the average profit return of about $10 per contact ($1000 total profits from 100 calls) wouldn't be worth calling for, but keep in mind that those are just *first year* annual profits. If the retained customers were treated well and if they kept their accounts for seven years, the average profit contribution would be $70 per contact.

Only two-tenths of 1 percent of the called customers indicated that they didn't want to be phoned. The overwhelming majority actually enjoyed and appreciated being contacted by their bank. The bank's senior management team calculated that saving just 5 percent of its customers could increase profits by 100 percent.

What Can You Learn from This Example?   John's experience taught him and his bank lots of lessons that you, too, can use in your own business:

- Customers don't mind being contacted when your aim is to strengthen their relationship. In fact, the overwhelming majority welcome the attention.

- Your customers probably do have questions and concerns that they haven't yet expressed. Customers are often more willing to discuss them over the phone than face-to-face. If you just call and ask them, most will tell you what their concerns are. If you don't ask, their unresolved issues will weaken your relationships with your customers.

- Calling to welcome aboard new customers solidifies their relationships and provides you with an opportunity to uncover their unasked questions. In an important way, the welcome call also provides an opportunity to increase the relationship's yield immediately through increased sales—as the bank learned with its credit card offer.

- The majority of involuntary closures often originate as voluntary. Some of your customers whose accounts are delinquent are trying to tell you something. They wish you would ask—and listen.

- It's well worth contacting customers whose accounts are in trouble—and *the sooner, the better.*

Example

AEI Music Network Listens between the Lines

Next time you're eating in a fast-food restaurant, listen. Hear that music? Chances are it's being piped in via satellite, and the story of how it got there is a perfect example of upside-down marketing in action. You've probably heard of Muzak, but may not know about AEI Music Network, Inc. AEI Music, the largest sound system design and installation contractor in the United States, is a $50 million company that provides business music for customers like Marriott Hotels, The Limited, United Airlines, Jack in the Box, even Air Force One, and a certain well-known national chain of fast-food restaurants.

The fact that you're hearing top-quality music while munching your lunch is testimony to the persistence, personality, patience, and perspicacity of Charlotte Wintermann, National Account Executive for AEI Music. She told me the restaurant chain's full story, and it involves one of the most difficult marketing situations any sales professional ever deals with: the smoke screen. Sales professionals encounter it all the time, but very few even realize they're caught in it, and far fewer have the stick-to-itiveness to blow the smoke away and get to the core problem.

Charlotte's story begins back in 1990, when AEI management became concerned about the company's churn rate. AEI had grown explosively in the 1970s and 1980s, with so many new customers coming in over the transom that management had paid little proactive attention to the cancellation rate. But when the flood of new business started to plateau, two of AEI Music's vice presidents decided to confront the situation head-on. They calculated that about 12 percent of their customers were canceling their music service each year, and that that figure was higher than the level of new sales.

Naturally the management team saw where the trend was taking them. They selected Charlotte as the company's account retention manager to deal proactively with any customer concerns that may have led them to request cancellation of their service.

Charlotte became the one person all canceling customers were routed to when they wanted to close their accounts. Her job was to pull out all the stops to save the accounts and also to find out exactly why customers were canceling so that AEI could address any deficiencies that might be driving customers away—or toward the competition.

Throughout 1991 she handled about 1000 customers who wanted to cancel service, and she succeeded in retaining about 75 percent of them. Most of the others canceled for reasons beyond her control, such as business closures or bankruptcies. A single small convenience store with an on-premise system or a satellite system might be billed between $39 to $130 per month, depending on the service provided and audio equipment installed. A large national airline or hotel chain receiving music via satellite at many locations would incur billings of many thousands of dollars monthly. In other words, many of the lost accounts were well worth investigating and pursuing.

One of the canceling customers Charlotte handled was a relatively new owner for an existing chain of fast-food restaurants. Though small, the chain was growing rapidly. Yet Charlotte kept receiving location closure notices from the chain's corporate office, as if the individual restaurants were having a hard time staying open. Each time she got one, it signified that AEI was losing another small customer. It just didn't make sense to her. If the chain was growing, why would so many of the restaurants be closing? So Charlotte started calling the managers at the individual locations. Guess what? They kept answering. The restaurants weren't really closing. They were switching to a competitor's satellite broadcast music system rather than staying with AEI's tape delivery system or converting to AEI Music's satellite system.

For some reason, customers are often reluctant to say why they're really closing their accounts. Perhaps they feel it would be embarrassing to explain and justify their decision to go with a competitor, so they just make up a reason that they think will avoid scrutiny. The chain's headquarters management hadn't been telling Charlotte the true story.

Determined to stem the exodus, Charlotte finally tracked down the purchasing manager, Jerry, who was one of the chain's corporate office managers with responsibility for approving music contracts for the individual locations. Without accusing him of lying, she innocently asked what was going on. He didn't claim that the restaurants were really closing, but he did offer plenty of other reasons why AEI's service was being canceled: "We never get our music on time." "Your people keep changing and we can't keep track of who's handling our account." "You always send us the wrong music."

Charlotte knew that these reasons weren't really true. AEI Music is the quality leader in its field, and their customer service department does a fine job of handling customer service issues. Jerry had no history of calling in with complaints; in fact, he hadn't been making any contact at all, except to keep on sending in those location closure notices for restaurant after restaurant. Whenever she asked him how things were going or if she could help in any way, Jerry had always responded, "Things are fine."

Charlotte had the distinct feeling that she was facing a smoke screen. She wasn't being told the truth. Each time Jerry justified his cancellations with an excuse, she addressed it directly and offered her personal guarantee that the problem, even if it had been true in the past, would never happen again. It didn't make any difference to Jerry. He still kept on canceling individual locations.

She knew that there was another factor that was preventing her from getting to the bottom of it.

At long last, after over a year of trying to determine what Jerry's real issue was, she realized that his unwillingness to work with her was based on a situation in the past, before Jerry had gone to work for the chain. He had at one time wanted to be a sound system resale agent to AEI. Because AEI deals directly with wholesalers, they did not have a need to purchase equipment through Jerry. Years later, it was apparent that this was the main reason for Jerry's smoke screen tactic. He was getting back at AEI for rejecting his proposal years ago.

Charlotte's instincts told her that there was no rational way to deal with Jerry's enmity, so she changed course and began to develop a relationship with another of the chain's purchasing agents, Jessica. Charlotte started all over again from scratch, treating Jessica as if she were a brand-new customer. She did all she could to strike up a friendly relationship. As Charlotte describes her efforts, she says:

> In every conversation I had with Jessica, I ended on a personal note—either mentioning something about myself in relation to something Jessica had said, or making a personal comment involving weekend plans, etc. I also always asked one question relative to moving forward in determining how their organization's decision process worked. I'd ask who authorized decisions for various operational aspects and try to identify any other players who might be involved. My objective was to place Jessica within the structure, to determine her level of influence, to gain her trust, and to develop an ally who had an interest in creating the best possible music solution for the business.

Charlotte's wooing of Jessica succeeded. After working hard to build rapport, respond to concerns, and circumvent Jerry without alienating him, she finally received no more location closure notices.

AEI Music has now successfully installed their satellite broadcast system for the restaurants. The chain has since grown to an excess of 200 locations, and their business is now worth several thousand dollars a month.

What Can You Learn from This Example?   AEI's marketing program and Charlotte's actions provide many lessons for companies who want to retain customer relationships:

- *Listen and pay attention.* The single most important factor was AEI management's recognition that customer cancellations were hurting them—and their subsequent decision to do something about it. Even if the rate of cancellations had been less than the inflow of new customers, they would have been losing out because of the high costs associated with winning over new replacement accounts. AEI has calculated that it costs them four times more to sign a new customer than to keep an existing customer.

- *Make somebody accountable.* It's easy to say, "We ought to have someone check on these cancellations and try to stop them." But nothing happens unless one person or team leader is personally responsible for changing things. In AEI's case, the whole organization was dedicated to turning these types of situations around, but it was Charlotte who had a personal stake in the execution. She was responsible. Fortunately, AEI's management team had the good sense to pick the right kind of person for the job.

- *Be suspicious.* I don't mean to suspect that people are lying to you, but do expect that you're not always hearing or seeing the complete picture. This is what Charlotte did when the expanding restaurant chain appeared to be experiencing a high rate of closures. It didn't make sense.

- *Avoid judgments and accusations.* If Charlotte had said, "Jerry, I just don't believe that those are the real reasons you keep canceling our services, and I know for sure that the restaurants you say are closing are really still open for business," he would have slammed the door in her face. But her focus was on her desired end goal: to find out what was really happening and create a mutually satisfying situation. She wasn't out to discredit her customer, even though she knew that he wasn't telling the truth.

- *Be persistent and indefatigable.* The whole process of resecuring this one customer's account took two and a half years. Was it worth it? Not if you think about a month's billing for one of the chain's original 40 locations that were affected when Charlotte first entered the picture. But she was thinking about the *potential* account: the total value of over 200 locations' monthly billings over the course of five years (an AEI customer's typical life span) is in excess of half a million dollars. *That's* worth it.

■ *Like what you're doing.* As I interviewed Charlotte, it was clear that she enjoyed getting to the truth. She viewed this situation as a challenge and rose to meet it. At no time did she sound like it was a drag to deal with Jerry's smoke screen. AEI management had selected someone who relishes dealing with canceling customers and handling objections. (Right after our interview, Charlotte sent me a fax that read: "I forgot to tell you about the customer who screamed and swore for over 20 minutes about a service misunderstanding—in Italian, mind you—but who still calls, as a very satisfied AEI customer, to ask when I will be in Chicago so he can treat me to lunch at his establishment!")

The Value of "Exception Reporting"

One of the most effective systems for preventing customer relationships from lapsing is what I call *exception reporting*. It refers to methods by which marketing managers can become aware of customers whose behavior is beginning to deviate from their normal purchasing pattern.

If I normally place an order with Quill Office Supplies every four to six weeks and for some reason I place no order for ten weeks, Quill ought to be concerned. Maybe nothing's wrong. Maybe I've just ordered so many supplies recently that the stockroom is full and I don't need anything. But maybe it's something else. Perhaps a competitor is wooing me. Maybe I'm unhappy about a delivery problem on my last order. It could be that I've just grown indifferent. In any case, a relationship with a customer is a valuable asset, one well worth hanging on to. You have to have some way of noticing when it starts slipping away.

I recently interrupted my normal ordering frequency with Quill because I got an unsolicited catalogue from one of their competitors, Misco. What the heck, I thought. Their merchandise and pricing looked about the same, so I'd give them a try. I had no loyalty toward or relationship with Quill. When the order arrived, I was satisfied with Misco's service and the supplies were fine, but I didn't plan to develop any particular loyalty toward them, either.

A few weeks after my first Misco order, I received a letter from its president, Terence Jukes, that read, in part:

> If there's one thing we like better than serving new customers, it's being given the opportunity to serve them again. I don't know why we haven't heard from you, but I do know this: we want you back, and to encourage you to order from Misco again, I have a very special offer.

The letter went on to offer me a $50 credit on any order over $150 I placed within the coming month. The back of the letter was a simple feedback form asking me to rate Misco's prices, courtesy, quality, etc. It was designed to be faxed back immediately, and it also gave me the option of requesting a callback from a Misco employee to discuss any of my comments. Their attention won my repeat business.

Federal Express has a great system for handling exception reporting. Not only are their computers constantly surveying changes in customers' account activity, their couriers are, too. When a Fed Ex driver notices that a customer is sending lots of parcels via UPS, for example, he alerts his sales department so that they can find out what's going on and give the customer a little extra attention. This happened to me recently when one of Fed Ex's phone agents noticed a steady decline in my shipping activity as she arranged a courier pickup for me. She courteously asked me how my business was changing. I explained that my customers pay the shipping charges for the books, audios, and videos they order from my office, and that I didn't feel right about charging them Fed Ex's high prices on shipments that weren't really urgent. I had changed my shipping policy so that routine orders went out via United Parcel Service's economical second-day air service.

A week later, Dawn Taylor phoned and introduced herself as the Fed Ex sales representative responsible for my territory. She offered to come by, meet me, and take the time to ensure that I was using the best price plan I could get with Fed Ex. When she arrived, she was clearly aware that I had shifted some of my allegiance to UPS, and she set out to win me back. Sure enough, she explained how Fed Ex could actually be less expensive than UPS if I consolidated my shipping activity and took advantage of volume discounts. Thanks to Dawn, I started shipping orders via Fed Ex again.

Avon Cosmetics has 110,000 women in door-to-door sales in Germany. Management there discovered that 20 percent of them dropped out and stopped ordering products in any given month. Since Avon's independent saleswomen are, in effect, its customers, the company now calls every Avon saleswoman who hasn't placed her order within five days after the close of each ordering period. As a result, the 20 percent monthly drop-off is down to 8 percent, an improvement worth $3.4 million in revenues.

Listening to the Silence

You can almost hear the silence in our typical customer relationships. Failing to establish and nurture an ongoing, two-way dialogue with your customers hurts your firm's success. I can say this with confidence because it's so extremely rare for an organization to have *too much* contact with its customers. As we've seen, they consistently react very positively to an organization's increase in personal contact. They have a lot to tell us, and they want to help if we'll just let them. You'll find many more strategies for developing this beneficial dialogue in Chapters 4, 5, and 6.

What Can You Learn from This Chapter?

- Most customers who stop doing business with any company leave quietly and simply stop buying. Collectively, they cost the company much more than the relatively few who complain and cause a fuss.

- Few companies have any effective system for detecting quiet defections. They're too busy dealing with the complainers and slow-payers.

- The leading reason why customers stop doing business with any company is that they feel neglected. Customers like more attention.

- Failing to actively seek customers' opinions and feedback is dumb, and costly.

- Many organizations simply delete inactive customers without taking the time to ask why they aren't ordering anymore. In doing so, they're overlooking a rich opportunity to rekindle those relationships.

- It's easy and highly profitable to implement a system which identifies any customer whose account activity has declined or ceased and alerts marketers to reestablish contact before it's too late.

- Huge opportunity costs result from an organization's failure to seek customer input about product improvements, process glitches, competitive moves, new products, and overlooked complaints.

- Waiting until a customer closes an account before paying more attention is waiting too long.

- Once your company identifies indicators which suggest a customer is about to defect, it's likely that a significant percentage of the vulnerable accounts can be saved, if action is taken soon enough—the sooner, the better.

- The best way to ensure that customers don't slip away unnoticed is to make somebody responsible for redeeming them.

- Instituting exception reporting procedures that flag accounts with declining activity and direct remedial attention is one of the most profitable courses any company can take.

Action Summary
What You Can Do *Now*

- Estimate how close you are to giving your customers *too much* attention. If you're not very close, start exploring how you can strengthen those undernourished relationships.

- If you use a feedback survey system, critically evaluate the forms and determine if they encourage both positive *and negative* comments.

- Carefully evaluate any compensation policies that link rewards to customers' quality ratings. Is there incentive for your employees to manipulate the results for their own self-interest?

- Find out if you're currently getting some form of to-be-purged report flagging inactive customers. Don't settle for automatic deletion until you've made contact with enough zero-dollar customers to determine that they truly don't offer any potential.

- Question the way you've always done it when it comes to cleaning up the company database and eliminating customers who appear unprofitable.

- Make it easier for your customers to provide their input on a 24-hour basis, including the availability of an after-hours suggestion line with voice mail or an answering machine.

- Avoid asking simple "Yes or No" questions when seeking customer input. Ask *how*, not *if*, you can improve.

- Make it easier for your customers to complain, and reach out to them, asking them what they're dissatisfied about.

- Launch a proactive calling campaign and chronicle customers' ratings of your quality. Then compare them with a control group that receives no proactive calls.

- Look for links between voluntary and involuntary account closures among your customers. Is it possible that the ones you kicked out wanted out in the first place? What can you do to prevent it?

- Make it difficult for customers to quietly slip away unnoticed by giving one person ultimate responsibility for tracking and stopping account closures.

- Seek staff members who are especially intuitive to hear between the lines when customers explain their cancellations.

- Talk with your MIS department and get them to institute an exception reporting system that will alert you when accounts show unusual changes in activity.

PART 2

Keeping Customers on the Belt

First, make sure that you've smoothed out the bumps on your conveyor belt and corrected the service and quality deficiencies that have been driving your customers away. Next, pay more attention to the customers who are still on your conveyor belt. Some of their loyalties are wavering right now. Others have new needs that you aren't satisfying because you don't know about them. Most of them aren't hearing from you nearly often enough, and they probably suspect that you don't value their business.

The customers who are already on your relationship conveyor belt are precious assets and can offer remarkable lifetime values. You can benefit from the full value of those relationships only by employing the strategies outlined in this section.

Take decisive action to solidify your current customer relationships, find out what your present customers want and need from you. Above all, stay in touch with them. The time to start is right now. Don't wait until you're certain that all the plans you began in Part 1 are well underway. The rough spots on your conveyor belt may take quite some time to smooth out. Meanwhile, ensure that your current relationships are getting stronger. Follow the examples of Airborne Express, Washington Mutual Savings Bank, IBM, and the other companies you'll be reading about in the three chapters that follow.

Seek to maximize the profitability of your current customer relationships by doing everything you can to keep them on your conveyor belt.

4
Know Thy Customer

In "Listening to the Silence," in Chapter 3, we focused on customers who have fallen off the relationship conveyor belt or are teetering at the edge. When the relationship breaks down and you endeavor to figure out what went wrong, you'll find that silence is often the culprit. Ongoing, active relationships, though, can also suffer from a lack of communication. Since we're now turning our attention to the customers who are still buying from us, who are still on the conveyor belt, let's see how we can increase and improve the dialogue in current relationships so that we can make them more vital, enduring, and profitable.

While you're salvaging lost relationships with customers who've stopped ordering, you may get some pretty good ideas about some of the more glaring problems that have already driven some ex-customers away. But you probably don't know about the less dramatic annoyances that may be irritating your current customers. Cumulatively, they may result in lost accounts; individually, they can prevent maximized relationships with customers. Thinking back to the conveyor belt analogy, what you are really seeking are customers who are centered right in the middle of your belt. You want buyers who are going to stay with you and whose loyalty is assured.

Starting New Relationships Right

Customers' views of their relationships with suppliers are *front-loaded*, meaning that what happens during the earliest stages of the relationship carries a disproportionate weight in shaping customers' opinions. It's especially important to start things off on the right foot in new relationships.

One of the most effective techniques is the welcome-aboard contact. Lots of companies are now sending out letters after customers place their first orders, and that's certainly a step in the right direction. If you're out to create a strong *personal* relationship, though, more personal contact is called for. A phone call makes a much more positive and effective welcome-aboard impact and also gives you the opportunity to ask your customers questions and then answer them.

That masterful relationship-building organization I've referred to earlier, US WEST Cellular, uses a special technique in this early phase of its customer relationships, too. When you first become a new customer and walk out of a Radio Shack store with your portable phone in hand or drive away from your car dealer with your newly installed car phone, you're eager to make that first call. You dial the number of your spouse or a good friend, eagerly anticipating the thrill of your first cellular connection. But who answers? A welcome-aboard specialist at US WEST! Their telephone switching equipment is programmed so that any new customer's very first phone call is intercepted and routed to the phone company's 24-hour customer service call center, and it's forwarded in such a way that the person who intercepts your call knows that it's your very first call. The representative congratulates you for deciding to go cellular and makes you feel welcome. He or she then verifies your account number, correct address, and so on, and uses this opportunity to be sure you have answers to the most common questions new customers ask.

Quite often the caller has just purchased the phone from a sales clerk in a department store or car stereo shop but has received no explanation at all about how to use it. The salesperson, eager to handle the next customer's purchase (and rack up another commission) has little interest in showing this customer how the phone works. The US WEST Cellular rep, though, is interested in the long-term relationship and will walk the new customer through the process of making and receiving calls and explain how to take advantage of the phone's special features.

Most organizations don't have the advantage of being able to meet and greet their new customers with such electronic expediency. Most new customers come to our attention in more traditional ways. They may be calling, faxing, or mailing in an initial order in response to a catalogue mailing. Or they may be responding to an 800 number displayed on their television screen. Or they may become new customers without even realizing it as the result of a company merger.

Example

Washington Mutual Merges with New Customers

Mergers and acquisitions are usually viewed as purely financial transactions with a focus solely on increased profits. What many organizations fail to recognize is the tremendous marketing opportunities and challenges that present themselves when two organizations consolidate.

One institution that's highly sensitive to mergers—and determined to capitalize on them—is Seattle-based Washington Mutual Savings Bank, one of the leading thrifts in the nation, and the largest independent bank in the state of Washington.

A major portion of Washington Mutual's customer growth over the last decade has come from the acquisition of smaller banks. The relationships that an acquired institution has developed with its customers are often its primary asset, potentially far more profitable than its real estate holdings or other financial assets. Letting those customers slip away is like buying a string of pearls and then letting 25 percent to 40 percent of them fall off the string. Washington Mutual sets out to keep as many of the pearls as possible.

When it acquires another institution, Washington Mutual's goal is to maintain 85 percent of the smaller institution's customers, even though the industry average for customer retention when one bank acquires another is only 60 percent to 75 percent. Using the teamwork techniques and targeting strategies described here, Washington Mutual is even exceeding that ambitious goal. When it comes to mergers, these folks are pros. In fact, one of the bank's most successful ad campaigns was built around the merger theme. Print and broadcast advertising targeted to reach retail customers used the headline: "Merge with Washington Mutual," inviting customers of other institutions to switch and become their customers whether their own banks were being acquired or not.

In a merger situation, the most useful viewpoint for marketers to adopt is that of the acquired customer. If you were a customer of Pioneer Savings in 1993, for example, your own bank wasn't likely to alert you to the coming change in ownership when Washington Mutual's acquisition was complete. You probably first heard about it on the evening news. Your immediate reaction was to wonder what would become of your accounts. What about your preprinted checks bearing the logo of the bank that's about to vanish? Would your CDs, IRAs, and loans be secure? Washington Mutual's first priority was to get a welcome-aboard package into your hands.

The kit began with a letter from the president and CEO, Kerry Killinger, explaining that you were now part of the Washington Mutual family. It included a comprehensive booklet offering side-by-side comparisons of Pioneer's account types and Washington

Mutual's. Copies of sample bank statements were included, along with thorough descriptions explaining what each section meant, including definitions of key terms.

The cover letter and booklet both featured toll-free and local phone numbers for customers to call so that they could get answers to their merger questions. But the bank didn't leave it at that. The corporate communications department, marketing groups, individual branches, and the bank-by-phone department all worked together to contact customers with personal outbound phone calls.

The bank's merging theme doesn't end when the new customer is absorbed into Washington Mutual's customer base. Proactively partnering—or merging—with customers is the ongoing theme of its relationship development efforts.

I arranged to interview Tom Boyd, manager of Washington Mutual's bank-by-phone sales operation in Seattle. Soon after I arrived at the downtown offices to learn the secrets of Washington Mutual's extremely successful bank-by-phone program, Tom and I walked up behind one of the phone reps, Ed Duff, who was wearing a telephone headset while working in his cubicle. At that moment, he was leaving a message on a customer's answering machine. Checking the account information displayed on his computer screen, we could see that this particular customer had a CD in the amount of $8600 that had just reached its maturity date several days earlier. The record showed that the funds had been automatically moved into a passbook account, earning roughly half the interest that the customer had been gaining from the CD.

Think about the impact that phone message had on the bank's customer. The reason for the call was not to sell something, but rather to alert the customer to a missed opportunity for his funds to work harder for him. That customer might otherwise have gone for weeks or months assuming that his funds were still working hard for him when, in fact, they were not. Ed's call was a tangible demonstration of Washington Mutual's interest in helping its customers gain the maximum value from the bank's services.

The bank-by-phone unit generates customer loyalty and big profits for the bank. Had Ed reached the customer himself rather than his answering machine, he would have begun by probing to find out about that particular individual's needs and then taken into account his age, investment objectives, and so on. That phone call might also have resulted in an annuity investment since the bank-by-phone agents are licensed by the state to sell such contracts. Agents may also introduce customers to an affiliate's representatives who hold licenses that permit them to sell mutual funds as well as stocks and securities.

Washington Mutual has recognized that a checking account is the cornerstone of a customer's relationship with the bank. Customers with checking accounts are more likely to keep a larger portion of their business at that institution than if they just have a loan or time deposit product. Employees throughout the bank-by-phone department are provided with incentives for strengthening customer relationships. Although these are not commissions per se, point values are assigned to various types of sales and services that can ultimately lead to incentive pay ranging up to 30 percent of an individual employee's total compensation.

Washington Mutual isn't just concerned about merging with its *customers*. Management also views the *employees* of the acquired bank as people with whom it also wants to cultivate relationships. Just as a customer relationship is viewed as a valuable asset, so is an employee relationship. Members of the acquired bank's retail sales team are usually hired by Washington Mutual and brought into a training program for a one year period during which they learn about Washington Mutual's procedures and, more important, its value system.

One of the keys to Washington Mutual's enlightened view of customer (and employee) relationships is the fact that each branch is run on a profit model. Individual representatives at the branch level receive incentives for achieving profit objectives, as do the telephone representatives. A typical representative might be paid $1750 per month as a base salary, and have the opportunity to earn $750 in additional compensation by achieving profit objectives. Examples of incentive pay run along the lines of a $100,000 annuity sale being worth one point, which ultimately translates to a $100 commission. Lower value sales have corresponding point values that translate to incentive pay. New checking accounts are rewarded with a $5 incentive.

Washington Mutual uses its excellent research department to help its employees know its customers. One typical project is a closed account survey. All customers are polled after they close an account and withdraw their funds from Washington Mutual. This survey is mailed monthly and can yield a valuable opportunity to renew relationships. The research department provides in-depth customer profiles for direct marketing letters followed by consultative phone calls to ensure that customers' current products are fulfilling their needs. Additional customer feedback is solicited for customer retention programs and new product development. All these efforts are ongoing activities, not one-shot projects. All are designed to help Washington Mutual know its customers.

Customer focus groups and service surveys also assist in achieving and maintaining Washington Mutual's high customer retention rates. "Secret shopper" results from face-to-face observation at branches and calls to the bank-by-phone department grade employees on how they are doing in relation to service and sales criteria. When a customer wishes to close an account employees will gladly assist, while probing to determine if there has been a problem. Additional activities like closed-account surveys and/or follow-up phone calls to customers with recent account closures are conducted monthly and bring many customers back.

What Can You Learn from This Example?   Lots of different teams and departments in your organization can work toward the goal of understanding and satisfying your customers' needs. It's not any one department's job. At Washington Mutual, individual branches, research, marketing, communications, and other groups share this common goal. Pull together a task force in your organization with interdepartmental representatives and take advantage of the synergy that results from a multifaceted approach.

Mergers and acquisitions present particularly fruitful opportunities to establish early loyalty—and prevent costly mass defections—by the acquired customers. Why buy a string of pearls unless you plan to ensure that only the barest minimum of the pearls drop off?

One of the most important lessons in this example is that you don't have to accept industry standards. Although other banks typically average up to 40 percent customer losses when they acquire another institution, Washington Mutual decided that that wasn't nearly good enough. They discarded the industry benchmarks and shot for a mere 15 percent loss. And, by setting that ambitious goal and stimulating joint cooperation, they've even bettered their goal. The ultimate profit differential is in the many millions of dollars. Don't accept your industry's standards in situations like these.

Friends and Partners Talk, So Why Don't Buyers and Sellers?

Right now as you're reading, a good many of your customers aren't centered securely on your belt. They may not be right at the edge, but they're definitely off-center. Although they may continue buying, they don't feel a sense of loyalty toward your organization. The relationship is simply not as strong as it could be. If you want to keep them on your belt, you must actively reach out and establish a dialogue to find out how they feel, rather than waiting for some incident to create a blowup.

Business relationships really aren't all that different from personal relationships. In fact, they *are* personal relationships. No company buys from another *company*. There are always at least two *people* involved. When marriages wither and couples seek counseling, the problem most commonly boils down to, "We just don't communicate anymore." Buying and selling relationships need improved ongoing communication, too.

Example

Thorndike Press Develops Unity with Librarians

Thorndike Press is a specialized publisher of large-typeface books for visually impaired readers. When their small company in Unity, Maine, was acquired by Macmillan, Thorndike executives feared that they might lose their traditional personal touch with librarians and the few specialized bookstores that buy books for nearly blind customers. The publisher wondered if some of its buyers might have had negative experiences with their new, much larger parent company. So, they started calling their buyers to find out how they felt about what effects the recent changes might have had.

Sure enough, the calls paid off. Not only were they able to reassure their customers that Thorndike would maintain its reputation for personalized, top-quality service, they also learned about a small glitch in Macmillan's procedures that could have driven Thorndike's customers off the belt. For years, the small publisher had included card catalogue kits with its books so that librarians could immediately update their card catalogues as shipments came in. Once Macmillan took over the shipping function, however, the cards were mailed separately, sometimes weeks after the books themselves. Few librarians had taken the time or the trouble to call and complain, but once Thorndike's representatives called them to find out if there were any problems, the librarians were quick to explain the annoying situation. The folks at Unity quickly alerted Macmillan's shipping personnel, changed the procedures, and averted a potential mass customer defection.

What Can You Learn from This Example? While it's a safe bet that your customer relationships would improve with more direct, personal communication *at any time,* there are certain key times in a relationship when closer communication is definitely called for. Change often precipitates doubts. Whenever you make changes that affect your relationships with customers, it's best to assume that they may be feeling a little alienated. Reinforce your relationships by picking up the phone and making direct contact. Ask questions that will make it easy for your customers to tell you if something is interfering with your relationship so you can get to work and improve it. *Know thy customer.*

Find Out What Your Customers Want

The basic reason why any buyer/seller relationships endure at all is because sellers meet buyers' needs. So, isn't it odd that sellers often rely primarily on guesswork to figure out exactly what their customers need? Oh, sure, many initiate various research projects along the way, but for the most part, companies do what they *have* been doing. They function habitually.

To maximize customer relationships, we have to constantly do a better, more thorough job of meeting customers' needs. The very best source of information about their needs is the customers themselves, of course. That's one of the primary benefits of the relatively new discipline called *relationship marketing*. I'm certainly not the first marketing advisor to point out the obvious need to establish and build a stronger dialogue with customers.

The Trouble with Newsletters

Do you really read all those newsletters you've started receiving in the last few years? With the advent of desktop publishing and the widespread availability of page layout software, it seems as though everybody is producing and sending out newsletters. While almost anything that helps establish an ongoing presence for your company may help strengthen customer relationships, newsletters suffer from one serious shortcoming: they're one-way communications. They offer scant opportunity to find out what your *customers* are thinking about.

Most newsletters are merely self-aggrandizing puff pieces. "Look at our new factory!" "We've expanded our shipping facility!" "We placed third in the industry softball championships!" What customers really care most about is *themselves*. Newsletters should be used to offer ideas about how to improve their businesses and their lives. Articles should focus on techniques for increasing profitability—sometimes (but not necessarily always) involving the products and services of the seller. Still, any newsletter's ability to stimulate customer feedback and questions is limited. One of the best newsletters I receive always includes a bright yellow faxback form designed to stimulate feedback. It's preformatted to be very easy to use. It includes just a few questions, like "What articles would you like to see in future issues?" and "What changes would you like to see in the format of this newsletter?" The form provides plenty of open space, so it's easy to quickly jot out answers and ask questions. The company's fax number is prominently displayed. It's out to make it very easy for its customers to respond.

Make Personal Contact and
Listen between the Lines

Two-way communication is what's needed. Sending out newsletters and other one-way communications won't tell you what your customers are thinking. While it may not be practical to contact every customer personally, it's well worth reaching a rotating random sample of them to strengthen those relationships and probe for unmet needs. Sometimes you don't have to call them because they'll call you. When you're in the fortunate position of having a customer reach out to make contact with you, leverage the time you're already investing to handle the question and respond to the customer's request. Go beyond the stated purpose of the call. Always be prepared to ask additional probing questions about unmet needs that your customer hasn't yet expressed.

Example

CareerTrack Listens for a Triple Win

If you're like 5 million other businesspeople, your mail includes seminar brochures from CareerTrack, the nation's leading seminar company, with burgeoning operations worldwide. Each year, CareerTrack mails out about 100 million individual brochures and catalogues to its customers and prospects. You can bet that some of the names on its lists are duplicates or are simply inaccurate. Most people who receive redundant direct mailings from any company simply throw the extras away and mutter about how wasteful direct marketers can be.

One of CareerTrack's customers, the Rock Island Arsenal in Illinois, took action instead of silently grumbling. Various staff members, including lots of people who were no longer even working there, routinely received up to 75 copies of each seminar brochure, far more than they wanted or needed. So, CareerTrack's primary contact, Helene Scott, a training specialist for the Arsenal, called to complain. "Isn't there something you guys can do to cut down on our mailings? Half the people on your list aren't even working here anymore, and most of the others have no authority to enroll in any seminars!"

Rather than simply brushing aside the customer's complaint, Greg Smith, CareerTrack's client service representative responsible for the Rock Island Arsenal account, listened. He wanted to satisfy his customer by eliminating some frustration, and he also wanted to save CareerTrack unnecessary mailing costs. Greg took the time to review the mailing list carefully, eliminating people who had moved on or who lacked authority to make enrollment decisions, and trimmed the list down from 75 names to just 5. Helene offered to serve as the clearing house for incoming seminar information and promised to disseminate notices to her colleagues via E-mail after identifying programs that would be particularly appropriate for their departments. This move alone saved CareerTrack about $500 per year in printing, processing, and mailing costs that had been going to waste.

As he listened to his customer, Greg heard more than just frustration about "too much excess mail." He also noted the remark, "And anyway, the brochures get here way too late." After probing for more details, Greg discovered that Rock Island Arsenal's planners determined their budget allocations long before the seminar mailings even arrived. He offered to prepare a quarterly listing of upcoming CareerTrack seminars in the Rock Island area, so that the budgeters could plan ahead and figure in registration fees for the programs that were of greatest interest to them.

Greg gained a triple payoff by listening to his customer's concerns, taking them seriously, and asking for more details, rather than brushing them aside as just another junk mail complaint.

- First, he reduced CareerTrack's mailing expenses (not to mention helping to cut back on wasteful consumption of paper and the generation of waste that would otherwise be clogging our landfills).

- Second, he increased the annual revenues CareerTrack realized from this single customer from $700 per year to $18,000 per year. Not a bad payoff for just listening, paying attention, and cleaning up the mailing list.

- And third, he helped *other* CareerTrack customers plan to allocate more of their budgets for CareerTrack seminars. After hearing Helene's comments about needing more advance notice of upcoming seminars, Greg asked some of the other client service representatives he works with to check with *their* customers. They also found that many of them shared Rock Island Arsenal's timing concerns. The result was the creation of a new, quarterly advance seminar listing that is now routinely provided to other large organizations that plan their budget expenditures well in advance.

What Can You Learn from This Example?   When your customer calls you or writes to express concerns about one aspect of your product or service, you're in an ideal position to leverage that dialogue by asking what else you can do to help. What you hear about meeting one customer's needs may be extremely helpful in dealing with others' needs too. Greg found that there were plenty of organizations that were glad to take advantage of the future seminar listing notices Rock Island Arsenal had requested. If Greg hadn't "listened between the lines," he wouldn't have picked up on this profitable idea. His customer's primary comments concerned the waste of too much mail. Timing was a side comment, but Greg picked it up and homed in on it.

Be sure that you hire people who are good listeners, and then train them to be even better. Customers can be extremely profitable sources of ideas if you listen to them carefully enough.

Benchmarking Won't Tell You Where to Go

Large organizations often hire specialized research firms to find out where they stand with their customers. This can be a very good practice, especially when the same study is repeated year after year, making it easy to detect trend lines and note how customers' perceptions of your products and services are changing. Most such studies, though, are limited to telling you how things used to be. There's often a lag of several months between the conducting of the research and the publishing and distributing of the results.

The fundamental shortcoming of benchmarking research, though, is that it gives little idea of what you must do to significantly change and improve what your customers think about you. You need benchmarking, and you also need more direct, personal research.

One of my clients, GTE, hired me to present a series of Business Customer Seminars for their small and midsize commercial customers in the western United States. In addition to hearing my presentation for the audience, the GTE customers also listened to a variety of the company's management representatives. But GTE's primary reason for the programs was to develop stronger customer relationships, and they couldn't accomplish that by doing all the talking. So during each seminar, senior managers faced the audience as a panel, available to field audience questions, which were often quite direct. ("How come you force me to buy ads in all three directories just because my flower shop is located right where your apparently arbitrary publishing boundaries happen to converge?") While the audience asked away, a member of the GTE team responsible for coordinating the seminars was writing down every question, because they provided excellent insight into what customers were wondering about and wishing for. From the company's standpoint, the audience questions may have been the most important part of the seminar.

Focus Groups Help Shy Customers Talk to You

GTE realized that it takes a certain kind of outspoken customer to raise questions when there are hundreds of other people present in the audience. Many customers with valid input and good ideas just won't speak up. So, after the seminar, about a dozen randomly chosen individuals were invited to remain for an informal focus group discussion over sandwiches and pop.

Greg Gardner, GTE's coordinator of employee involvement, was asked to facilitate the sessions because of his extensive training and experience in leading discussions during internal meetings. Right after the focus group meetings, he told me, "It's so hard to hold myself back in these focus groups. I want to lead, but my true role is to facilitate. I must remain neutral if customers are going to take the discussions where *they* want them to go." His aim was to create a safe place where customers could tell GTE—through him—what they think of the company overall and what they want to see changed.

In each seminar location the discussions were different. Some focused on equipment concerns, others on telephone network services, others on billing procedures, still others on directory advertising policies, and so on. After starting things off with opening questions about the value of the seminars and of GTE's overall service, Greg let the discussions take their own direction. GTE needed to hear what the customers wanted to talk about, not what the company thought was important. Greg took careful notes on large flipchart pages, which were all saved, transferred to a more practical format, and then distributed to senior management along with summaries of customers' concerns.

Some of the customer suggestions validated moves that the company was already making, and others were completely new, creative ideas with real merit. Customers said they wanted to be able to visit a demonstration center where they could see GTE's Centranet service in operation and learn how to take advantage of its advanced features. So GTE is proceeding to build just such a center in Long Beach, California. They said they thought GTE should cosponsor seminars and events with local communities and specific industry groups, so GTE is looking into doing so. The company had never before considered, for example, offering a seminar on how real estate agents can do a better job of communicating with their clients, but the idea has tremendous merit. Other customers complained about their complicated, hard-to-read phone bills and pointed out that the confusing format forces them to call GTE's customer care center for explanations, thus further clogging the lines and slowing service for others. So GTE is moving ahead with a billing simplification project. One of the most frequent comments from customers was right in line with the main thrust of this book you're now reading: "How come I get so much attention *before* I buy a new service, and so little *after* I've signed the contract?" (Would *your* customers say the same thing?)

You Are the Best Researcher

Over and over, I've worked with large organizations that wanted definitive research and guiding input about where they should be heading. They hire researchers, conduct competitive analyses, boil them down to Executive Summaries, and then do little with them. Formal research tends to be fairly cold. Statistics, tables, correlation values, trend lines, graphs, and bar charts don't really give you much of a feel for what your customers want. There's no substitute for direct, personal contact.

Put MBCC to Work for You

Tom Peters popularized the acronym, MBWA, which was a very simple and powerful concept: you can't manage people if you don't get out there and Manage By Walking Around. You have to talk with employees, ask them for their ideas, find out about their morale, and let them ask you tough questions, if you truly want to manage effectively.

Well, if you want to *market* effectively, you have to do the same thing. I'm an advocate of MBCC: Market By Calling Customers. It's way too easy to become completely preoccupied with managing your own employees, reading industry journals, and commissioning research. You end up by merely glancing at Executive Summaries, while generally losing touch with the people who really determine your future, your customers.

You need to get out there and talk with them. Fortunately, there's a very efficient tool for doing so: your telephone. Whatever your role is in your organization—president, chief financial officer, manager of finance, or anything else—you simply *must* stay in touch with your customers. Never let a day go by without talking with at least one customer. Stop right now and ask yourself, when did you last encourage a customer to tell you what he or she wanted your organization to change?

It's not critically important that you talk with any particular type of customer. Whether the customer is big or small, old or new, what's important is that you make direct, personal contact, and listen. No formal script is necessary. Just be genuinely interested. Get a printout of your current customers, flip open to any page, stop midway down the list on that page, and dial.

Hello, Mrs. Zunsser. My name is Bill Lane, and I'm the (president/vice president/accounting supervisor, or whatever) at XYZ company. You've been buying (fan belts/slides/carpet cleaning, or whatever) from my company, and I want to thank you for your business. Sometimes we get so busy that we forget to check in with our customers, and that's why I wanted to talk with you for a few minutes. I'd like to find out how you're feeling about how we serve you now, but more important, I want to find out what we can do to improve. There are probably some rough spots in our service or perhaps a couple of improvements we should make to the products you buy. Maybe you wish we'd start making or selling something altogether different, something you have trouble finding elsewhere. In other words, I'm all ears, and I want to listen. For starters, if there's one thing we should focus on to do a better job for you, what is it?

It's best if you *don't* sound all polished and smooth and researcherlike. Be yourself, genuinely care about what your customers think, and just listen. Even if you get no ideas at all, you will have made a powerful, positive, personal impression on your customer, because you made contact.

Now just a minute. Are you thinking that this would be a good thing for someone else to do? I'm writing for *you*. Whatever your formal role is, you work for your customers, and it's always a good idea to check in with the boss to find out how you can do a better job.

Middlemen Can Isolate Your Customers

Whenever there's an intermediary separating you from your customer, communication tends to suffer. That buffer may be a professional research organization, your own field sales force, or simply your corporate hierarchy. In some cases, it may be your current channel of distribution that's preventing an open flow of customer ideas and feedback.

Example

Clinipad Finds Out What It Didn't Know It Didn't Know

You don't know what you don't know. And it's very hard to fix customers' problems if you don't know what they are. While it's a challenge for any sales professional to stay close enough to customers, it's especially difficult when there's a third party involved between the seller and the buyer.

In the medical supplies field, and in many other industries, a manufacturer's products are often sold exclusively by a dealer who may also represent many other noncompetitive products. When this is the case, the dealer's sales reps may be the only ones who maintain (or don't, as is often the case) ongoing contact with the manufacturer's ultimate customer. As you can imagine, the result of surrendering complete control to a middleman can be disastrous, so many manufacturers employ a team of their own sales reps to stay in touch with the dealers *and* some of the larger end-user customers.

One such company is The Clinipad Corporation of Guilford, Connecticut. While they manufacture and market a broad line of consumable medical supplies, perhaps their best-known product looks like those little pre-moistened towelettes that come in your bag of Kentucky Fried Chicken. I say looks like because the medical version of those towelettes is a quite different product. The medical community's quality standards are very different from the colonel's. Before you're jabbed with a needle at the doctor's office, the nurse tears open a little packet and swabs your arm (or some less comfortable part of your anatomy) with an Antiseptic Alcohol Prep Pad. If you're wheeled into an emergency room with a cut or abrasion, the first person who attends to your lesion will rip open a little Poridone Iodine Antiseptic Swabstick pouch to immediately disinfect your wound. These little pouches, and many other varieties, are turned out by the zillions at Clinipad's charming and historic converted clock factory turned medical manufacturing facility in a lovely New England seaside town. From there, the pads are shipped to dealers, who in turn ship them to hospitals, doctors' offices, and other medical facilities across the country.

I became acquainted with Clinipad when the company's president, David Greenberg, hired me to present a seminar at the firm's annual sales meeting. I had planned to talk about the upside-down marketing concept and asked for a list of the sales representatives who would be in the audience so that I could make some calls to interview them and customize my speech.

After talking with several sales reps, I began to feel uncertain about the main thrust of my speech. As I questioned them by phone, I'd ask each rep, "During my speech, I'd like to share some real examples of how some Clinipad sales reps have saved customers who decided to stop ordering Clinipad's products. What stories can you tell me about some of the accounts you've won back after losing them?"

Nobody had any stories to tell. In fact, they all insisted that they had never lost a single customer. I had been asking them to tell me about the business they knew they had lost. But they didn't know of any, because they didn't know what they didn't know. Their primary contacts were the dealers they called on, and the Clinipad reps often had little access to or direct contact with the ultimate end-user customers.

I called David Greenberg to say, "Maybe we should change the topic for the meeting. It seems that none of your reps lose any of their customers."

Right away, David responded, "No, that can't be right. I know we're losing business. Go ahead as you planned, and I'll do some further research."

On the morning of the meeting, just before I went onstage, David handed me a sheet of paper with a summary of the business he *knew* had been lost during the previous year. The total came to $1,100,000, about 3 percent of Clinipad's total annual sales.

The sales reps had been unable to tell me about their lost business, because they didn't know about it. The dealers' sales reps had acted as buffers, insulating Clinipad's representatives from their own end-user customers. When David revealed the startling lost-business figure, he captured his sales force's attention, and everyone collectively focused on getting closer to their customers so they could find out what they hadn't been finding out.

The results of this ongoing effort were surprising and very rewarding. To keep the sales force's attention focused while cross-pollinating their ideas, the president asked all the sales reps to write up synopses of what they were finding out. Rep after rep, story after story, the themes were consistent. Once they got closer to their customers, the reps found that plenty were in danger of falling off the belt, and lots more had already fallen. But, most important, they found that it wasn't all that tough to get them back on.

Tom Joyer, Clinipad's sales rep in the El Paso, Texas, market, wrote about one customer who had purchased $80,000 worth of various types of towelettes in 1992, but was planing to switch all the business to one of Clinipad's competitors in 1993. Why? Because the dealer's sales rep covering the account had left the company, so the customer was getting no attention. Once Tom, as the new rep, was in place, his welcome from the customer was a barrage of quality-control complaints. They weren't just once-in-a-while complaints; they were constant. Clinipad is proud of its reputation for superior quality control, so the dealer's rep discounted the customer's complaints, assuming that the customer was simply being difficult.

When Tom got closer to the customer, though, he found that the customer's concerns were bona fide. To Tom's surprise, he discovered that Clinipad had recently changed the foil packaging it used to keep the pads sealed and sterile, and that indeed, the new material was troublesome. Suddenly the customer was taken seriously and began to be treated as an important partner in assuring quality control, rather than as just a bothersome, ill-informed complainer. The buyer got genuine attention from the dealer's rep, the Clinipad rep, Clinipad's sales manager, and Clinipad's president himself. The defective products were immediately replaced, and the dealer's sales representative made a commitment to see the customer on a more regular basis.

Looking back on the experience, Tom wrote:

> This has worked out so well. Had we not had this quality-control problem, we may have lost this business. A competitor was already in there undercutting us on our pricing. And we had been thinking everything was going along fine. By being made aware of the problem, we were in the forefront

of their thoughts and we forged a partnership. They think we're great now. In addition to the $80,000 they bought from us last year, they brought in another $40,000 opportunity that they had been getting from another supplier. Here is an account we had ignored for a while. Then we had a horrible quality experience with them, and they were ready to switch away from us. We turned it around and picked up more business—which amounts to a 50 percent growth.

This situation, of course, also benefited Clinipad's relationships with other customers, because the manufacturer was alerted to a quality problem that was not yet widespread. Once it knew about the problem, it was able to fix it.

You can only fix what you know about.

One of Clinipad's newest sales reps, Tom Popescu, hadn't sold through dealers in his former job, and he was worried about trusting someone else to sell his products to the end-users. It turned out that his mistrust was warranted. After a prior unpleasant relationship with another manufacturer's sales rep, one particular dealer viewed Tom—who, as far as the dealer was concerned, was just another new manufacturer's rep—as a threat to its business. Tom wrote, "The dealer was stabbing me in the back, taking shots at me and Clinipad, and it was definitely falling off the conveyor belt.

After considering a variety of sales strategies, Tom decided to ask the dealer's national sales director what he could do to make the dealer's job easier.

When I asked him that question, he was speechless—which was a first for him. He thought about the question a long time. Finally he said he thought the best opportunity was to work with his reps and only promote his products. I started to keep in touch with him more, phoning more, writing letters, follow-ups, etc. I had a wonderful meeting with some of the top management people at this account and we came up with some more strategies for a better working relationship by having biweekly meetings. We started to communicate on a more personal level, and these people started to really believe in me. I took interest in them as people, also.

When you decide that you want to find out about what you don't know about, a very good starting place is to ask your customer.

Still another Clinipad sales rep, Jeff Jones, decided to approach a customer who was already completely off the conveyor belt. There were no longer any sales at all to this account. Without adopting a defensive posture, Jeff made a forthright approach to the customer and openly asked why the company had stopped buying from Clinipad. Jeff reports that the answer was simple:

They left us for one reason only: our competitor was doing a big study with them and the customer felt that they owed them the business. The competitor offered them a low price (it was kind of a payoff) but they never came through with service in the long run. They had no character; they were good at the start when it was exciting but, over the long run, gave them no return. Now, I'm giving them good pricing and making them feel very special by providing a high-quality product and excellent value. They are back with us again, and are very, very happy. This is what the conveyor belt idea is all about.

What Can You Learn from This Example?   You must stay close to your customers to keep them on your conveyor belt. It's not good enough to blindly trust a middleman to maintain close contact. Third parties may consciously shield your company from customers' dissatisfaction, and they're almost certainly unconsciously filtering out valuable feedback. Your own salespeople are probably unaware of the business that's being lost, and they have a vested interest in minimizing the apparent magnitude. Calculating an estimate of the actual losses is well worth senior management's attention.

Buying relationships thrive on contact and communication. If you're not staying very close to your customers now, you can be certain that you're losing plenty of business, and are about to lose more. There's simply no substitute for making direct, personal contact with customers on an ongoing basis. You don't know about what you don't know about.

What Can You Learn from This Chapter?

- Customers who have stopped buying from your company aren't the only ones with valuable ideas that can help your company improve. Your present customers will be glad to offer their suggestions, but you have to ask for them.

- Your welcome aboard contacts, if you make them, carry disproportionate weight in shaping a new customer's view of your company. It's well worth ensuring that all new customers immediately sense your organization's intention to form a strong bond.

- Any company participating in a merger faces a particularly ripe opportunity to establish a fresh relationship with the acquired company's customers. The existing customer base should be courted as if they were brand new buyers, or else they're likely to feel little loy-alty toward the acquiring organization.

- Your industry's common guidelines for customer retention don't have to apply to your company. Set much higher retention goals, and implement whatever means are necessary to attain them cost-effectively.

- Whenever significant corporate changes affect your customer rela-tionships, your organization should make deliberate plans to estab-lish enhanced dialogue with your clientele to ensure that the changes are having positive effects.

- Most customer newsletters are far less effective than they should be because they focus on newsy boasts about the company, rather than delivering ideas of value to the readers.

- Relatively small customer complaints can lead to significant market-ing enhancements, if your customer contact representatives are trained and encouraged to listen between the lines, probe for ideas, and take responsibility for seeing them through to fruition.

- While focus groups and other formal research forums are valuable, there's no substitute for talking with customers firsthand. If you want to really know your customers, call some of them yourself.

Action Summary
What You Can Do *Now*

- Focus on the first impression new customers gain of your organiza-tion, and make any changes necessary to make sure those hard-won relationships get started on the right foot.

- Begin making welcome-aboard phone calls to new customers. Be sure they get personal attention immediately after their first transaction.

- Think of merging with your customers as a way of summarizing your relationship aims. Seek to form alliances and customer partner-ships.

- Throw out your industry's habitual rules of thumb and set more ambitious goals for your customer retention efforts.

- Whenever you're involved in a merger or business acquisition, think of the acquired firm's customers as pearls and then do all you can to ensure that they don't slip off the string once you've completed the purchase.

- Make thorough plans to welcome aboard any customers you acquire. Start with a welcome kit and be sure that you include a personal phone call in your program.

- Start a calling program that reaches out to current customers for the purpose of making certain that they are taking full advantage of your product or service. Don't call just to sell something, but be prepared to do so.

- Form affiliations and alliances with other business organizations that can team up with yours and meet more of your customers' needs than you can meet alone.

- Merge with employees as well as customers. Relationships with employees are potentially even more valuable than those with customers and will impact many, many customer relationships.

- Explore some form of incentive pay or recognition for employees who successfully strengthen relationships with customers.

- Create an interdepartmental task force to explore how your various teams can work together and create synergy to build a stronger customer retention program.

- Assume that there is always a large contingent of your customers who have something to say to you but who are waiting for you to contact them. Initiate the contact yourself and they'll gladly tell you what they've been thinking.

- Critically evaluate any newsletters you now send out. Are they touting your company or are they really helping your customers? Are they being read?

- Incorporate some form of feedback like a faxback form or voice mailbox to solicit input from your customers as they read your newsletters.

- Train your colleagues in active listening, and encourage them to hear between the lines when customers offer suggestions.

- Reevaluate the timing of your communications with customers. Ask them if they currently get your information when and how it's most useful to them, in a format they really find useful.

- Be sure that your benchmarking studies always show trend lines tracking changing performance over time, as well as your relative rankings with competitors. Don't, though, expect them to tell you where you need to go.

- Plan a series of customer seminars based on your desire for *two-way* communications, and be sure to include an executive panel to field customers' questions.

- Record the questions and provide them to your whole management team. This is what your customers are wondering about and wishing for.

- Conduct ongoing focus group discussions to allow your less outspoken customers to tell you what they want from you.

- Regardless of your formal personal role, conduct your own customer research daily. Invest three minutes and call a customer right now.

- Commit yourself to Market By Calling Customers (MBCC) on a daily basis.

- Jump over any middlemen that insulate you from your customers. Make direct, personal contact, and reevaluate how you can eliminate or neutralize whatever institutional obstacles serve as buffers.

- Approach distributors and dealers as partners. Ask how you can help them stay close to customers. If they don't want you to be in contact with their customers, maybe you need some new partners.

5

The Critical Value of Staying in Touch

The single best—and easiest—way to keep customers on your conveyor belt is simply to stay in touch with them. They must perceive that you want to have a relationship with them and must feel that the relationship is mutually beneficial. Of course you're sending them invoices and they're sending you checks. That, though, doesn't constitute a maximized relationship. In order to fully capitalize on your relationship, they have to feel that they're getting more than just a product or service for their money. Surprisingly, very few marketers do much to stay in contact with their customers except to periodically ask them for new orders.

We've already discussed the limitations of newsletters and the basic limitation of their being one-way missives. No newsletter can be as effective as a personal phone call. To make customers feel that you take a personal interest in them, you've got to do more than send out mail. US WEST Cellular does just that with the proactive calls described in an earlier example. Their calling campaign has generated an important—and quite unexpected—benefit: customers who receive periodic courtesy calls believe that their cellular phone service is better.

More Contact Brings Better Ratings

When cellular phone users complain about poor service, it's usually the result of specific, measurable quality problems. There's a lot of static during calls; or you can hear other people's conversations; or your call is simply cut off while you're talking as your transmission is handed off from one cell site to another. US WEST now routinely monitors customers' assessments of their call quality. Soon after the company began its proactive calling campaign, its researchers noticed something very interesting. Customers who received the courtesy calls became convinced that their call quality was improving.

Comparing the service quality ratings of customers who had recently received a proactive call with those who had not, the company tracked a 20 percent across-the-board increase in quality ratings. That is, the customers who received relationship-maintenance calls *thought* they were getting better service than those who didn't receive the calls. The comments customers offered were along the lines of:

> You people have sure improved the quality of your network lately. I used to get a lot of static, but it's much better now. And I used to notice errors on my bills, but you must have completely revamped that department, because there are no more mistakes. I also used to notice that I had a lot of dropped calls when I went behind the big hill near my house on the way home from work. That's much better now, too. Did you install a bunch of new antennas out here?

As a matter of fact, *no!* The customers who were given the proactive attention and rated the company's service 20 percent higher in all categories were using the same network, the same antennas, and the same billing department as all the other customers. They rated the service better, though, largely because they *felt* better about their partnership with US WEST Cellular.

The Halo Effect

What had the company done to reduce static? Nothing! The only difference was that they had started making the personal calls to show customers that they cared about them. A kind of halo effect took place as customers started thinking "It's unusual and quite nice that US WEST Cellular calls me now and then to check up on me. They're a good company. They care about me. Their service *is* good." Quantitatively, customers who receive the company's periodic proactive calls rate US

WEST Cellular's call quality 20 percent higher than those who use exactly the same network facilities but don't get the calls.

It pays to stay in touch with customers. You contribute to their perception of your good service, you have the opportunity to gain an early warning signal if problems are beginning to develop, and you also enhance the customer's feeling of loyalty. Very few companies do it, though. This is a ripe and easily captured opportunity for you.

The relationship-maintenance call should be made with a specific customer-oriented objective in mind. All too often, such calls are poorly received because it's clear that the marketer is calling with only a selfish motive in mind. Often, you can almost hear the calling employee saying:

> Oh, hi there. We haven't heard from you in a while, so I just thought I'd check in and see how things are going with you. Is everything OK? Would you like to place an order, as long as I have you on the line?

Here's my rule of thumb for making relationship-maintenance calls. If the customer hangs up feeling glad that you called, you're on target. Ask yourself just before you dial, "What am I going to do in this call that will make the customer feel glad that I called?" Think of your customer's secretary saying, "Deborah, I have Jason on the line for you." Your aim is to have Deborah think: "

> Oh, good. Whenever Jason calls, it's worth my while to talk with him. He usually has some good news or a suggestion for me.

Most of the time, if we could hear our customers' thoughts, they'd be saying:

> Oh, *him.* He's probably calling to ask for another order. Probably getting close to his month-end sales contest deadline again. What a bother. I'm too busy for him.

Naturally, customers can sense when our motives are purely selfish, and they resent it.

A Tip of the Day Keeps Resentment at Bay

One solution to this situation is to have a *tip of the day* in mind when you call. Think of yourself as an expert business consultant who is constantly in contact with many companies whose operations are much like this next customer's—the one that you're about to phone. You hear about many customers who are doing well, and you often hear about the good ideas that led to their success. Often—but not always—those ideas involve the use of your products and services. Without divulging any competitor's proprietary information, your aim is to pass along a suggestion or two in each contact with your customer. Remember, the more successful your customers are, the better able they'll be to buy more of what you're selling.

Your tip of the day might be along the lines of:

> Steve, I was talking with one of my other customers last week, and I picked up an idea that I think you may want to use. This customer is a manufacturer like your company, and my contact told me about a new inventory control technique they're using to reduce their overhead costs. I thought of you because of the similarities in your operations. Let me tell you about how it works, and you can see if it has some merit for your company.

Note that the idea you pass along may or may not involve a sale or use of your product or service. If it always does, your customer will soon recognize that these are veiled attempts to sell more of your stuff. As a genuine partner, you want to help your customer thrive, and your scope of suggestions will extend well beyond your own personal interests.

Contact Continuity Counts

An effective customer-contact program should be ongoing and multifaceted. In actuality, most are halfhearted and short-lived. It's amazing when you think about it. I suspect that as you read this you're thinking, "This isn't revolutionary but it makes a lot of sense. Surely everybody does this already." Now, ask yourself, "Which are the companies I buy from that give me ongoing, far-reaching, beneficial attention?" Having trouble coming up with many examples? Your customers are just like you; they also don't have many suppliers giving them the kind of attention we're talking about.

Example

Brock Control Systems Practices
What It Preaches

All too often, consultants and companies who are in the business of advising others don't follow their own advice. We all know the parable about the cobbler whose own children went without shoes. In researching *Upside-Down Marketing,* I came across one software marketer whose success story has been built on showing other companies how to maintain close contact with their customers. *And this company follows its own advice!* Much of its success is based on the fact that it uses its own software system—the same one it sells to clients—to run its own business. In fact, revenues for the last four years have grown at an annually compounded rate of 37 percent, while profits have grown at 54 percent annually.

Richard Brock is the founder and chairman of Brock Control Systems, a software solution provider based in Atlanta, Georgia. Only to hear Richard tell it, software is only the tangible evidence of his company's true business: partnering with customers.

In fact, Richard says, "If somebody doesn't want to be a partner, we don't want to sell them software." Brock sees his organization as being filled with expert business counselors who want to work on behalf of their clients. The many modules of the software they sell are intended to revolutionize (or, shall we say, turn "upside down") the way Brock's customers do business. This starts off with a module called "Database Marketing Activity Manager," and carries right through with telemarketing and field sales automation, culminating in the module named "Customer Care Activity Manager." The whole series emphasizes relationship responsibility. Using Brock's software, no lead, prospect, or long-term customer can ever fall through a crack unnoticed.

It's remarkable that so many marketers are so loose—or shall we say, sloppy—about sales accountability. Brock aims to help them tighten up. For example, *The Wall Street Journal* published the results of a five-year study conducted by Performark, a Minneapolis specialist in sales and marketing services. The research company mailed in thousands of responses to advertisements for goods and services costing at least $5000. You'd think that the price tag would make it worth the advertisers' while to react responsibly to prospects' inquiries. However, Performark found otherwise. It took an average of 58 days for the requested pamphlets or brochures to arrive, and nearly 25 percent of the inquiries went unanswered. Only one in eight inquiries generated a follow-up sales call—an average of 89 days after the inquiry!

Brock's software is designed to change all that, and the emphasis on accountability and responsibility begins at home. Not only does Brock's own sales process maintain a tight rein on leads with detailed follow-up reports spelling out exactly what happens to every lead and who's responsible. It also recognizes that the typical traditional sales representative just isn't very good at following up.

Another important part of Brock's marketing plan is the idea that Brock Control Systems must respond to human nature, rather than try to change it. The reality of human nature is that sales reps who concentrate on and excel at landing new accounts just won't stay as close to their customers as would be most beneficial for the customers and for Brock Control Systems. In recognition of this, the account is handed off to the customer-development representative and the commission is split between the original selling rep and the person who will have ongoing contact with the customer. Very few other businesses face the fact that new-account reps simply won't maintain contact with old customers. There is too much hand-holding involved. Brock *does* recognize this reality of human nature, and its solution to the problem is paying off well.

Brock began using customer-development representatives—staff whose responsibility was to service only the existing installed customer base—in 1991. The program has been so successful that Brock Control Systems now has seven customer development representatives to whom accounts are handed off once the 14 new-account representatives have completed their sales. They use a teamwork approach involving four individuals:

1. The new-account rep who originally made the sale

2. The customer-development rep who is responsible for ongoing customer retention

3. The customer

4. The professional service person who assists with the actual implementation of the software

Among those team members, the customer is often the greenest, least-knowledgeable individual.

After installing the software, customers are encouraged to purchase an annual maintenance plan that entitles them to software updates and ongoing training and consultation. The annual cost amounts to 18 percent of the original software price. In a recent campaign, Brock Control Systems sought to find out why some customers had gone off their maintenance programs. They implemented a maintenance amnesty campaign and were successful at getting some major customers back on the plan. Under this amnesty program, customers who had not upgraded in a long while could get back onto the maintenance program and install the current system without undergoing the expense of the several incremental upgrades they had passed up.

It's interesting that Richard Brock describes the situation with the following language: "If they didn't buy the maintenance program, it's because *we* failed to demonstrate its value." This is exactly the kind of terminology that shows Brock's acceptance of responsibility when a sale isn't made.

One of the things Brock discovered during the maintenance amnesty program was that its software was so good that most customers who did not go on the maintenance plan were continuing to use the program and were quite happy with it. The shortcoming was on Brock's part because it had not effectively demonstrated why it was worth taking advantage of the extra value offered through its annual maintenance program. This led to a renewed emphasis on long-term partnering with customers.

Brock Control Systems has also discovered that the relationship is not just between the software buyer and Brock but must also be with the people who actually use the software, particularly since there is a relatively high level of personnel turnover among their customers. About 50 percent of the people who come to Brock's Atlanta headquarters for training were not at all involved in the original software purchase decision and do not fully understand the objectives of the marketing campaigns Brock Control Systems software is intended to help with. Sometimes they have just been sent to the class without any real understanding of Brock's partnering role with the customer.

Brock has recognized that it's important to develop a personal relationship with all members of the team, not just with the person who made the decision to purchase Brock Control Systems in the first place. Richard uses some great visual analogies. A good doctor doesn't just give you a prescription for medicine. He makes sure that you take it. You can't let a child run amuck and eat whatever she/he wants. As a parent, your role is to make *sure* they have a good diet. If you have a health club and someone comes in to lose 10 pounds when they really need to lose 40 pounds, your responsibility is to show them what they need to do and help them do it. Brock Control Systems takes this same view with customers. They are partners in the success of the customer.

"The better we know our customers, the stronger our relationship will be." It's very embarrassing for Richard to speak at a conference and encounter a customer who has had internal turnover that Richard doesn't know about. This is one reason it's so important to have the customer-development representative stay very close to the customer.

Customer referrals are Brock Control Systems's very best source of business, so they have an excellent referral system that places a high value on referrals and includes a reward structure. It's kind of like a frequent flier program. Customers get points for providing referrals, and they're mailed a quarterly statement showing their point totals. These points may be redeemed for training and consultation services, documentation, or registration at the annual users conference.

Customers are particularly delighted with the follow-up aspect of the referral program. They are quite happy to give references because they are pleased with the product and service. What they like most of all, though, is hearing what happened to their references, so Brock makes it a point to send update letters to customers who provide referrals. They tell the customer what actually happened to the referral and describe the outcome. This is exactly the kind of positive reinforcement that gets people to keep giving more referrals.

Richard says that customers often don't know what hardware and software configurations they should be using, and Brock Control Systems has the internal expertise to act as an effective guide and partner. If a customer changes hardware or operating systems, Brock levies no charge for changing out the software.

Brock Control Systems does not settle for an annual customer satisfaction review. It does it weekly, surveying a cross section of their customers to make sure they are doing well. Brock sends a $10 reward to everybody who fills out a survey for Brock's professional services organization—the fastest growing part of their business—which is responsible for presale consultation and postsales customization and implementation. The company has even started surveying its telemarketers' calls to make sure that they are effective.

Brock Control Systems has been particularly successful with banking customers. Many of them are using Brock Control Systems software to become much more proactive in response to customer inquiries and to sell additional services to their customers. The Bank of Montreal is one good example. It has an outbound teleservicing group that has been able to generate an 18 percent increase in CD renewals. During the renewal calls, the reps notice if the customer has no line of credit or no credit card, and proceed with cross sales.

Lenders are also using Brock Control Systems to facilitate refinancing of their borrowers' loans. Realistically, customers are probably shopping for refinancing options anyway, so Lincoln Services, a full-service mortgage banking company with mortgages in 48 states, doesn't wait for customers to start contacting competitors. They call their customers first. This makes customers happy, so they stay with Lincoln Services.

What Can You Learn from This Example?   Salespeople who are charged with the responsibility of bringing in new business probably won't do such an outstanding job of maintaining the relationship once it's begun. You'll probably be better off, and your customers will, too, if you turn newly acquired accounts over to specialists whose primary interests are in developing long-term relationships.

Structuring a sales organization built on teamwork and shared goals will yield your biggest profit payoff. The initial salespeople and those with primary responsibility for account development must remain in close contact, and they should have a common stake in building the long-term customer relationship.

If your partnerships with customers aren't as strong as you'd like them to be, there's only one party to blame: your own organization. The responsibility for nurturing the relationship rests with you, not the customer. If it's not strong enough, you have the power to make it stronger.

A referral gathering program can be highly profitable and rewarding to both your company and your customers. The vital feedback loop is what most companies overlook. Be sure that your customers know what became of their referrals and are given incentives for helping to establish relationships with new buyers.

Customers will build strong partnerships with you if you approach them on a long-term basis. Sporadic, short-term programs won't build the level of relationship that's most beneficial for both you and the customer.

Example

IBM Becomes More Attentive

One fortunate result of upside-down marketing is that it can produce win-win outcomes that you never even expect. Many propitious ventures begin with a program conceived to achieve one objective and end up succeeding in quite another way. Consider the genesis of IBM's version of an upside-down marketing program, called their After-Market Group. Back in 1990, IBM realized that some of its relatively low-revenue customers were just too costly to contact in the conventional face-to-face way. So, they set out to experiment with phone-only attention for some of IBM's smaller customers. The program started as a test in the Denver office with one client support team serving a trading area of several western states.

Theorizing that there must a lower cost coverage strategy for customers who weren't in IBM's top tier, a small group of pioneers set out, as researchers, to contact the targeted customers and find out how they'd feel about being contacted more regularly, exclusively by phone rather than by a field sales rep. As would be the case with nearly any company that took the trouble to find out, IBM soon discovered that lots of its customers were falling off the belt. Sure, the field sales reps maintained close contact with the largest, most active customers. But when it came to the smaller and midsize accounts, contact was often infrequent at best and sometimes altogether absent.

When IBM's phone-based researchers called the smaller accounts, they often encountered customers who hadn't had any contact with IBM in over a year. And we're not talking about tiny buyers who just purchased a couple of PCs. These were business customers with midrange computers who may have originally spent $25,000 to $75,000 on IBM hardware and software and then lost all contact with their sales reps.

Alana James, one of IBM's Client Support team coleaders, recalls her initial call to Wallace Vacuum, basically a mom-and-pop specialist in the vacuum cleaner business. "Why," you may ask, "would a little vacuum cleaner company even be *on* IBM's customer list?" Well, this relatively small company had originally leased a $40,000 IBM AS/400 mini-computer to manage all its business affairs. Ironically the company founders, a husband and wife team, were both ex-IBM employees.

When Alana first called, though, the reaction she got ran along the lines of, "How dare you call us! Now that we're your customer instead of employees, we hate IBM and we never want to talk to you guys again." In their own minds, these customers had "lost $40,000" on IBM equipment. The original computer hardware had been sold along with COBOL software as its programming language. Wallace Vacuum, though, was never able to use it. The owners had understood the original IBM sales representative to say that COBOL would run the various business applications the company needed with a minimum of adjustments. In actuality, the software needed lots of adjustments for Wallace Vacuum's applications—*so* many that the company simply wasn't using the IBM computer and had instead acquired a competitor's system to run the business. On the day of Alana's call, though, *that* computer had just crashed, so the customers' emotions were rather frayed.

Wallace Vacuum didn't immediately buy lots more IBM hardware and software. But there was a positive outcome of another sort: IBM successfully neutralized a highly vocal and very negative client who would otherwise have had a negative affect on many other customers and prospects. Perhaps even more important, IBM learned from the situation and realized that Wallace Vacuum wasn't alone, and that its concerns were valid and needed attention. This one situation dramatized the plight of many other IBM customers. Lacking after-sale contact, they were finding that nobody at IBM was readily available to help them solve their problems, so they were fuming in frustration instead.

In addition to seeking actual solutions to their problems, customers wanted something very basic: attention. Kendra Lee, IBM's project leader, was surprised to learn how much and what type of contact they said they wanted most. During the research phase of the program, fewer than 1 percent of the customers expressed a preference for face-to-face visits, while 82 percent said they wanted periodic phone contact. Rather than "stop calling and bothering me," customers were saying, "I'm glad you called, I hope you won't wait so long next time."

Acting on her customers' desires, Kendra has spearheaded IBM's after-market group strategy with an emphasis on giving customers what they want. Of course, the starting point is to *find out* what they want. So, that's the basic approach taken by IBM's telephone reps. They begin their contacts by asking customers what they want.

"We're calling to find out what business concerns you're facing and how IBM may be of service."

Telephone reps begin with a baseline survey and ask customers how often they want to hear from an IBM representative, what kind of contact they prefer, how happy they are with IBM, and whether or not they would recommend IBM to others. Starting with IBM's target guideline of one contact with every customer at least once every 70 days, they let the customers dictate whether they want more or less frequent calls. About 35 percent actually want to be called more often.

Customers typically express surprise at getting a call from IBM, and quickly add that they're happy to be getting some attention. They *want to communicate.*

Fortunately, they also want to buy. While the representatives' primary goal is to increase contact with customers and give them an opportunity to communicate any concerns or needs they may be feeling, they also find plenty of opportunities to sell additional products and services to these existing customers. Remarkably, customers are quite happy to make significant purchases by phone without face-to-face contact. Typical sales range from low-end terminals costing $800 to $2000, to high-volume printers costing $5000 to $10,000, and even AS/400 computer upgrade packages costing up to $50,000—all exclusively by phone. And all because IBM took the time to ask customers what they wanted, then listened and acted on what their customers told them.

As you might guess, the cost of generating sales by phone is lower than those involving face-to-face contact. IBM hasn't left it to guesswork to estimate how much less costly the telephone sales channel is. Their financial analyses have confirmed that telesales is the least costly, most profitable way to satisfy customers' needs. Even if you disregard the long-term benefits of strengthening customer relationships and uncovering and addressing problems and concerns, the reduced sales cost alone is a compelling reason to service existing customers with more frequent phone calls. The net profit margin on a sale consummated by a field rep working with an industry remarketer (IBM's term for an industry specialist reseller, or business partner) is as low as 4 percent (going up to 11 percent in the infrequent best-case scenarios), depending on the specifics of the sale and the level of support needed. With the telephone-based after-market group, however, the same net profit on the sale can reach 17 percent.

What Can You Learn from This Example?   The lessons IBM has learned will most likely apply to your business, too:

- Small and mid-size customers are probably getting too little (if any) attention from your field sales force.

- Those same customers typically welcome more attention and are probably feeling neglected because of their present level of contact.
- Given the choice, most would probably prefer periodic phone calls rather than face-to-face contacts.
- Those same customers are also quite likely to buy more products and services once you establish ongoing phone dialogue.
- Your net profits from phone sales are going to be much higher than through traditional direct sales channels.

The bottom line is this: You'll profit by giving customers what they want, but you can't tap that potential unless you first find out what they want, and to do that, you have to get in touch with them.

Customers Welcome More Attention

Repeated examples in a very wide range of industries and business situations continue to show that customers respond favorably to more frequent contact, so long as it's the type of contact that is of benefit to them. In earlier chapters you've read the profiles of Washington Mutual Savings Bank, AAA, Graphic Controls, Thorndike Press, and others. There's always a common theme to their success. The closer they get to their customers, the more they and their customers benefit.

Err Toward Too Much

But, how much is too much? Isn't there some point at which customers will feel bugged by your attempts to be attentive? Yes, of course, it can be overdone. But it's being so vastly *underdone* right now that I wouldn't worry much about smothering customers with too much attention. The frequency of contact should reflect the intensity of your relationship and your capacity to help customers. If you can't do much to benefit them and the type of purchase they make is typically an annual situation, twice a year may be enough. If they buy from you frequently and you can be a real help to them, perhaps your contacts should occur twice a month. As a general rule, though, aim for at least quarterly contact. If you're not now initiating quarterly contact to poll your customers for feedback, suggest ideas that will help them, and probe for unmet needs, you're definitely not overdoing it.

If They're Not Complaining, Increase Your Contact

Example after example has shown that customers want and appreciate more frequent contact, and that they'll show their positive response by increasing their purchases. If you reach the point where you're giving your customers too much attention, they'll let you know. We've explored many ways to forge stronger links with customers, including feedback-gathering focus groups, more formal research surveys, and MBCC programs. If you're overdoing it, your feedback will alert you.

Continue Contact, Even When Buying Wanes

Another aspect of buying/selling relationships that we've seen again and again involves variability. Relationships don't stay the same. Sometimes our customers need us more, sometimes less. Our relationship-nurturing efforts should not be dictated solely by the frequency of orders we receive. It often takes a very long time to maximize relationships, and there will be lulls in purchase activity along the line.

For example, I've always been curious about real estate professionals' relationship-developing efforts with buyers and sellers. Right now, as I write *Upside-Down-Marketing,* I have eight condominium units that I want to sell, and I also want to buy some recreational property. Who's going to help me? I don't yet know. In the last five years, I've worked with six different realtors on various purchases and sales, but not one of them maintains contact with me. I don't even get a one-way newsletter from any of them. Doesn't it make sense that someone with real estate investments is likely to do some buying and selling again in the future? Wouldn't it be easier for those who've already served my needs to invest in our relationship and patiently wait in the wings for my next transaction? I'm sure that there are some agents out there who are conscientious about keeping client relationships strong, but I'm afraid they're the exceptions.

Relationship Means More Than Just Exchanging Money

If you're to have a viable relationship with customers and clients, it must persist even when money isn't changing hands. The real estate agents I've dealt with have each stopped helping me when they cashed their commission checks after a completed transaction. Don't they realize that I can't view them as long-term partners if they just wait around for their checks and then disappear? Sound relationships are based on long-term service and exchanges of ideas even when there isn't a commission check hanging in the balance.

Example

Celestial Seasonings' Great Tea, Plus Something from T

What do you get when you open a box of Celestial Seasonings tea? Great tea. And nothing else.

That was true from the early 1970s until 1994. But the next time you open one of the 40 million boxes of Celestial Seasonings tea that American consumers buy each year, you may get something more. It's all because T Taylor decided to give something more to Mo Siegel, founder of Celestial Seasonings.

T (It stands for nothing, so there's no period; he changed his name from Robert after discovering there were six other Roberts in his fifth-grade class.) is known for his extraordinary creative talents. He's also known as a man who is committed to his principles and to doing the right thing. After 11 years as a founding member and creative director at CareerTrack Seminars, he followed his vision and started his own agency, The Creative Alliance. Never one to let himself get too comfortable, he was leaving the security of a 32-member, highly acclaimed group to enter the uncertain world of entrepreneurship. It took guts.

Mo Siegel was an herb-growing, tea-loving hippie back in the 1970s. He cultivated his crops, concocted unusual teas and herbal mixtures, and sold them to health food stores in his home state of Colorado. Although he wasn't really aiming to become a packaged-goods giant, the business exploded. By 1988, Kraft, a division of The Philip Morris Companies, was impressed enough to pay $55 million for his company. Mo moved on, followed his heart, and started Earthwise, a company dedicated to producing biodegradable dishwashing liquids and other environmentally correct household cleaning products.

Introduced by a mutual friend, Mo and T originally crossed paths in 1990. They quickly discovered they had a few things in common, including their principles and love of marketing. T's new agency did some design and creative projects for Mo, and Earthwise quickly became The Creative Alliance's biggest account.

By this time, Celestial Seasonings had been sold to a new owner who realized that it wasn't just another packaged-goods company. It had great potential, but it required a great leader. Celestial needed Mo's "heart and vision" to tap its true potential, so he was enticed back as CEO of the company. T thought, "That's great for Mo, but there goes the Earthwise account. Not good for the agency."

Struggling, with three young children and $38,000 in debts, T knew that The Creative Alliance's business future was on the line. He had enjoyed great personal rapport with Mo at Earthwise, and now T desperately needed some major assignments to keep his agency afloat. Mo's position back at the helm of Celestial Seasonings offered that opportunity. But how to reach him?

As a busy CEO of a major company, Mo's time was totally committed and a veritable shield of assistants blocked out distractions and kept him focused on the daily operations of the company. T was unsuccessful at breaking through to actually speak with Mo. Thinking about what they had in common, T realized that he and Mo had both relied on their spiritual convictions to shepherd their businesses. Having grown up with strong Christian values, T sums up his business philosophy in this way: "Have faith and do good. The money will follow."

T decided he would do whatever he could to help Mo. When he came across a particularly effective catalogue, ad, or promotion from any company competing with Celestial Seasonings, he sent it to Mo along with suggestions to help Celestial Seasonings improve its advertising and marketing.

For example, when T's colleague and new partner, Russ Minary, noticed a *New York Times* article about the burgeoning iced tea industry, they sent it to Mo with a little note saying, "Why isn't Celestial Seasonings in this article?" When a local newspaper profiled Mo's successful career, T faxed him a copy of the article with a note of congratulations.

In other words, T kept in touch. He didn't pitch the business or even ask for anything. Although Mo was no longer his client, he offered ideas, suggestions, and congratulations. He relied on the Golden Rule and did what he would want someone to do for him. He focused on giving.

Then, one sunny day in Boulder, Colorado, T was dropping off some materials at Celestial Seasonings. There was a commotion in the parking lot, which turned out to be an outdoor photo shoot. As T made his way across the lot, a man on roller blades broke free from the crowd and skated over. It was Mo. He said, "I've missed you, T." They quickly made arrangements to meet in Mo's office. In the next few days, T outlined a plan of creative ideas in preparation for the meeting.

At the meeting, T began by asking his friend a single question: "Mo, how many boxes of tea do you sell each year?"

"About 40 million."

"And what's in those boxes?"

"Tea."

"Nothing else?"

"No, just great tea."

"Mo, what if each of those boxes contained *something more?*"

And T went on to outline a plan that could literally quadruple Celestial Seasoning's sales, using the products, customers, and vehicles that were already in place—just by adding one small thing to each and every box of tea.

T compares his relationship with Mo and other associates to a courtship. In interpersonal relationships, it's common for people to give each other a lot during the early stages. You want to impress each other, so you may send flowers, write thoughtful notes, offer fun ideas, and generally emphasize giving rather than getting. Then, in most relationships, the giving part fades away and both partners think more about what they are doing than what they are giving. That's when relationships fizzle.

What Can You Learn from This Example?   To succeed in personal relationships you have to give more. To succeed in business relationships, the same principle applies. And when you give because you care, not just because you want to get something back, good things happen. This may take a long time. A relationship can go through long lapses with little sign of life. But your instincts should tell you if there's potential for long-term mutual gain even if it's not likely to pay off on your financial balance sheet soon—or even ever. The next time you open a box of Celestial Seasonings tea, look inside. You'll find great tea, sure. But you'll also find a little something extra, courtesy of Mo Siegel and T Taylor.

Three Business-Based Relationship Builders

I haven't meant to imply that your relationship-developing programs should only benefit your customers, or that generating increased revenue for yourself isn't important. It not only *is* important, it's a sign that your relationship is healthy and beneficial to the customer.

The following five business-based, revenue-yielding techniques will strengthen customer relationships while increasing your profits. Each is underutilized, and highly profit-leveraged.

1. Upgrade Volume for Your Customers' Benefit

Increasing the volume of the business you do with your customer benefits you for sure and also benefits your customer. If you're one of several nurseries supplying plant materials to a landscaping service, and you can increase the level of business by helping the landscaper consolidate more of her purchases with you, your customer benefits. If your pricing policies make any sense at all, you'll be able to offer better pricing on larger volumes. The benefits, though, go far beyond lower unit costs. Having a buying relationship with any additional supplier means more paperwork and overhead costs for your customer.

Reduce the High Cost of Buying. Several of my larger clients have discovered that their internal administrative costs to initiate a single purchase can range from $40 to $100. Somebody prepares a purchase order; it gets handled by a couple of clerks; the receiving staff watches for the shipment; it's routed to the correct department; the documentation is sent to the accounting department; they watch for the invoice; somebody correlates the original purchase order with the receiving report and sends it through to bookkeeping; and so on. Each person, each step in the process, adds to the cost of the purchase. It costs about the same, administratively speaking, to buy a ream of copy paper, a case of it, or a truckload. As the order size increases, though, the portion of the total cost that's wasted in administrative overhead expenses decreases. If your customer is buying a $5 ream of paper from you, and expending $50 in administrative costs, you're helping him go out of business. If you're able to upgrade that order to a $500 shipment, you're helping your customer reduce his expenses and assisting him in being more profitable. (Of course your costs for handling each order are also high, so larger outgoing orders are very beneficial to you, too.) If you are ultimately able to increase that order to a blanket purchase order that constitutes a standing order for tons of paper, you're further reducing your customer's administrative costs and are likely to also pass along much lower per-unit pricing.

Use Incremental Costing to Encourage Upgrading. Always seek to upgrade your customers' orders for their own benefit—and for yours. One of the most effective techniques is to quote incremental pricing. A client of mine recently asked me to offer a variety of my audio and video tape programs to a seminar audience with discounted multiprogram pricing. The ordering sheet included seven different programs, each regularly priced at $79.95. For the seminar audience, though, any one package was discounted by 24 percent to $60. Each additional program was further discounted. Rather than quoting the total price only, we highlighted the incremental cost. Four programs, for example, carried a total discounted cost of $205. Five programs totaled $240. If I weren't using incremental costing, the most logical way to describe the discount would be to say: "Any four programs are $51.25 each; any five are $48 each." The incremental costing approach, though, is much more persuasive, and encourages the upgraded quantity: "Any fifth program is just $35." A buyer who's planning on getting four at $51.25 is already planning to invest $205. A fifth program will increase the total order to $240 (six times $48 each). It's the *incremental cost* that should be the customer's primary concern. Look at it this way: if the customer has already decided that the programs are worth $51.25 each to him, and you're willing to add another program for just $35, aren't you doing your customer a *disservice* if you don't make it very easy for him to increase his order?

Always cite the incremental cost for increasing your customers' order volumes. Make it very clear that the incremental per-unit cost of the additional items that will get the order up to the next quantity price break is comparatively small. All the while, you're also reducing your customer's total cost per item by spreading the administrative costs of processing the order out over a larger number of units.

There's another, even less obvious benefit of upgrading customers' orders. In addition to the actual product costs and the administrative costs, there's also a time cost associated with making purchases. You have to hunt around for a reliable supplier, invest the time necessary to build up a level of trust, and take time to get comfortable with each other. If your customer is already buying from you and you're able to help satisfy more of that customer's needs, you're saving him the time costs of finding and dealing with another supplier.

For reason after reason, it's in your customer's best interest—and yours—to upgrade the current buying relationship in terms of quality *and* quantity.

2. Practice Cross-Selling for More Hooks

You'll remember that John Bartholomew's banking clients find it very profitable to offer credit cards to current customers (the associated credit card fees and interest earnings are relatively minor considerations). Tom Boyd's teams at Washington Mutual want to help customers with multiple products and services in addition to their basic checking accounts. Again, it's not the direct profits from any one sale that generate the primary benefits of these *cross-sales*. The main benefit of increasing the variety (as opposed to the volume) of products and services that your customers buy is that each new product serves as a further hook connecting you with your customer. If a customer has a checking account at one bank, an equity loan at another, and a retirement account at a third, all three banks' relationships are vulnerable. If all of those banking products are provided by a single bank, their relationship with the customer is much more secure.

One of the best ways to intensify your relationships with customers is to broaden them. Look for additional products and services that you can provide for your customers. The best sources of ideas, of course, are your customers themselves. When talking with them firsthand as you proceed to Market By Calling Customers, when commissioning research companies to poll customers, and when conducting focus groups, always seek to find out what additional services and products your customers would like you to provide. The more hooks you provide, the more secure and long-lasting your relationship will be.

3. Bond with Referrals

Attend almost any sales seminar, read any book on sales techniques, and you're sure to be reminded of the value of gathering referrals from your customers. Yet, when is the last time that someone who sells to you asked you for referrals? Although the practice makes all kinds of sense and is easy to do, very few salespeople put the technique into practice. The normal approach to referral gathering stresses the benefits to the salesperson. Certainly they are considerable. Referred prospects are much more receptive to a salesperson's approach, are much more likely to buy, and also tend to become more valuable customers who place larger orders for a longer time. But these aren't the primary benefits of referral-gathering. Asking for and following up on referred leads is another way of strengthening relationships with the referring customers and keeping them on your conveyor belt longer.

I often think back to a very effective referral gathering technique used by the company that used to insure my cars when I lived in California. This particular company accepted only customers whose driving records were unblemished and who drove cars with low accident rates. If you'd had a couple of DUIs and drove a Porsche, this company wouldn't insure you at any price. They catered to the very lowest-risk population of drivers, and their rates were always the lowest available anywhere. For as long as I lived in California (the only state the company is licensed to insure in), I was a steady customer, and one day one of their salespeople called me and said:

> Mr. Walther, you're exactly the kind of driver who makes it possible for us to keep our rates so low. You should be very proud of your driving record because I see that you've had no moving violations, ever and have never been involved in any kind of accident either. There aren't many drivers who can say that these days. We want to keep on providing the lowest possible rates for you and other safe drivers, and I'd be happy to contact any of your friends who also drive very safely. This will help us keep serving you well, too, by ensuring that we only cover people with the lowest risk of filing claims. That's what keeps our rates low for you. I'll be happy to call them directly. Among your friends, who are the two or three very safest drivers you can think of who also drive low-risk vehicles?

Since he put it that way, I was happy to provide a couple of referrals, and I also felt a closer partnership with my insurance company. You can use a similar approach to get the same positive results with your customers. Follow the simple steps outlined below.

Tell Customers Why You're Asking *Them* for Referrals. Let's face it, you have some customers who you wish would go away and quit buying from you. They're more trouble than they're worth and they're unpleasant to deal with. Getting them to pay is like extracting molars, and they're just no fun. You shouldn't ask *them* for referrals, because their friends and associates will probably also be a pain to deal with. Only ask your very best customers if you want to get referrals who will be a pleasure and profitable to deal with.

Now, if you're going to be selective and ask only your very best customers for referrals, how are they to know that? Tell them! Start right off by letting your good customers bask in the attention they deserve. Just as the insurance agent congratulated me for my outstanding driving record, tell your customer why he or she is so valued by your company. I'm not talking about buttering him up with false flattery. I mean *sincerely* telling your customer why you like dealing with him or her.

> Mr./Ms. Olson, I deal with quite a variety of customers in my work, and very, very few of them are as pleasant to deal with as you are. I probably haven't told you often enough why I appreciate having you as one of my accounts. You're always open-minded when I make suggestions, you're prepared with all the details when you call in to place your orders, and you make sure that your bills are paid on time. As a company, we appreciate you, and I myself appreciate you most of all.

Of course your customer is in a positive frame of mind now, and feels good about your relationship for good reason.

Point Out How Referrals Benefit Your Customer . The insurance rep who had called me explained that my rates could be kept low only by finding additional very safe drivers to insure. What he didn't say, but what turned out to be true, is that my friends appreciated my referrals, and I benefited through their appreciation. The company saved me a lot of money on my insurance premiums. When I referred friends and they saved a lot of money, too, my friends were glad that I had referred them.

When you call to ask for referrals, be sure to show your customer why it will be of benefit to him to help you.

> I feel that we've developed a good relationship and I will always do my best to be as helpful as possible. I'd like to help some of your colleagues, too. I concentrate my attention on a relatively small number of customers whose relationships I value highly, so I can give them top-quality attention. I'd like to give some of your associates that same level of quality.

Ask for *Specific* Referrals. The insurance representative didn't call and say, "Hey, know anybody I can call to try and sell some insurance to?" The question was very specific. He was only looking for "the two or three very safest drivers you can think of who also drive low-risk vehicles." This makes it much easier for your current customer to think of exactly the right kind of referrals to offer you.

When prompting referrals from your customers, make it easy for them to cooperate by asking specific, clearly-defined questions:

> Among your colleagues, there are probably a few purchasing agents at other companies who come to mind when you think of people who are a pleasure to do business with and whom you respect as being very conscientious. I'd like to call them and see how I can be of service. Who are the two or three people you'd recommend I get in touch with?

Referral gathering is a very profitable and rewarding way to sell. But the practice also benefits your existing relationships by strengthening the partnership bonds you want to nurture with your customers. The specific way you prompt referrals determines how successful you'll be at getting them.

Staying in touch with customers pays off with stronger, more enduring relationships that are worth more—to both of you—now, and over the long haul.

What Can You Learn from This Chapter?

- The best and easiest way to keep customer relationships active is to stay in touch. To maximize profitable relationships, customers should perceive that they have a connection with your company.

- More frequent contact leads to higher perceptions of quality. A customer who feels that your company cares enough to stay in touch and provide helpful information thinks you are a better company.

- When customers think more highly of your company, they also rate your product and service better, thanks to the halo effect.

- When making contact with customers, it's important that the information conveyed benefits the customer, such as with a "Tip of the Day."

- Traditional salespeople are oriented toward initiating customer relationships, rather than maintaining and extending them. Your company will probably be better off if it places the responsibility for nurturing alliances with individuals other than the original salespeople.

- A surprisingly high proportion of any company's customers probably want more frequent contact, particularly by phone. IBM found the figure to be 82 percent for its customers. What about yours?

- It is possible to contact your customers too much. But it's extremely unlikely that your company is in that situation. Odds are overwhelming that you're currently giving your customers too little attention.

- Increasing sales to your customers benefits them by reducing their cost of buying, as well as their unit costs.

- Using incremental costing is the best way to dramatize the savings inherent in increasing order volumes.

- Cross-selling strengthens bonds with customers by positioning the marketer as a more indispensable business partner/supplier.

- Soliciting referrals also builds relationships between sellers and buyers, if it's done right.

- When soliciting referrals, first explain why you're asking this particular customer for referrals, then point out the benefits to the customer, and be specific about exactly what kind of referrals you seek.

Action Summary
What You Can Do *Now*

- As you continue to track customers' perceptions of your quality, correlate their ratings with your frequency of contact and notice that quality ratings increase as contacts increase.

- Before calling any customers, be prepared to provide an idea or suggestion that will make them feel glad that you called.

- Prepare a series of "tips for the day" to use when calling customers. Build an internal system and reward structure for employees to craft these customer-benefiting ideas.

- Balance your tips and suggestions, ensuring that some do not directly benefit your company with increased sales.

- Ask yourself and your employees to think of actual examples of companies that provide you with high-quality ongoing attention. Use their techniques as models when developing your own systems.

- Honestly assess how your organization responds to sales leads, and compare the results with the Performark study.

- Evaluate your sales management system's ability to ensure that new-business salespeople have sufficient incentive to provide ongoing support after the sale is made. Consider instituting a cadre of customer development representatives.

- If you sell any type of ongoing service plan, experiment with an amnesty program designed to get lapsed customers caught up and back on your belt.

- Use descriptive language that appropriately acknowledges your firm's responsibility for the failure to convince customers to buy what you're selling.

- Seek relationships with end-users in addition to the purchasing decision makers to strengthen relationships with your customers.

- Build a reward system for customers who provide referrals.

- Implement a feedback loop so that your customers are advised of the outcome when they do provide referrals.

- If you use written surveys, provide substantial incentives to customers who take the time to complete them.

- Launch an internal analysis of the cost of covering your small and midlevel customers with your current sales program. Compare those costs with a phone-based program.

- Notice how few of your customers complain about getting too much attention; find out how many would like more of it.

- Find out if customers who currently receive face-to-face attention would prefer a different kind of attention.

- Ensure that your customer contact programs continue even during lags in purchase activity.

- Track your own internal costs for processing orders and estimate your customers' administrative costs for generating them. Focus on reducing the per-unit costs for both parties by upgrading order quantities.

- Cite incremental costs to move customers to higher purchasing volumes.

- Constantly seek logical cross-sales that will help strengthen your relationships with customers by increasing their reliance on you to satisfy more of their needs.

- Look for areas of your business where you can stimulate customer referrals, and be sure to tell customers why you're asking *them* for referrals, point out how referrals will benefit them, and ask for *specific* referrals.

6

Strengthening Partnerships by Meeting Needs

When you seek enduring, long-term relationships with customers, your constant aim should be to deepen and strengthen your ties. The more needs you meet, the deeper will be your customers' reliance on your business partnership. To maximize relationships with customers and capture their full profit potential, you must constantly analyze their changing needs so that you can meet more of them.

There's a rule of thumb in the insurance business that illustrates what I mean. If an insurance agent sells you one policy, let's say term life, there's a slightly better than 50/50 chance that you'll renew it next year. But if he sells you two types of coverage, perhaps a term life policy and homeowner's insurance, the odds of renewing both policies next year are more like 75 percent. And if he sells you three types of coverage—say life *plus* homeowner's *plus* disability—the odds shoot up again to something like 95 percent. Increasing the *breadth* of the needs you satisfy deepens the relationship and strengthens your bond.

That insurance guideline isn't very surprising when you think about it. The same line of thinking applies to the banking business, as we've seen in previous examples. If you have a checking account at one bank, a CD at another, and your savings account at a third, your relationship with each bank is relatively inconsequential and vulnerable. It's easy to move one account away from any one of the banks, and you probably don't feel a strong sense of loyalty. But if all of your banking business is consolidated at a single institution, you're much less likely to move elsewhere. If for no other reason, it would be just too big a hassle. The more needs are met, the stronger the relationship.

The same basic principles that apply in banking and insurance also apply in *your* business. Whenever a business is able to satisfy more needs for its customers and whenever its customers buy more of a given product or service, the relationship between them deepens and strengthens. If you own a travel agency and a client books her flights herself and only occasionally calls you for special hotel values, your relationship is weak. If that client regularly asks you to handle all hotel arrangements, also books flights through you, and has you handle her rental car reservations as well, your relationship is much stronger.

When it comes to strengthening relationships by satisfying more customer needs, the primary limitation is our failure to recognize and uncover those needs. If you want to be truly successful at building strong and enduring relationships with your customers, you must uncover more of their needs and then meet them.

Don't Ask Unless You're Going to Act

Of course, the most effective way to find out what your customers need is to ask them directly. Whether you use focus groups, mailed questionnaires, or phone calls from the CEO's office, it's absolutely necessary to analyze what your clients' needs are if you're to satisfy them and become an indispensable long-term partner. The analysis, however, will be worthless unless you follow through and take action on what you've learned. Making promises that you'll meet more needs and then failing to do so will only damage your relationships.

Analyzing Customer Needs Is an Ongoing Imperative

The kind of direct contact with customers that is designed to uncover and analyze needs must not be viewed as a one-shot or periodic effort. It must be constant and ongoing. Customer requirements are changing all the time and you have to keep asking your clients about their needs over and over again to keep abreast of and anticipate their developing wants.

Whose Department Is It?

Yours! The constant search for and satisfaction of customer needs is the very essence of marketing, and every single person in your organization can play a role. Even employees who never directly talk with customers can contribute by recognizing their own personal needs when they're acting as customers and suggesting ways to incorporate them into your firm's offerings. What you want to develop is an organization in which everyone is aware that they come to work each day in order to uncover and satisfy customers' needs. If that's not done, there will be no job for anybody.

Example

Airborne Is Big Enough to Deliver, Small Enough to Listen

When you see an Airborne Express courier dashing to her truck, or spot one of those black and red shipping pouches, you probably assume that Airborne is just like the other air express companies. Not quite. Airborne is highly specialized and concentrates on serving the needs of fast-growing businesses with high-volume shipping needs. This keeps Airborne's costs down, and also helps it keep its sights fixed on customers' needs. Airborne's single most important business advantage is its size. It's big enough to benefit from economies of scale and small enough to listen to its customers—*and act on what they say.* Airborne's core marketing strategy is to find out what its target shippers want, and *deliver* what they want better than anybody else in the business.

Is this approach working? Airborne is the fastest-growing air express company in the country. They're in their fifth decade of international service, with shipments to 200 countries. One of Airborne's handling stations was the first transportation facility in the United States to receive certification for meeting the super-stringent ISO 9000 international standards for quality service. On a station-by-station basis, Airborne continues to pursue the ISO 9000 certification for all of their facilities systemwide.

Everyone at Airborne—at every level of the company—is acutely aware of the partnership role they play with their customers. Needs analysis is the cornerstone of Airborne's corporate culture. Sales reps and district managers meet regularly with key customers and ask, "What do you need from us? What could we do to strengthen our partnership? How can we help?" An internal telesales group is charged with the responsibility of not just growing their business but also conducting informal research. They, too, constantly ask customers what they need and ask if Airborne is meeting their expectations.

Airborne offers shippers a multitude of innovative programs that
have grown directly from customers' past suggestions. One of their
largest national accounts is a medical testing lab that specializes in
the rapid analysis of blood and urine samples. Of course their
samples have to be fresh, but it's also critical that they be secure.
AIDS awareness, the potential for medical contamination, and the
legal implications of drug testing all combine to make a chain of
custody absolutely essential. Traditional tracking procedures
weren't secure enough for this customer, and normal shipping
pouches didn't offer adequate safeguards. Airborne listened and
went to work, creating a new type of tamper-proof packaging called
a Lab Pack and a highly sophisticated tracking system for these
sensitive shipments.

When IBM awarded a huge contract to Airborne giving them the
exclusive right to expedite all of its shipments under five pounds,
Airborne listened carefully to the shipper's needs, and ended up
adding extra aircraft to their nightly schedules at key IBM shipping
locations to ensure that no package or pouch would be left behind.

A wide variety of changing market conditions and customer
suggestions led to the creation of Airborne's third-party logistics
subsidiary, Advanced Logistics Services (ALS). Many of ALS's
services for customers take place in the fast-growing Airborne
Commerce Park, a 447-acre business and industrial park being
developed adjacent to the parent company's privately owned, all-
cargo airport in Wilmington, Ohio. The park includes nearly a
million square feet of warehousing space. ALS oversees extensive
warehousing and distribution capabilities and provides state-of-the-
art information and technical support.

If your sophisticated equipment breaks down in Java, you can ship
it to the Airborne Commerce Park's foreign trade zone, send in your
technicians to diagnose and repair the fault, and then ship it back to
Indonesia without ever clearing U.S. Customs or paying
international duties. The facility even offers a service called Central
Print to enable the American Express Lifeco Travel service to have
its clients' airline tickets and travel itineraries printed out at
Airborne's facilities as late as 2 a.m. Eastern Standard Time and still
have them delivered the same morning throughout the continental
United States.

Several industrial equipment manufacturers answered Airborne's
needs-analysis questions by explaining their requirements to get
replacement parts shipped in a hurry when their equipment failed in
the field. Airborne's response was to create the "Stock Exchange"
system—essentially a network of Airborne Express warehouses filled
with its customers' coded emergency parts—ready for immediate
loading onto Airborne's jets.

As you might expect, Airborne offers overnight morning and
afternoon deliveries, as well as economical second-day service and
special handling for large shipments. But next-morning wasn't fast

enough for some of Airborne's customers, so it instituted a *same-day* shipping service by offering a door-to-door express arrangement through its Sky Courier subsidiary. Why? Because customers said they needed it. Airborne listened *and took action.*

Other customers complained about the administrative overhead associated with handling Airborne's shipping invoices and processing them for payment. Airborne's response was to do away with invoices for these customers. Some of its shippers never get what you think of as a regular invoice. Instead, their shipments are itemized and debited electronically; even the payments are electronically shifted to Airborne's accounts receivable department without anyone needing to print out checks and stick them in envelopes. Innovations like this automatic billing and payment system might seem to have little to do with getting customer's packages delivered on time. But Airborne doesn't just view itself as a shipping company. Its aim is to form strong partnerships with customers to meet their shipping-related needs and deliver outstanding satisfaction even if this means changing the way Airborne does business.

What Can You Learn from This Example?   Listening to your customers pays off, but only if you're prepared to take action based on what you hear. At Airborne, listening and acting is part of the corporate culture. Management inculcates every employee, and practices the same disciplines at the top. Expand and reframe your thinking about the partnership role you play with your customers. At Airborne, it would have been easy to say, "We pick up documents and packages, put them in airplanes, and deliver them to consignees. We're not in the warehousing business and we're certainly not going to print up travel itineraries for our customers' customers." That kind of limited thinking, however, would have meant totally overlooking some of Airborne's most successful innovations at Commerce Park. *Your* guiding aim should not be to narrowly stick to the business you seem to be in, but instead to meet more and more of the needs your customers express.

They'll Talk If You'll Listen

Customers aren't the least bit reluctant to help marketers improve their products and services, it's just that we don't often ask for their input. I have yet to encounter a company that sincerely sought its customers' ideas, and ended up saying, "Gee, they just wouldn't give us any."

Where's Your *Real* Product- Development Department?

Your customer base constitutes your real product development department. If you're positioned as a long-term partner with your customers, you'll seek out their opinions.

Some companies go to extreme lengths to find out how their customers would improve their products. One of the great software success stories comes from Intuit, Inc., publisher of Quicken and QuickBooks. Both are programs that dominate their respective categories: home and small business accounting. In addition to their excellent traditional telephone service operation, focus groups, and formal surveys, Intuit uses *follow-me-home* research, in which Intuit calls retailers to get the names of customers who have purchased Intuit's programs. Then researchers go to the customers' homes to watch them actually using the software so that they can see what hang-ups may occur for the average user.

Cofounder and CEO Scott Cook says:

> In a consumer-driven company, the *R* in R&D is lots of customer research. In order to meet the needs of customers, you have to be very good technically, but you get to the technology through up-close-and-personal contact with the consumer.

Example

High-Tech Firms Stay Attuned to Their Customers

There you are, piloting your 747-400 on its final approach to Hong Kong's Kai Tak airport and thinking, "I'd really rather be landing my Cessna 182 in Renton." You can be. Because the company that made your software is listening to its product development team: *you* and all the other avid fans of its flight simulation computer program. The airports and aircraft used in the software are not selected by some product designer, but by customers who are called for their ideas and requests.

Some of the world's leading high-tech companies are fanatical about staying in tune with their customers' needs and wishes, and they do so by contracting with ATTUNE, a Bellevue, Washington, marketing services company that maintains a constant vigil for them. (ATTUNE's clients are understandably mum about their secret marketing tool, so their identities are disguised here.) When a new software program or significant upgrade to an existing program is released, product managers at one of the most famous West Coast computer companies hold a daily staff meeting on the project's progress. The meeting takes place at 4 p.m. and everyone involved knows what customers have been saying all across the country right up through 3 p.m. that same day! ATTUNE's researchers are on the phone, calling customers for their feedback until 3 p.m. (6 p.m. on the East Coast, where most business users have already completed their full day of testing the software). ATTUNE's array of personal computers calculate quantitative analyses of the customer research, quickly interpret the results, summarize the qualitative comments, and modem the comprehensive reports to the product management teams daily at 3:45 p.m. for distribution at the 4 p.m. meeting.

When you compare these high-tech companies' stunning growth records over the last decade with the relatively mediocre performance of most low-tech companies, think about what their respective marketing managers are saying. The high-techies may be grumbling: "It's three forty-five and we still don't have the new national research analysis. Our meeting starts in fifteen minutes; we have to know what our customers think!" The others are saying: "I wonder when the latest national research analysis is going to show up. It's already May, and we have our planning session for next year's product launch coming up next month, already." Don't you suppose that a significant part of the high-tech companies' success has to do with their managers' consistent, urgent preoccupation with customers' opinions?

As PC users around the world are installing version X.0 of their operating systems, ATTUNE is already making daily research calls to beta testers who are using version X.1, and are helping to plan the features of version X.2. There is no possible way that a fast-moving software company can test every possible unusual use of its products, given the variety of computers and software packages that its customers use every day. So they do their very best internal research, and then turn to their external research team, *their customers.*

Another one of ATTUNE's successful clients sells the leading high-end graphic display system that's been used by Boeing engineers to design the 777, by Michael Jackson's video producers to create captivating effects, and by Steven Spielberg to conceive computer simulations of DNA manipulations for *Jurassic Park.* This company thought it might be nice to follow up and talk with its customers after system engineers visited their sites to fix computer system technical problems. In the beginning, a few employees tried to do this during their already busy day, or stayed late and made some evening phone calls. As a result, the company discovered that its sophisticated customers were delighted that someone cared enough to follow up and talk with them. Now, the company says, "We don't consider a job complete until the customer has been called and asked for feedback about our engineer's visit." J. D. Powers is well known for publishing the leading customer satisfaction rankings in the automotive industry, but in the computer industry, that authoritative voice is Dataquest. Dataquest ranks ATTUNE's client in the number one spot—ahead of that for Sun, IBM, Digital Equipment, and Hewlett-Packard. And the client is determined to stay in front of its competitors in the sophisticated computer graphics workstation marketplace.

This company recognizes that customers' perceptions of its field service are the direct result of specific experiences with the individual engineers who make the service calls. They're not leaving the engineers' performance to guesswork. Thanks to ATTUNE's system, all the systems engineers know exactly where they stand compared with their colleagues, as well as knowing what their rating trend has been over the last nine months and what the three-month projection of where it's headed looks like. Each individual systems support engineer gets his or her own monthly customer satisfaction survey, including both the quantitative results of customers' rankings ("How would you rate the engineer's technical abilities?" "Response time?" and so forth), and a summary of qualitative comments.

What Can You Learn from This Example?   Companies that are moving fast and advancing in quickly changing business environments don't rely on customer initiated feedback only. They actively seek it themselves—and quickly. You give yourself a tremendous competitive boost when you decide to stay close to your customers. The faster you hear from them, the wiser your product development decisions will be. It's not enough to wait for them to make contact with you. The most profitable position is to take a proactive stance and reach out to customers, treating them like product-development partners. Consider forming a long-term, ongoing relationship with a third-party marketing firm that has already developed expertise in this field. You may find that your customers are more open when they talk with a third party, too.

Think Beyond Your Product

It's easy to think of "needs satisfaction" as being linked to your product. As Airborne Express's example shows, programs you initiate and changes you make to satisfy needs may go way beyond your current offerings and may be only indirectly related to the business you seem to be in.

Step back from your current business and ask, "What are my customers really buying? Why do they do business with me in the first place? What is it they want?" Toyota asked itself and its customers those questions back in the early 1980s and realized that buyers want ownership satisfaction, not just good cars.

Example

The Lexus *Concept* Includes a Car

Lexus isn't just the name of a car. It's the name for a conceptual product that embodies superior customer satisfaction and aims to delight customers and convert them into advocates. It sprang from the fertile imagination of an American car man named John French who suggested one critically important word change at Toyota.

You may have thought that the Lexus was designed in Japan. It was. The *automobile* was engineered by a Japanese man named Suzuki. The body, engine, interior, and dashboard all came from Japan. But they are not what sets the Lexus automobile apart from other fine automobiles.

More than anything else, the Lexus is a customer satisfaction *concept* that just happens to include a vehicle that delights customers. The actual car is just one facet of the conceptual package. You buy a Lexus because you know that the dealer who sells it to you is going to take care of you. You buy it because Lexus is consistently ranked at the top of customer satisfaction surveys. You buy it because the name connotes luxury in both the automobile and the care you will receive as a customer. You buy it because you've had a friend tell you that his dealer washes and waxes his Lexus without charge when he takes it in for an oil change. One of my colleagues talks enthusiastically about the time he took his Lexus in for a routine tune-up and found, on picking it up, that the dealer had—without charge—repaired a parking lot dent in the driver's side door. The car itself is certainly top-notch, but it's Lexus's way of making you feel cared for that is unsurpassed.

On a flight from Los Angeles to Dallas, I had the good fortune of sitting beside John French, the person who actually came up with the name Lexus, and he told me the story of the car concept's beginnings.

John grew up in the car business, working both at Ford Motor Company and at a Ford dealership in Portland, Oregon. Later, he moved over to Toyota, again working in a variety of capacities in the field organization, dealership network, and at the national headquarters. He told me about a monumental change at Toyota that hinged on changing a single word in a dealer performance index. That one word change led directly to the genesis of the Lexus concept.

In the early 1980s, John was responsible for Toyota's customer administration department, and he presided over its owner satisfaction budget, or OSB. This was a management-budgeted sum allocated to cover repairs for Toyota customers with unusual

circumstances. If you bought a Toyota that had a problem and you
brought it in for repair within the warranty period, there was no
question that the dealer would have it fixed, and would bill Toyota
for the costs. But if you didn't experience the problem until after
your warranty expired, you might not be so lucky. If you were
sufficiently insistent and persistent, you might still get Toyota and
the dealer to fix the car without charging you. The dealer would in
turn charge these unusual repairs to Toyota, which debited them
against the dealer's OSB.

In 1982, Toyota budgeted for these customer satisfaction repairs,
and measured and evaluated dealers based on their adherence to the
budget. If a customer came in with a problem after the warranty
period, Toyota and the dealer could decide to fix it and charge it to
the OSB, all in the name of customer relations. But if the budget was
used up, and another customer came in with the identical problem,
the repair might not be approved. "The way to be a hero," John
recalls, "was to come in under budget."

John reasoned that this policy was rewarding the wrong behavior.
Toyota's field representatives and Toyota dealers were being
rewarded and favorably evaluated for turning away the customers
who represented Toyota's future success and reputation. Short-term
behavior was hurting the company in the long term. Since dealers
had been trained to mind budgets rather than customer
relationships, John implemented "The Toyota Touch" concept in
1984. This concept referred to an arrangement whereby the corporate
customer relations folks could step in and take over if a Toyota
customer was not satisfied. The focus was now clearly to be number
one in customer satisfaction.

John started thinking about the implications of the word *budget.*
As businesspeople, we're conditioned to think of the all-important
budget as the maximum amount we should spend. But he didn't
want dealers to *spend.* He wanted them to *invest* in customer
satisfaction. So the fund's name was changed from Owner
Satisfaction Budget to Owner Satisfaction Assistance. The familiar
OSB line item in the budget became known as the OSA. The
manufacturer's role, John reasoned, is to assist dealers in creating
satisfied owners who will buy again and speak highly of Toyota to
their friends.

It worked. Dealers began investing in assisting customers rather
than coming in under budget. And, in the process, the company was
investing in long-term customer satisfaction ratings that led to a
dramatic rise in Toyota's rankings in customer surveys when
compared with the figures for competing cars. Toyota's management
teams in Japan and the United States noted that the brand was
showing strong growth in customers' satisfaction and in their
indicated intent to buy Toyotas in the future, even though the car
itself had not dramatically improved.

This scenario led to some important what-if thinking. What if

Toyota were to create a new division to build and market a superb car that came with unsurpassed customer care? Thus John French became the first employee of this project and commissioned a New York creative agency to conceive a name for a new company and product. The moniker specialists came up with a list of 30 potential names, later narrowed to 24 finalists. One of the names presented by the agency was Alexis Motorcars. *Alexis* didn't sound right to John or present the feeling or image he had in mind. So John dropped the *A* and substituted a *U* for the *I*. Now he had a name that presented an image of high technology with a feeling of luxury. After much testing and focus grouping, the project team ended up with *Lexus* and with Toyota management's okay, it was finalized. In 1989, the first Lexus automobile was sold in the United States, and if you have a friend who owns one, you'll already know that Lexus customers rave just as much about their customer care as they do about the automobile itself.

Toyota's success with the Lexus project stems not so much from the technical excellence of the car itself, as from the superb job the company did of analyzing, understanding, and meeting car owners' needs.

What Can You Learn from This Example?　As you review your current systems for satisfying customer needs, be on the lookout for small things, like the word *budget*, that may be subtly distracting your employees and colleagues from their goal of creating satisfied customers. Sometimes satisfying them requires adding a completely new service or product line or even establishing a new brand, as Toyota did with Lexus. Just tweaking your current service policies and improving your product may not be a dramatic enough change to win enduring relationships with a whole new base of customers, particularly if your current reputation is only so-so. As you analyze your customers' needs and seek ways to satisfy them, think well outside your current brand and product. Look for new ways to use your resources—like automobile factories, for example—to meet customers' needs. You may come up with a whole new product concept, and maybe even a new company.

A Promise Is a Promise

When you discover what your customers' needs are, be very cautious about promising to meet them and then failing to do so. Breaking a promise is much worse than making no promise in the first place.

To avoid falling short of customers' expectations, *manage* those expectations. A big part of customers' opinions of our companies stems from a comparison of our performance with their expectations. Where do those expectations come from? Often they begin with us and the promises we make. If you place an order with me toward the end of the day and I think there's a chance it'll still go out today, it's tempting for me to tell you that I'll get it right out. You hear this as a commitment. If, as happens all too often, things don't go quite as smoothly as I had hoped and your shipment doesn't go out until tomorrow, you're disappointed with me for falling short of your expectations. I'm much better off to say your order will ship within 48 hours, and then *still* do all I can to get it out today. Although your initial reaction to the 48-hour commitment may be slightly negative, you'll be delighted when your order arrives "early" or at least "on time."

To put yourself in the best possible light, make commitments that you're positive you can keep but are also quite confident you can beat. This sets realistic expectations for your customer, avoids disappointments, and provides you with the opportunity to exceed those expectations, creating delight.

Example

How Apple Underpromised, Then Overdelivered

The photography field has changed dramatically over the last few years, thanks largely to new technologies that permit computer manipulation of photographic images. Using digital imaging and retouching, a computer-savvy professional photographer can alter almost anything in a photo, given the right combination of hardware and software. Apple Computer is the standout leader in this highly specialized, fast-growing technology market segment.

When the Professional Photographers Association, or PPA, began making preparations for its 1993 annual convention to be held at Nashville's Opryland Hotel, they assumed that they could once again count on Apple's support. For years the computer company had made sure that seminar leaders had the latest computers on hand at the photographers' convention to use for live demonstrations of new techniques. Apple didn't charge the association to use the equipment and, of course, the association's implied endorsement of Apple's product line as the de facto standard for photographers helped Apple's image and sales with this important market.

The year 1993 was another tumultuous year for the computer industry, and it was especially tough on Apple Computer. Due to staff cutbacks and general disorganization at the company's Cupertino, California, headquarters, the PPA's convention planners got nothing but a runaround when they called to arrange for the equipment loans. Their old contacts had moved on, and the new people in charge of this type of promotion seemed unaware of Apple's long-standing commitment to support the photographic industry. They were not at all helpful.

So, the photographers tried to get help from Apple's regional people in Chicago, where the association is headquartered. Again, no help. The convention committee started to get nervous as the show date approached. Without Apple's support in the form of computers for the seminar classrooms, they'd have to cancel some of the scheduled programs and use technologically inferior non-Apple machines for the others.

Planning a major event like this one, with 5000 professionals expected to attend and dozens of seminar sessions to coordinate, is a daunting, time-consuming, complicated task, to say the least. Apple's failure to provide the expected support was the last thing the planners wanted to deal with. With only one week to go before the convention's opening session, they finally found someone at Apple who was willing to listen, and act.

Steve Turner is Apple's market development executive, based in Nashville, the site of the convention. When the PPA's electronic imaging coordinator finally tracked him down, Steve describes the photographer's disposition as "frustrated, desperate, and panicked." The PPA representative said, "Look, we're trying to help Apple maintain market leadership by giving you great exposure at the convention, but absolutely nobody will cooperate." Steve's first reaction was to put himself in the customer's place. The Professional Photographers Association wasn't charging Apple for the publicity and they weren't looking for any gifts or handouts. All they wanted to do was borrow several computers for a few days during the convention so the seminar instructors could showcase Apple's technology and teach other photographers how to use it. After all, Apple had routinely done exactly the same thing for past conventions.

Steve knew it was well worth helping the PPA, and he had a pretty good hunch that he could get them at least partially out of their jam. So he asked them exactly what they needed.

> What we need is ten of Apple's top of the line machines, each fully loaded with twenty megs of RAM. And each one must have a large, top-of-the-line color monitor with a video accelerator board installed.

That was a tall order.

As he listened to their request on the phone, Steve was looking at three top-end computers right there in his office. But he had no way of lining up seven more. So, rather than going out on a limb and making a promise he might not be able to keep, he said only:

> I'm going to do my best for you, but I can't make any firm
> promises right now. Tell me, though. Would it help you out if I
> were somehow able to line up two or three machines for you?

At least this would mean that they could proceed with their most
critical seminars, forcing the cancellation of only a few less
important ones. Hopeful of averting a complete disaster, the PPA
representative said:

> You bet it would. I think we can make some adjustments to
> get by with two or three machines.

The photographers had already been disappointed by Apple, so
Steve was extra careful not to let them down again. He made sure he
didn't overpromise and underdeliver. In fact, he did just the
opposite. He underpromised so that the customer's expectations
would be realistic. And then he got to work trying to exceed their
expectations by overdelivering.

After much hurried scrounging, Steve Turner came up with not just
two or three, but five high-powered machines. And he phoned a contact
at RasterOps, manufacturers of top-quality monitors, to plead for some
displays. Everything came together, and the Professional Photographers
Association had five powerful computer systems delivered to the
Opryland Hotel's Convention facility just in time for the seminars.

The PPA had been disgusted with Apple, but now they were very
appreciative. Steve credits his practice of underpromising for the
complete change in how the PPA views Apple. As he puts it, "If delivery
equals expectation, it zeroes out." He didn't want to zero out, he wanted
to delight the photographers. So he promised less than he knew he could
deliver, anticipating that they would set lower expectations for
themselves and then feel truly delighted when he overdelivered.

What's most important about this incident between Apple and the
Professional Photographers Association is not the convention itself,
but the relationship. Looking back, Steve says:

> These are nice people. They didn't yell at me, and they
> wouldn't have written any nasty letters complaining about
> their treatment by the corporate office staff. But I'm sure glad
> they tracked me down because otherwise they would have
> just quietly gone away feeling very frustrated about Apple.
> IBM, or Compaq, or somebody else would have been sup-
> portive at next year's convention, and after a while, the whole
> photographic industry could have slipped away from us.

What Can You Learn from This Example?   Once again, the relationship theme comes through loud and clear. When you turn your
marketing priorities upside down, you can better focus on the value of

your long-term relationships. That's much more important than the resolution of any one incident. Valuable long-term alliances can be damaged—at great cost—by bungling seemingly small episodes.

Whenever you're presented with a situation in which the customer needs *big* help, and you're fairly sure you can come through with a *little* help, be sure to underpromise. This lowers the customer's expectations to realistic levels and puts you in the position to overdeliver and create satisfaction.

Your ultimate success in maximizing customer relationships depends on your ability to analyze, understand, and meet the needs of your customers. That's what will keep them on your conveyor belt.

What Can You Learn from This Chapter?

- To maximize customer relationships and capture their full profit potential, you must constantly analyze customers' changing needs so that you can meet more of them. The more needs you meet, the deeper will be your customers' reliance on your business partnership.

- Direct contact with customers that is designed to uncover and analyze their needs must be constant and ongoing.

- Listening to your customers pays off only if you're prepared to take action.

- If your company sincerely asks customers for their ideas, they'll readily follow through and provide them.

- Your best product development ideas will always come from customers who are actually using your products and services. They're the only ones who can reliably suggest what's needed to improve what your company does. Ask them.

- The standard for "fast feedback" has dramatically shortened in the past few years. Getting input about customers' opinions last year or last quarter is no longer fast enough. Aim for real-time feedback. The more quickly you know, the faster you can react.

- Sometimes it's best to rely on an outside vendor who specializes in securing quick, objective feedback from your customers.

- If your company renders a service, consider reframing your definition of when the service is complete to include a direct follow-up contact as part of the service process. The service isn't complete until the customer has been contacted and polled.

- Your customers are in the best position to provide candid feedback about the performance of your people. Ask them.

- If your company has a "budget" item for customer satisfaction, the inherent implications of the word probably encourage your people to minimize expenditures in this area. You'll be better off to think more in terms of investing in customer loyalty.

- A broken promise to act is much worse than no promise at all.

- In order to better manage customer's perceptions of their own satisfaction, it's best to underpromise and overdeliver.

Action Summary
What You Can Do *Now*

- Make a candid audit of the number of needs you meet for your customers. Are you, like the vulnerable insurance companies and banks, meeting just a couple of needs rather than developing breadth and depth in customer relationships?

- Track down the ideas that have *already* been submitted by your customers and find out their status. Is somebody working on them right now? Before launching a campaign to get more ideas, are you confident that there's a smooth system in place for acting on the ones you have already received?

- Get the word out in your company's internal newsletters, E-mail, and voice mail reminding everyone of the role they play in soliciting and *acting on* your customer's needs.

- When brainstorming internally or with customers, think way beyond your current product and business. Are there additional or innovative procedural or administrative needs you can satisfy for customers, as Airborne did?

- Honestly assess how welcoming you are regarding your customer feedback. Do you give your clients the cold shoulder and permit obstacles to interfere with their input? Do you simply accept their suggestions passively? Or do you actively reach out to your customers?

- View your base of customers as your product development department and conduct a departmental audit to determine how much performance you're getting from that department. If it's falling short of the same expectations you set for other departments, is it their fault, or yours? What can you do to change it?

- Measure the time it takes for your organization to hear and analyze customers' feedback about their needs. Do you get it daily, as in the example of ATTUNE's clients, or annually, or only sporadically?

- Make sure that your mechanism for soliciting, analyzing, and acting on customers' needs functions on an ongoing basis, not merely in response to some temporary push for a needs analysis.

- Given that customers' perceptions of how well their needs are being met tend to be formed during individual encounters with personnel, are you doing anything to monitor your people so that you can spot trends and identify any corrective action that might be needed?

- Think about the *concept* that your customers are buying from you. Could a new division, brand, name, or even company deliver it better?

- Survey procedures that encourage behavior *other* than satisfying customers' needs, and change them. Remember Toyota's change from Customer Satisfaction *Budget* to Customer Satisfaction *Assistance.*

- Make sure that you personally underpromise so that you can overdeliver, even if what's involved is some small commitment like saying when you'll complete a report or arrive at another office for a meeting.

- Encourage changes in your company's policies so that you under-promise as a matter of corporate habit.

PART 3

Getting Customers on the Belt

Don't read this section unless you're confident that you are already doing all you can to stem the loss of customers who are falling or jumping off your relationship conveyor belt. Then make sure that your current relationships are secure. From a profitability standpoint, both goals are far more highly leveraged than the aims of this last section.

Yes, the strategies you'll read about here will improve the efficiency and effectiveness of your prospecting and selling efforts as you seek new customers. But any gains you make in those arenas will have far less impact than your efforts to strengthen current customer relationships and salvage ex-customers who no longer buy from your company.

I've written these last three chapters *not* because I want this to be yet another comprehensive sales training manual, but because your actions in coaxing new prospects onto your conveyor belt do influence how long they'll remain with you. By employing the strategies outlined here, you can do a lot to lengthen customer relationships even before they begin.

You can conserve your resources while prospecting and qualifying leads so that your best prospects for long-term, highly profitable relationships receive your highest-quality attention. That's the best way to get relationships started on the right foot.

7

Al Dente Prospecting and Qualifying

One of Peter Drucker's most useful contributions to the lexicon of business is his clear differentiation between the words *Efficiency* and *Effectiveness*. Efficiency is doing things right. Effectiveness, Drucker reminds us, is doing the right things. Balancing the two is a major challenge in any commercial enterprise, particularly when it comes to prospecting.

The biggest shortcoming of most sales prospecting activities is that they are very inefficient and, at the same time, very ineffective. They employ the al dente approach familiar to pasta chefs everywhere. Fling a lot of noodles (or leads) at the wall or ceiling, and see if some stick. If so, you've succeeded! The pasta is ready; you've got a prospect! If nothing sticks, keep flinging more and more up there until something sticks and your efforts pay off.

Marketers pursue a large number of potential leads, send out heaps of costly sales literature, schedule many face-to-face sales calls, and clog up their appointment calendars with multiple phone contacts. All of this attention goes to leads that are largely unqualified. Very few are really likely to ever buy anything and should really be thought of only as "suspects."

When pursuing a large volume of unqualified leads, this system is both inefficient and ineffective. The pasta chef's approach results in salespeople who are so busy chasing all those unqualified leads that they fail to give quality attention to the relatively few leads who might actually become qualified prospects.

Prospect for Relationships, Not Sales

If your firm's eventual success and profitability is measured by its ability to keep customers on your conveyor belt for many repeat purchases, then you should be prospecting for relationships, not sales. A marketing campaign that pulls in 10,000 onetime buyers is much less profitable than one that produces 2500 customers who each buy four times and have the potential for remaining active customers for years.

As you design and modify your prospecting system, your goal should *not* be to produce leads. Your aim should be to produce leads that turn into sales that turn into relationships. Every time you produce a lead that *doesn't* go on to become a sale and a long-term relationship, you're costing the company money, not producing profits.

The High Cost of Lead Fulfillment

One of my clients, an otherwise sophisticated marketing organization in the Midwest, won't permit me to use its name because of the embarrassing answer one of its representatives gave to this simple question: "How much does it cost you to provide your fulfillment literature as follow-up to sales leads?" The response went like this:

> Gee, I'm not really sure, but I have a feeling it would make me sick if I knew. Let's see. The leads come in to the fulfillment center, then they get sorted and logged. Then they're sent over to marketing, where they get separated by sales territory and product interest. Then they go over to the data entry department and sit around for a while until the clerks have the time to give them coded mailing labels. Then the mailroom clerk chooses the right brochures according to the coding of the request, and finally, they go out in the mail. Altogether, I'd say about $25 in handling costs, plus maybe $4.50 in printing and supplies. Plus postage. So, around $30 each. Yikes!

The answer I got to my follow-up question—"And then what happens?"—was even more disturbing:

> Well, every week or two we bundle up a stack of little cards showing the source codes and all that we know about the leads, and we mail them off to the field sales reps, and hope they follow up on them. But we really don't have any way of knowing for sure what they do with them.

I know what they do with them. And you can guess, too. The bulging pouch arrives, gets put at the bottom of the mail stack since the sales rep knows what's inside, and then the reps all have some coffee and talk.

> Geez, those guys at the home office must be really busy. My leads envelope is thicker than ever. Where do they get those names, anyway? None of them ever amount to anything. I get college students working on school projects who just want samples of our brochures, competitors checking out our pricing, and some people who have no recollection at all that they ever even saw our ads. I think they're just bored and start asking for free literature. I'd never have time to sell anything if I followed up on all those stupid worthless leads they send us.

(I hope, as you read this, that you're certain it doesn't apply to you. And I hope you're right.) If you're making use of the newest contact management and sales lead-tracking programs, you may have a good handle on what's happening to your leads. If you truly do, you're part of a very small minority and I congratulate you. But that's still no guarantee that your lead program is effective. One of my clients has a semisophisticated lead-tracking system that's based on little postcards that field offices are supposed to return. The cards make it very easy to indicate the outcome of the lead, including purchase intent, types of products of greatest interest, likely purchase date, and so on. Fewer than half are returned, and my client is puzzled. The company's offices are independently owned and the local office managers are saying to the home office, "We don't want your leads, even though they're free!"

One thing's for sure. Your leads are costing you plenty. Remember, the cost of fulfilling the leads is minor compared with the cost of generating them in the first place. Divide all your lead-gathering costs by the number of leads you get, and that's your per-lead generation cost. Remember to figure in those costly trade show exhibits. And the people who staff your booth. And the magazine ads. And all those very expensive radio and television commercials. And on, and on, and on. Your average cost per lead generated and fulfilled probably exceeds $100, and many organizations expend hundreds of dollars per lead.

Why Companies Seek Leads

I'm convinced that there are three main reasons why most companies seek sales leads:

1. It's common knowledge that you have to get new leads. Everybody knows that.

2. Lead generation is easily measurable, so it's satisfying to see the fruits of your efforts.

3. You need new leads so that you can get more people on your conveyor belt, which you have to do, since so many are falling off.

As for common knowledge, I think it's always a good idea to challenge what everybody else is doing. Maybe you don't need any new leads at all. I'm not necessarily advocating that you stop advertising, but what if...What if you gave your customers so much attention that none of them ever stopped buying from you? What if the resources you invested in lead generation and fulfillment were instead allocated to intensifying your relationships with your current customers? What if you won absolutely no new customers next year but kept all of your current customers and were able to increase your sales to them by 15 percent overall? What would that do to your bottom line?

I'm not seriously suggesting that you should abandon your lead-gathering programs. I definitely am suggesting that you turn things upside down and take another look at how you're allocating resources. Do you have to put so much attention into lead gathering, or could you allocate far fewer resources in that direction and end up with fewer but far more valuable leads? Isn't the big majority of your lead-generation investment wasted?

It is easy to measure the quantity of your lead-generation results. Keep in mind, though, that having lots of leads means nothing and a high volume may indeed be counterproductive. As long as the numbers of leads are easy to measure, though, they will be the rewarded goal of prospecting systems. Stop measuring the quantity of leads; focus on the quality of the results they produce.

And finally, as you turn your marketing efforts upside down, you'll find much less need to get new recruits onto your conveyor belt because you'll be keeping your current customers on the belt rather than churning them so that they need to be replaced with new ones all the time.

The Role of the Media and Advertising Agencies

I have a personal confession. Fresh out of business school, I worked in the ad business. One of my clients was a catalogue publisher who ran ads for small companies that couldn't afford to advertise in more traditional media. My client gave me this assignment:

> Small business owners advertise in our catalogue because we produce sales leads for them. All they really care about is generating lots of leads. If we produce lots of inquiries, they'll buy another ad next year. The *quality* of the leads doesn't really matter, because they'll blame themselves or their salespeople if business turns out to be bad. But they'll blame us—and cut us out of the ad budget—if we don't produce a big *quantity* of leads. What I want you to do, George, is redesign this catalogue so it will produce more leads for our advertisers.

This turned out to be a fascinating project. I finally realized that my only real goal was to stimulate people who received the catalogue to open it, tear out the reader service card, or "bingo" response card, and start circling lots of advertisers' ad numbers to request more information so that they would be inundated with leads.

Since this was the goal, making the catalogue pretty didn't matter. Rather than commissioning a handsome, creative cover, we ended up with a really ugly cover showing an illustration of a big hand holding a pencil and circling numbers to request more information. Inside the cover were really big instructions: "1. Tear out the card right now. 2. Get a pencil. 3. Begin circling numbers." We even included a blown-in postcard, the loose kind that falls out on the floor when you open most magazines. (Incidentally, they're *supposed* to fall out on the floor, so you'll pick them up and look at them. They generate about twice the results of bound-in or perforated cards.) Our blown-in card had big instructions printed on *it*, too: "Now that you've picked up this card and are holding it in your hand, reach for a pencil and start circling numbers so that you can send it in." The publisher even promoted a prize drawing that everyone could qualify for—if they circled some numbers and mailed in their response cards. The entire program was a huge success—for the publisher, anyway. In a single year, responses to the advertisers increased by 342 percent! The publisher was immediately overwhelmed with advertisers' requests to run even more ads next year. They paid in advance to make sure they would be included in this superefficient advertising vehicle. We sent a positively towering pile of reader response cards to the data-entry vendor to be converted into mailing labels for the advertisers' literature packets.

The project produced far more reader inquiries, and the publisher was delighted. He sold his catalogue to another publisher, retired in his early forties, and is now living quite happily. But were the advertisers successful? I don't think so. True, they were inundated with a huge quantity of leads. But what about quality?

That wasn't our concern. Advertising agencies and media representatives know that their clients like to quantify results. The people who buy advertising aren't sales professionals; they're marketing people. They have no accountability for producing business, only for producing leads. If they don't pan out—if the pasta doesn't stick—they blame the sales force. Meanwhile, the sales force blames the marketing people for sending them so many lousy leads.

In the end, the marketing folks, advertising salespeople, and agency account executives are all happy because they really delivered those leads. And the sales force is quite happy ignoring them.

Always remember that the media is interested in proving to you that they can deliver a large quantity of inquiries. What happens after that is your business. You've probably heard the old saying, "I know that half of my advertising is working, and half of it isn't. I just don't know which half." It's a nice quote, but it's nowhere close to accurate. *Maybe* 10 percent of your advertising and lead-generation budget is producing leads that are really prospects who could buy. Most of your leads aren't really prospects at all.

The Importance of Saying "No"

The single best piece of advice I can offer to salespeople whose concentration is on winning new customers and getting them on the conveyor belt is to *stop!* It's easy to get so caught up in the activity that the activity itself seems to be the goal. When a sales manager asks, "How is your prospecting coming along?" the *wrong answer* is:

> Great! I'm sending out hundreds of catalogues and brochures. I feel sure that there's some good business waiting out there.

It's much more effective and efficient to say:

> Great! I've had conversations with most of my 100 current leads and have narrowed it down to about 25 who look like good prospects. I'm giving those 25 close personal attention, and have sent a quick form letter to the other 75 who don't look so hot.

One of my clients is a very large insurance company that constantly urges new agents to schedule as many sales appointments as possible. I created a custom video training program for the company that shows their agents how to be more persuasive at convincing "suspects" to set aside time to sit down for a personal meeting (they call appointments "sits"). My client was surprised when the scripts I prepared included an out that let agents *not meet* with potential customers who showed little likelihood of eventually becoming policyholders. The results? Agents feel better about their work, don't waste time (and suffer from lagging morale) because of having to meet with people who just aren't going to buy. Instead, they concentrate their attention on doing a much better job of preparing for sales calls with real prospects and are more conscientious about their follow-up activities.

Do You Want Busy-ness or Business?

Steve Miller, trade show consultant and author of *How to Get the Most Out of Trade Shows* (NTC Business Books, 1990), points to the widespread misconception that an exhibitor's success can be measured by observing how crowded the booth is and asking salespeople how busy they've been. *Busy* doesn't mean effective; in fact, there may be an inverse correlation between busy-ness and business. One of Steve's key challenges is showing companies how to be less busy and get more business. Average costs per trade show lead can run as high as $400 to $500, so we're talking about leveraging some very significant investments.

Weyerhaeuser's DRIpride adult diaper marketers, for example, are well represented at the American Healthcare Association's trade show each year. Administrators of extended-care facilities are prime sales prospects. Before Steve revamped his client's trade show plans, they were delighted to generate 1800 leads from the show. The trouble was, the follow up was dismal and company insiders joked about the piles of business cards sitting on someone's desk back at headquarters. In the year when Steve guided their efforts, the number of leads gathered plunged by two-thirds, to only 600. But these were *quality* prospects, who generated $6.5 million in documented sales within the next 90 days. The leads were far fewer in number but far higher in quality. As a result, they got attention, rather than being added to some dusty pile.

Steve instructs the personnel staffing his clients' trade show booths to ask direct, specific questions that will qualify the booth visitors immediately. If, after asking four questions (to determine job title, buying authority, company size, and so forth), you don't get four affirmative answers, Steve advises you to politely thank the visitor for stopping by, honestly explain that there probably isn't a good fit with what your company sells, and suggest that the visitor shouldn't waste his or her valuable time by lingering any longer.

You've been to plenty of trade shows at which exhibitors have a big fishbowl at their booth and you're encouraged to drop in your card to qualify for some drawing or contest. U.S. Bank used the fishbowl technique to get leads at boat shows, hoping that some boat buyers would finance their yachts through the bank. The bank's booth personnel did succeed in getting hundreds of business cards but produced little traceable revenue. At the first boat show after Steve came on board, the fishbowl was gone. The bank's booth personnel made direct eye-to-eye contact with visitors, asked qualifying questions, and solicited cards from only 180 *qualified* leads who were willing to commit to a next step (meaning a quote, an office visit, or a completed loan application). U.S. Bank lost the fishbowl, but gained $3 million in new loans within 30 days.

Who Benefits When You *Disqualify* Prospects?

Saying "No" to people who really aren't qualified prospects benefits you as well as your current customers and your future customers. If you and your organization aren't squandering scarce resources by throwing pasta up on the ceiling, mailing out expensive brochures, burdening the field sales force with low-quality leads, and keeping the fulfillment clerks busy sending out costly stuff to people who aren't going to become repeat customers anyway, you'll be in a position to concentrate on the much more profitable tasks of nurturing current relationships and salvaging relationships that have gone awry.

Your current customers will also benefit because they'll be the beneficiaries of that attention. Remember, they *want* more attention and value closer bonds with you.

Your future customers will benefit, too. Rather than spinning your wheels and attending to marginally qualified suspects, you'll be concentrating quality attention on prospective buyers, helping them reach good decisions, and giving them the follow-up attention that will convert their single purchases into long-term repeat buying relationships.

My Own Qualification System

I used to send out information about my services as a professional speaker to anyone who asked for it. There's a widespread belief in my profession that prospects may be scared off if they know your speaking fees before they've read your brochure, seen your video, and know your reputation. Many of my colleagues will refuse to quote a fee in an initial conversation.

I've come to recognize that only a very tiny percentage of people who call and ask about my speeches and seminars are ever going to be in a position to hire me. I use my fee as an early step in the qualification process. I want prospective clients to know my fees before we even talk, so I've set up a voice mail information system that tells callers exactly what I charge for my services. If their budget is much smaller and we never talk, fine. We wouldn't have been able to work together anyhow. I conserve my energy for my clients.

When I do talk with prospects firsthand, I ask them exactly what they want their speaker to accomplish during the presentation. If I can't meet their goals, why would I want the assignment? I ask what other professional speakers the client has particularly enjoyed working with in the past. Since I know most of my colleagues, their personal presentation styles, and their fees, I get a very good idea of what makes this client happy. If we don't have a great fit, let's not work together. The client would just end up unhappy, and I'd end up refunding my fee.

I think of my follow-up mailings as $100 bills. A bona fide prospect will want to review my books, tapes, and videos, as well as read my brochure, so the package I send will contain a lot of valuable materials. But it's my attention that's worth the most to me. My estimate of $100 is conservative, considering the opportunity cost of using my time to write another book or serve a current client. I don't like to throw away a lot of $100 bills, so I'm very careful to qualify prospects before agreeing to send out information.

You shouldn't want to make a sale to just anyone. You want to have new customers who stand a good chance of becoming long-term clients who will buy again and again and talk you up in the marketplace, helping to produce more long-term relationships. If a prospective onetime customer is likely to end up unhappy because your product or service wasn't really what he or she was looking for, you'll end up making an enemy who can do you great harm.

Think of your follow-up lead-fulfillment system as a way of dispensing cash. Maybe $100 is the wrong figure for you; perhaps your follow-up is only worth $20, or even only $10. Do you really want to squander a lot of $10 bills?

If you're not going to pursue a semivalid lead quite vigorously, you're better off not to respond at all. Save your energy and resources for those few prospects who are worth handling right.

There is a risk that you'll overlook some highly qualified prospects when you adopt more stringent qualification procedures. But there's a much greater risk that your organization will flounder in a sea of unqualified leads if you don't.

Salvaging Value from "No Sale"

I'm certainly not saying that you should ignore leads or slam down the phone if unqualified leads don't answer your questions in a way that makes you think you have a shot at building a long-term relationship. You already have the lead, so make the most of it, even if that doesn't involve making a sale.

Make Prospects Feel Glad You Won't Pursue Them

When you tell a prospect, "No," make sure you do it in a way that leaves him feeling good about having contacted you. Suppose you sell a computer consulting service, and this prospective client's needs aren't right up your alley. You specialize in networking Apple machines, and this prospect needs her Novell PC network reconfigured. It's not going to sound too good if you say, "Look, I'm not going to waste my time on you, since I'm not going to end up with the job, anyway." Instead, phrase your wish to decline in positive terms:

> Serena, based on what you're telling me about your needs, I'm not the consultant best suited to help you. Rather than take up your time and attention by having you meet with me or even read my brochure, let me make a couple of suggestions and steer you toward somebody more qualified to tackle your kind of project. I know several qualified Novell specialists, and I'll be glad to give you their numbers.

And then offer the referrals. You'll benefit from the professional courtesy by forging stronger relationships with your colleagues, and those relationships in turn are likely to result in referrals from them when they come across prospects who are just right for you. But even more important, you will have done the right thing for the prospect, and I'm personally convinced that that's always your best course of action.

Attempting to sell your product or service to someone who isn't likely to be happy over the long haul is only going to bring you and your customer dissatisfaction and discord. Oh, I realize that there are some readers who will laugh at this paragraph and say, "Are you kidding? I'm going to take any sale I can get, and then get outta there!" But I choose to believe that their numbers are small and that they aren't going to succeed in the long run anyway. Ethical business people who put their customers' needs first win in the long run.

Getting Leads from Unqualified Prospects

When you tell a prospect that what you sell doesn't fit well with what they need and then proceed to help them with a referral, you're ideally positioned to ask for their referrals, too. In the preceding example, it would be entirely appropriate to continue and say:

> The three people I've suggested are all qualified, and I'm sure you'll get the help you need for your Novell network. My specialty, as I said, is Macintosh systems, and I'll bet that some of your associates operate on Apple networks. Although I'm not in the best position to help you, I may be able to help one of them. Who are the two or three people who come to mind when you think of colleagues who use Apples?

You've already demonstrated your sense of honor and you've already invested the time to get this far in getting to know your prospect. Leverage that investment by asking for qualified leads yourself.

Your aim is *not* to make the maximum number of onetime sales if you're really interested in profits. Invest the time to identify highly qualified prospects—those who may develop long-term repeat-purchase partners—so that you can concentrate on providing a higher quality of sales attention to a smaller quantity of solid prospects.

What Can You Learn from This Chapter?

- Efficiency is doing things right. Effectiveness is doing the right things. Most companies' prospecting systems are both inefficient and ineffective.

- Your company's prospecting system should aim to produce profitable relationships rather than mere sales.

- The cost to fulfill unqualified leads and inquiries is shockingly high and is likely to negatively impact profitability unless you implement stringent qualification and follow-up procedures early in the fulfillment process.

- Ad agencies and media representatives have a vested interest in documenting a large quantity of leads, even though they may be of very low quality. It's wise to be very skeptical about marketing programs that emphasize the production of many leads without ensuring that they are of high quality and are likely to produce profitable relationships.

- An effective sales force should be trained to gracefully decline giving further attention to unqualified prospects.

- Reducing the amount of attention paid to unqualified prospects helps your current and future customers by allowing the reallocation of wasted resources toward satisfying their long-term needs. Nobody wins when a company dedicates too much attention to prospects who are unlikely to evolve into long-term customers.

- When you determine that a prospect is not qualified to receive concerted sales attention, you can still derive benefit from the contact by seeking more qualified referrals.

Action Summary
What You Can Do *Now*

- Aim for a balance between efficiency and effectiveness. Both are essential to successful prospecting.

- Honestly gauge your own prospecting system. Are you just throwing pasta up on the wall, hoping some will stick?

- Revamp your lead-acquisition systems and be sure your efforts are designed to secure relationships, not sales.

- Determine what it costs to fulfill literature requests with your current system and then ask yourself whether that investment is warranted, considering the follow-through system you have in place.

- Regard advertising agency and media claims with great caution when they start telling you about the quantity of leads they produce but they disclaim any accountability for the quality of the ultimate business results.

- Encourage and reward sales professionals in your organization who say "No" to leads that aren't highly qualified prospects. Celebrate their decisions to concentrate on more profitable allocations of energy with recognition, so that other salespeople will know that it's okay to drop poorly qualified leads.

- Evaluate your trade show exhibiting plans. Are you aiming for busy-ness instead of business? Get rid of the fishbowls; coach your personnel to screen out unqualified visitors right away and concentrate instead on those with good prospects for long-term buying relationships.

- Stress the need to leave unqualified prospects feeling positive about your organization even though you may not be giving them direct sales attention.

- Routinely incorporate referral-gathering questions into the dialogue you have with leads who do not turn out to be highly qualified prospects.

8

Time Is
of the
Essence

More than ever before, time is of the essence in the marketing world. When an organization goes to the trouble of generating a lead and qualifying a prospect, a *quick* follow-up is essential. How a salesperson behaves during the initial sales process sets the customer's expectations about the kind of attention he'll get later on. If a lead is followed up slowly and sloppily, the prospect assumes that he would get the same type of inadequate service if he became a customer.

Checking Yourself Out

Your starting point should be a self-audit. How quickly does your organization follow up as things stand right now? Don't ask some marketing specialist or a salesperson, find out yourself. The only accurate way to know is to test yourself by becoming your own prospect.

Formal research studies periodically show the awful norm. Remember the Performark study published in *The Wall Street Journal?* (See Chapter 5 for details.) It took an average of 58 days for requested pamphlets or brochures to arrive, and nearly 25 percent of the inquiries went unanswered. Only one in eight inquiries generated a follow-up sales call—an average of 89 days after the inquiry! I wouldn't have believed such research if I hadn't verified it myself using my phony department code technique.

Sleuthing with Phony
Department Codes

See for yourself. Respond to your own advertising. When filling out
the response card or giving your address to the person who handles
your phone call, add a phony department code to the mailing instructions. If you're responding to the ad on February 17, 1995, add a line to
your address that reads Department 2175. That way, as soon as you
receive the envelope, you'll be able to quickly compare the postmark
date with the code in your mailing label and tell how long it took to
get the literature in the mail. I've done this with many clients and the
overwhelming majority are shocked by the results. Do it yourself if
you're prepared to be disgusted.

Better yet, call an accomplice somewhere else in the country, or in
another country. Make a pact and agree to ruthlessly critique each others'
follow-up efforts. Coach your partner about how best to pretend that he's
a plausible buyer with real potential so that he can pose as a hot prospect.
Then do the same for him. Later, debrief each other on exactly what happened. How long did it take to get your follow-up literature? Did it
answer the questions you asked? Was there a neat cover letter that made
a positive first impression and guided you toward the next step in reaching a purchase decision? Did anybody call? Did you get more literature or
other attention? (I hope you won't be shocked, but I suspect you will be.)

Checking yourself out in a simulated real-life scenario is the only
way to know for sure how things stand right now. But how are things
changing? For that, you'll need to keep on checking, and you should.
My aim in writing *Upside-Down Marketing* is not to get you to take
action now and then forget about it. I want to see your business turn
things upside down and keep them there. It's all too easy to conduct
an internal audit, feel shocked at the true state of affairs you find, rat-
tle some cages and shake things up, and then let them slip back to normal. *Keep checking.*

First Impressions Set
the Tone

The quick follow-up techniques I recommend aren't just intended to
help big, well-funded sales organizations with lots of technology at
their disposal. In fact, informal personal attention can be even more
effective. I love flying and had to visit an FAA-certified physician for
my required physical exam before I could be licensed as a private
pilot. My flight instructor referred me to Dr. Richard Pellerin in West

Seattle. Two days after my physical, I received a quick handwritten note jotted on a postcard-size slip of paper: "Dear George: Nice meeting you and good luck flying. You're welcome here any time as a patient.—Doc." I don't normally think of physicians as salespeople, but his quick brief note definitely sold me, and will bring me back.

When I present seminars on upside-down marketing I dramatize the concept by positioning a long table up on stage. At various points in the speech, I'll act out the three main phases of initiating, nurturing, and salvaging relationships. For the first stage, I actually step up onto the table, which is a big, awkward, shaky step. Later in the speech, I'm back on the table, walking steadily forward step by step to demonstrate the need to keep relationships moving forward and continually reinforce the customer's position on the center of the belt. Finally, I wobble unsteadily on the edge of the table and ultimately jump off, dramatizing the demise of a long-standing relationship that should and could have been saved.

When I began doing this balancing-on-the-table/conveyor belt shtick, I found a great way to dramatize first impressions, too. I'd say to my audience:

> Just before seven this morning, I was down here in this hotel ballroom making sure everything would be ready for our seminar and I noticed that this table isn't very steady. So I asked myself, "What if it collapsed right in the middle of my speech. What would I do?" (At this point, I hold up the local Yellow Pages phone directory.) I'd call an attorney, of course!

And then I proceed to tell the audience what happened when I called several local attorneys early that morning. (Everyone likes to laugh about attorneys if they're made to look like fools.) Many lawyers don't even have an answering machine. Should new clients make sure they only have accidents during office hours? Others have terrible answering services whose operators can't even pronounce the attorneys' names (which can, admittedly, be a mouthful. "You have reached the law offices of Polito, Merrill, Shucklin, VanDerbeek, Moschetto and Koplin. May I take a message?") Is this any way to get new clients on your conveyor belt? After making hundreds of such calls, my two favorite examples represent both extremes.

Before a seminar in a Los Angeles suburb, I opened the Yellow Pages and thumbed through 174 pages of attorney listings. (No joke. With 174 pages of attorney ads and listings, no wonder we're in trouble!) I called one whose ad looked promising: "Personal injuries! On-the-job accident claims! Recoveries over $320 million! Call now." My call was answered on the first ring by a gruff male voice.

"Hello."

"Good morning, is this an attorney or an answering service?"

"Attorney."

This was not very encouraging, but I persisted: "Well, thank you for taking my call so early in the morning. My name is George Walther and I'm about to present a seminar on how to make positive first impressions on prospective clients. I'd like to find out if you get a lot of calls this early in the morning, and how you proceed to turn them into appointments."

"No comment. I won't answer any questions."

This response was followed by his hanging up on me. Not quite the impression that would make me want to be a client.

At the other end of the spectrum was an attorney in the island of Maui. My calling scenario was the same. I flipped open the much thinner Yellow Pages directory, found an ad that indicated a lawyer specializing in the area of personal injury, and reached a recording. It was clear, distinct, thoughtfully prepared, and began something like this:

> Thank you for calling my law offices. My name is Paul Yamato, and I'm sorry you've had to call. Most people who phone attorneys are in pain, or have been treated badly, or are involved in some kind of dispute. I'm sensitive to whatever circumstances made you feel you needed to call me, and I'll do everything I can to make our meeting much more pleasant than the situation that prompted your call. I've been in practice 17 years right here in Hawaii and have received many awards for excellence both here and on the mainland. But what's important right now is whatever has happened to you. As you've been hearing this recorded message, my telephone system has already paged me, and I'll be happy to talk with you right away. I'm standing by now. After the tone, just key in your own phone number. It'll show up on my beeper, and I'll call you myself within two minutes.

Now *that's* how I want to begin a relationship with an attorney (if I must). Obviously, this attorney is both sensitive and fast-moving. In a situation like a personal injury case, time is certainly of the essence.

If You Deliver Slowly Now, What About Later?

Earlier in *Upside-Down Marketing*, I commented on the front-loaded nature of relationships. What happens early on in a relationship carries disproportionately more weight in shaping a customer's opinion of you and your organization than what happens later. If your first impression is a negative one, you probably won't give the firm a second chance. If the same negative experience happens after a year of otherwise positive experiences, you'll be much more forgiving and understanding. If it takes a very long time for a company to respond to your initial request for information, it's natural for you to assume that the company would be sluggish later on when it's time to ship their products or provide service.

As you audit your own response procedures and check yourself out, pay particular attention to how rapidly your organization works to convert a lead into a qualified prospect into a sale. The most economical and effective method is to quickly make direct phone contact with inquirers. It's amazing how simple and impressive a quick phone call can be. One of the marketing directors I interviewed for this book insisted on anonymity when citing her study results, but her findings are typical. This company sends inquirers everything they need to send in an order: careful instructions, a little booklet explaining how to do it, an order form with the person's name and address already filled out. During the company's follow-up tests, some of the inquirers were called one week after the start-up kit arrived. The call wasn't a high-pressure urge to place an order. The caller simply said, "Just want to be sure you got the kit and had a chance to look it over. I'll be happy to answer any questions. Thanks for contacting us." That call alone generated a 30 percent increase in orders from the people who were contacted. Of course the company now makes sure it calls every prospect right after the kit is sent out.

Technology Can Accelerate Your Relationships

There are plenty of commonly available, inexpensive technological tools that will help you make quick, positive first impressions. They're simply tools, though. *You* have to make the decision and commitment to react quickly and implement the system for doing so, whether it includes technological help or not. A fast handwritten note, like Dr. Pellerin's, is much better than nothing.

How MCI Won My Business

When I joined the throngs of Californians who moved to Seattle in the late 1980s, my new business telephone number was published on some kind of new listings hot sheet. I know this because all of a sudden one day I was overwhelmed with telemarketing calls from fast-moving companies that had all just gotten the list. In the same 24-hour period, three different long-distance companies contacted me and asked to be designated as my preferred long-distance carrier.

The first call came from Sprint, and the caller did a fine job. She explained all about Sprint's fiber optic network, clear transmissions, low rates, and detailed billing. It sounded fine to me, so she said:

> I'll send you our brochure, and I'm going to staple my business card onto the cover. After you've looked it over, give me a call, and I'll be happy to get you signed up so you can start saving money.

Later that day, a salesman from American Network called from Portland, Oregon. Although I'd never heard of his company, he assured me that it leases transmission capacity from Sprint, AT&T, and other network companies, but because it doesn't have to maintain the facilities his company could offer lower rates. He, too, talked about the excellent quality of the transmissions, clear billing, and so forth. It sounded as though I might save even more money with American Network, so I said, "Sure, send me your information." He responded:

> I know you're very busy and you travel a lot, so I'm going to make this convenient by filling out the authorization form for you. I'll also enclose a pre-addressed envelope so that after you've looked over our brochure, you won't even need to call me back. Just sign the authorization form, pop it in the mail, and you'll be switched over within a week.

My third call was from MCI. This guy said the same things. Fiber optics, clear transmissions, detailed billings, low rates. But he also said something quite different:

> Mr. Walther, based on the size of your current long distance charges, you'll want to start taking advantage of MCI's savings right away. What's your fax number?

I told him the number, and within seconds, as we continued talking, I heard my fax machine ringing down the hall. He said:

> Oh, I think I hear your fax machine in the background now. I'll be happy to hold on while you go get the form I've sent you. (I went and got it.) Now, all you need to do is sign that authorization form and fax it back to me, and I can begin the switch-over for you immediately.

Now, wait just a minute. You don't think I was going to let him get off that easily, do you? I'm a trained consumer, and I know exactly what to say when I feel myself getting dangerously close to reaching a decision: "I'd like to think about it; can you send me some more information?" I'm the kind of customer who likes to look at the little maps with lines between cities showing call-rate comparisons. I like to study those tables that show my savings at various times of day. I like more information. My request didn't slow him down.

> Yes, of course, I'll be happy to get you more detailed information. Let's plan to talk again (I heard my fax machine ringing already) this afternoon. Does 2:30 look good, or would you like me to call you a little later?

Who do you suppose won my business? The MCI representative was no better at presenting his company's benefits than the other two telemarketers. I assume that the service and prices of the three are roughly comparable. Yet, since the day of that call, MCI has benefited from my rather large monthly long-distance charges.

We're all inundated with way too much information. The Sprint representative probably did send her brochure, and it was probably beautiful and persuasive. But as far as I'm concerned, her information is still out there floating around. John Naisbitt wrote about *information float* in his first big business book, *Megatrends* (Warner Books, 1988), in which he urged business people to reduce the time it takes to get the right information to the right people so they can act upon it.

MCI's key to success in winning my business was that the rep got me the information I needed very quickly and captured my attention by nailing down a specific appointment for follow-up action *fast*.

Fax-on-Demand

Sending sales literature out in the mail is simply not fast enough any longer. It's worth commissioning a designer to create fax brochures for your company so that you can get them into qualified prospects' hands immediately. Make them clear and easy to read (and respond to) by designing them specifically for fax transmission and storing them on your computer's hard disk. There's no reason to send printed brochures through standard desktop fax machines.

As I write *Upside-Down Marketing*, I'm printing out the original manuscript on a superb Hewlett-Packard printer. I have the machine because I saw an H-P ad describing how I could hook it up to both my PC network and my Macintosh computers simultaneously. The ad included an 800 number I could call 24 hours a day for detailed information about the printer's specifications. When I called late one night, the recording asked me to punch in my own fax number to receive the literature. Within seconds, my fax machine rang, and the information I needed to reach a purchase decision was in my hands. The technology that makes this possible is called *fax-on-demand*, and it's reliable and inexpensive. Take advantage of it.

Voice Mail

I know there are plenty of people who hate badly executed voice mail systems, and I'll grant that it's almost always preferable to have a wonderful, knowledgeable, friendly, persuasive, tireless human being to handle inquiry calls. But just in case you don't have a team of such specimens available 24 hours a day, at least use voice mail as a backup. We're no longer living and working in a nine-to-five world, and your prospective customers want access *when they need it.*

John Haynes is a regional manager for AT&T and is responsible for every single product and service AT&T sells, from long-distance service to PBX equipment and satellite services. His particular marketplace is the consulting community and his customers kept telling him how hard it was to get attention from AT&T's competitors and from many of AT&T's own divisions, too. So, John had the back of his business cards specially printed with the line: EASY TO DO BUSINESS WITH, followed by six phone numbers: office, home, cellular, fax, AT&T electronic mail, and voice mail.

Use voice mail, fax-on-demand, and whatever other technological tools you can find to make yourself easy to do business with. Respond quickly, cut information float, and remember that time is of the essence.

Problem Resolution Is Especially Time-Critical

Quick response is increasingly important at every stage in business relationships, and it's particularly critical during problem resolutions. As you review the earlier sections of *Upside-Down Marketing* looking for opportunities to turn your unhappy, complaining, ex-customers back into your *best* customers, remember that your timing is very important. A solution to a customer's problem creates a much smaller positive impact if it's delayed and the customer is left wondering whether you're going to follow through or blow it again.

Kathy Shrovnal sells cleaning products and odor eliminators for Neutron Industries, based in Phoenix, Arizona. She showed me a letter from one of her customers thanking her for her quick follow-through when Neutron accidentally shipped apple-scented odor eliminators, rather than the orange-scented ones the customer had ordered. Of course Kathy sent the correct product right away, but the original credit charge was overlooked, so her customer was incorrectly billed twice. Concerned, he faxed her his credit card bill, which prompted her to run downstairs to the accounting department, to have the credit issued that same day. The California customer was grateful enough to quickly type out a thank-you letter. He didn't write about the great product or the fragrant scent or even that he was pleased to get the credit. What impressed him was that she arranged it so quickly. People expect action quickly, particularly when they're annoyed.

Whether you're resolving a complaint for a long-standing customer or making a first impression on a new one, time is of the essence. There are plenty of new technological tools to help you speed things up, but the most important step is your recognition that fast action is important.

What Can You Learn from This Chapter?

- The impression your organization makes during the initial sales process sets your customers' expectations about the kind of attention that's likely to follow. If a lead is followed up slowly and sloppily, the prospect assumes that he or she would get the same type of inadequate service after becoming a customer.

- Independent research shows that slow and sloppy lead follow-up practices are the awful norm for most companies. Is yours poor, too?

- The best way to find out how prospects are impressed when they respond to your advertising is to pose as a prospect and find out for yourself.

- Quick, personal telephone contact with inquirers is the least expensive and most effective way to qualify prospects so you can determine the amount and type of attention that should be dedicated to their requests.

- It's wise to survey your own sales response procedures and look for ways to speed them up. Using fax-on-demand, voice mail, and other new technologies can help you respond more efficiently and effectively.

Action Summary What You Can Do *Now*

- Check yourself out by becoming your own prospect and noting how quickly or slowly you are pursued.

- Use the phony department code technique to measure your follow-up timing, but don't just do it once. Team up with colleagues in other parts of the country to audit one another on an ongoing basis.

- Identify the individuals in your organization who make the most first impressions on prospects and customers. Recognize and reward the critically important role played by people like your operator and receptionist.

- Make follow-up calls after fulfillment literature goes out so that you can answer questions, stimulate immediate purchases, and determine what type of sales support is appropriate for each prospect.

- Put fax-on-demand technology to work for you so that customers can secure detailed information whenever they want and need it.

- Using voice mail, make it easy for prospects and customers to contact you when they want to, not just whenever your organization is ready to respond.

- Pay particular attention to the time it takes to respond to problems and pull out all the stops to settle matters quickly.

9

Selling—
Breathing
Life into
Relationships

Here you are, at the very end of *Upside-Down Marketing*, and you notice that we haven't yet really talked about selling. Remember, this book takes the upside-down approach. The *last* thing you and your organization should be doing is selling to new customers. That's not to say you won't always be seeking new relationships and growing your business by getting more customers onto your conveyor belt. But new customers should be your last priority.

The one area of sales and marketing that has traditionally received the most attention is the technique of closing the sale. In the context of getting customers onto the conveyor belt, closing is not tricking, pressuring, or coercing the prospect into buying something. Instead, the focus is on beginning relationships. In fact, if there's little likelihood of developing a long-term, repeat-buying relationship, a sales professional who embraces upside-down marketing will *not* close the sale. Since prospecting and acquisition costs are usually much higher than profit margins on initial onetime sales, the profit-minded salesperson realizes that it's better not to go to the trouble of getting customers on the conveyor belt unless they're likely to remain on it for many repeat purchases or renewals.

What Does *Selling* Really Mean?

Before you check your dictionary for a definition, remember that dictionaries reflect common usage; they don't determine it. What you see in the dictionary is simply a representation of how regular people (not academicians) define a word.

Nevertheless, look up *sell* in any good dictionary, and you'll find some rather unsavory definitions. *Webster's Ninth New Collegiate Dictionary* includes these: "to deliver or give up in violation of duty, trust, or loyalty; betray; to deliver into slavery for money; to dispose of or manage for profit instead of in accordance with conscience, justice, or duty; to impose on: cheat."

Hmmm. Not quite how you want to be identified? Unfortunately, many salespeople have convinced buyers that selling is all about manipulation of others for the salesperson's own benefit. Abused customers say things like:

> Salespeople wear you down with a lot of talk and won't let you get a word in edgewise. They use every trick in the book to get you to sign the deal just so they can get their commissions.

Customers don't dream these things up; they've encountered salespeople who behave in exactly those ways.

In order to avoid negative associations, many sales organizations will call their salespeople anything *except* salespeople: account executives, customer consultants, applications specialists, territory managers, and so on.

Closing Sales versus Opening Relationships

Here we go with those labels again. The words we use to describe events shape our views of them and help to determine how we'll behave in any given circumstance. [For thorough coverage of how to change your life by changing your language, be sure to read my book *Power Talking: 50 Ways to Say What You Mean and Get What You Want* (Berkley, 1992).] So, what do salespeople themselves say to each other about the process of selling?

> I nailed another one today! I led that sucker right up to the dotted line and used my smoothest pitch. It gets 'em every time. I laid him out cold.

My apologies to the professional salespeople who read this and feel offended. Salespeople are certainly not all like that. But a good many are, which is why the public at large holds a generally negative view of salespeople. I've even worked with sales managers for large, reputable firms who were unaware that their use of terms like *kill ratio* to mean closing percentage was shaping their salespeople's thinking and behavior.

As with the term *deadbeats* back in Chapter 2, I recommend that you eliminate all counterproductive labels. Your aim is not to terminate customer relationships, so why talk about closing sales? You want to bring relationships to life, or open them. Why not simply substitute *opening techniques* for *closing techniques?*

Vitalizing Relationships

Amid the plethora of sales seminars, books, and video courses, there has been one particularly promising trend in the last decade, and that's the rise of the *consultative selling* concept. The basic idea is that salespeople should be *consulting with* their customers instead of *selling to* them. This approach positions the sales professional as a problem solver, which is, after all, the ideal position for developing long-term partnerships with customers.

Success in sales and marketing stems from the number and vigor of the customer relationships we're able to bring to life and nurture rather than from the number of sales we can make. For this reason I like to use the acronym CPR—with its echoes of life-giving CardioPulmonary Resuscitation—to sum up my belief in Consulting, Personalizing, and Recommending as the three keys to sales success.

Consulting to Discover Needs

The *C* in *CPR* stands for consulting. That's the first and most important step in developing any buying relationship. When I'm called upon to help organizations train their people to sell more effectively, managers often ask, "Can you help us with some scripting? We want our newer people to know what they should say." I decline. To start selling relationships off on the right foot, representatives shouldn't be *saying*. They should be *asking*.

All sales encounters should begin with questions designed to do three things:

1. Show prospective customers that your focus is on them and their needs, not on yourself and what you're selling.

2. Gain some immediate insights about your prospects' preferred styles of communication, so that you can tune in and match them.

3. Uncover your prospects' most immediate concerns.

Keep in mind that there are three varieties of questions: open, multiple-choice, and "Yes"/"No." Let's dispense with the least useful variety first. If you're asking any question to which the answer may be "Yes" or "No," change your question. These monosyllabic answers just don't give you much information to work with, and you also don't get your prospects truly involved in a dialogue.

Suppose you sell motor homes. You don't learn much, for example, if you query a prospective mobile home buyer this way:

> Do you plan to make a lot of long trips? Are you going to be taking along a lot of passengers?

Don't use any "Yes" or "No" question, except in very special circumstances. Perhaps you've encountered many decision delays, for example, and have provided lots of follow-up attention, literature, sales visits, callbacks, and so forth. Your gut tells you that you're being strung along, that this prospect is never going to make a decision and buy anything. There comes a time when it is appropriate to ask, "Mr. Cowan, are you really serious about buying a mobile home, or not?"

The multiple-choice-type question is much more useful than the "Yes" or "No" type.

> Do you plan to take a lot of short weekend trips, or will you be making a few longer journeys during the year, or perhaps both?

Multiple-choice questions give your prospect an easy way to help steer you toward the benefits that are of the greatest interest to him. Still, they're not the very best place to begin, because the answers tend to be short, giving you little information about this person's preferred style of communication. Moreover, you don't really know which multiple-choice questions are most appropriate until you know your prospect's needs a little better.

The best place to begin is with open-ended questions:

> Tell me about the plans you have in mind for your mobile home. How will you be using it? What kinds of trips will you be taking?

Listening attentively to the answers gives you valuable insights about your prospect's most important concerns and also shows you the style of communication that's most likely to be effective with this person. [For comprehensive recommendations on how to get on the other person's communication wavelength, refer to my book *Phone Power* (Berkley, 1987).] Your actions show that your primary interest is in your prospect's needs, rather than in your own particular inventory of products or services.

After a couple of open-ended opening questions, you should be prepared to home in on more specific needs with a series of multiple-choice questions:

> Will you and Mrs. Cowan be traveling alone most of the time, or will you have guests or grandchildren with you? Will you be away from shower facilities for several days at a time, or will you probably have regular access to motels or private campgrounds? Will you need to tow a boat or car, or will you be traveling with just the mobile home?

If, after asking good questions and carefully clarifying your prospect's answers, you detect a good fit with what you offer, you're ready to move ahead. If not, say so. If the products and services you offer aren't likely to be a good match for this prospect's needs, it's best to refer the sale to an associate or offer to be of help in some other way. This is also a good time to ask for some referrals. (Refer back to "The Importance of Saying 'No'" in Chapter 7.)

Personalizing to Demonstrate Alignment

If you do find a good fit, though, you're ready to personalize, the *P* in *CPR*. Match your prospect's answers to your benefits so you can demonstrate their alignment:

> Based on what you've been telling me, Mr. Cowan, it sounds as if you're really looking for a sort of retirement home on wheels. You plan to take a lot of extended trips so you want good driving characteristics and plenty of room. Your grown children may join you during some of their summer vacations, so you'll need comfortable sleeping space for at least two more people beside yourselves. You plan to stay in motels every couple of nights and will probably also stop at private campground facilities, so having a full bath isn't critically important for your needs. Considering what you're looking for, I will definitely be able to help you.

Recommending What's Good for the Customer

Now, put that consultative selling philosophy into practice and make specific recommendations for your customer. The *R* of *CPR* is the step that leads to results in sales: Recommending.

> I recommend that we concentrate on the 30- to 34-foot motor homes. We have two Paces, an Airstream, and a Holiday Rambler I'd like to show you. Let's start with the 34-foot Pace because it meets every one of the needs you've been telling me about.

Whether you sell stocks and bonds or truck-cleaning supplies, or cameras, or locksmith services, or athletic club memberships, or motor homes, you can use the same approach to vitalizing relationships.

Consult. Begin with an open-ended question or two that gets your prospect to open up and tell you about his needs, primary concerns, and communication style.

Personalize. Match your prospect's needs with your benefits if there's a good fit. If there isn't, find another way to help him and move on to serve a prospect who's qualified to enter a long-term relationship with you.

Recommend. Provide counsel about the solution that you believe will best serve your prospect's interests. Use the word *recommend* to remind yourself of your consulting role and to show your prospect that you're thinking of him.

The initial sale is the beginning, not the end, of the relationship. Always seek to maximize the total lifetime value of a buying relationship by starting it off on the right foot and concentrating on the CPR approach. Your aim must be to bring the customer's needs to the surface so that you can meet them. And never hesitate to abandon your selling effort with this prospect if there just isn't a good fit. Remember, selling something to somebody who isn't likely to be happy over the long haul exposes you to many costly risks, including negative word-of-mouth publicity in the marketplace, a tarnished image, and the emotional drain of having to deal with a genuinely dissatisfied customer.

Emphasizing the long-term goal of creating positive relationships with lots of repeat purchases benefits the salesperson, the company, and the customer. From the salesperson's perspective, it's both more rewarding and much easier to pursue customers who are likely to remain on the conveyor belt for many repeat purchase cycles. The company is much better off, too, since revenues that result from future repeat purchases are much more highly profit-leveraged than those from the first order. The high initial acquisition costs can be amortized over all future transactions, so the original marketing expenses, when spread over many sales, may become negligible. This allows a much higher proportion of the revenues to fall to the bottom line as profits. The customer also benefits by concentrating his buying relationships with the vendors who will serve as long term. Think about your own experiences. Isn't it easier and more enjoyable to do business with vendors who have served you well for a long time?

Shifting your organization's marketing emphasis from closing sales to beginning, nurturing, and rekindling repeat buying relatinships will benefit everybody involved in the marketing process.

What Can You Learn from This Chapter?

- When dealing with prospective new customers, it's best to adopt the aim of fostering a mutually profitable relationship, rather than selling somebody something.

- If a new customer is unlikely to become a long-term, repeat buyer, it may not be worth pursuing the first sale. Considering the high costs of the prospecting and acquisition processes, you're probably better off using your resources to seek more qualified prospects.

- Using words and phrases that refer to traditional sales closing terminology interferes with the upside-down approach to developing long-term profitable relationships. Rather than talking about *closing sales*, think and speak in terms of *opening relationships*.

- The most important starting step in any sales process is that of probing to find out what a prospective customer's needs are.

- Open-ended questions are particularly effective because they show prospects that your attention is focused on their needs rather than on your own company or products.

- Carefully chosen multiple-choice questions help prospects steer professional salespeople toward the benefits that prospects most want to know about.

- If prospects' answers don't align with the benefits a salesperson can realistically offer, it's best to decline further sales attention and seek referrals, rather than proceeding to force sales.

- An effective selling process should culminate with recommendations that benefit the customer. Use the word *recommend* to stay on track.

Action Summary
What You Can Do *Now*

- Review the labels you use in sales training and informal conversations about selling. Eliminate any that have negative or derogatory connotations.

- Replace closing techniques with opening techniques and be sure that your sales professionals are focused on *beginning* relationships, not on *closing* sales.

- Read *Power Talking: 50 Ways to Say What You Mean and Get What You Want* for many more ideas on using supportive and persuasive language.

- Be on the lookout for "Yes"/"No" questions and eliminate them from your sales dialogues.

- Kick off an informal incentive program to help members of your team focus on eliminating habitual "Yes"/"No" questions. Consider offering some reward to individuals who catch colleagues in the act of using such limiting questions.

- Brainstorm with your sales professionals to conceive useful open-ended and multiple-choice questions for use in sales dialogues.

- Train members of your team to follow the CPR steps in initiating customer relationships.

- Use the word *recommend* to motivate action.

Epilogue

What's the difference between your company's relationships with its customers and your personal relationships with friends, employees, colleagues, your spouse, or anybody else *outside* your business life? Not much.

We meet a potential spouse or life partner after a lot of prospecting, knock ourselves out during the courtship phase to close the sale and get them to say "Yes." Then we gradually begin taking them for granted, give them less and less attention, stop asking for feedback, and ultimately—all too often—hardly notice when the relationship begins to deteriorate and fall apart. But, never mind, there are plenty of appealing new prospects out there, so we set out to get *them* to say "Yes," without even really taking the time to diagnose what went wrong with the first relationship.

New friends cross our paths. We invite them over, find that we have a lot in common, and strike up a warm new friendship. But before long, we both get busy, neglect each other, and soon find ourselves saying, "Whatever happened to the Lackeys? I really liked them, but we sort of lost touch last year."

We hire new employees, train them, invest in them, give them lots of attention, and then slip into a policy of benign neglect. Rather than reaching out to see what we can do to solicit new ideas and improve the way we work together, we get busy with pressing projects, forget to show our appreciation, and allow resentment to compound. In the end, they quit or we fire them with little more than a cursory exit interview, and then we start prospecting for new employees.

We buy books about business and become determined to improve our customer relationships and really nurture them to make them as profitable as we can. All the while, our personal relationships may be faltering. Isn't it absurd to think that we can become skillful at establishing, nurturing, and salvaging relationships with customers while giving little attention to our personal relationships?

I don't want *Upside-Down Marketing* to be *just* a business book. Oh, sure, I hope you and your organization will profit from the simple principles I've written about here. But I really want you to apply them to your personal relationships, too.

I'm concerned about the apparent dichotomy in our professional and private lives. I seek *balanced* success in my life, and I hope you do too. Here's my invitation to you. Start using the upside-down marketing principles at home as well as at the office. Visualize the important people in your personal life as if they are on your conveyor belt. When your relationships with your kids or with your parents aren't as strong as you'd like them to be, invest the time to get back on track. When they teeter at the edge, knock yourself out to get the relationship back on a solid, positive footing. The sooner you face the music, find out what's needed, and set about meeting those needs, the greater your chances will be for resolution and renewal.

Focus on the personal relationships you already have. Are your spouse, friends, and relatives getting all the reinforcement they deserve? Can you find new ways to be of service in your relationships with them? Are you taking the time to reinforce the relationships that are important to you now? How about sending some flowers or a card to someone you love, today, just to practice showing appreciation?

Reach back to the people with whom you *used* to have important relationships, just as you might renew contact with a customer whose account has been inactive for a long time. While writing this book for you, I decided to reach way back, and tracked down my eighth-grade teacher to thank her for doing such a marvelous job. Back on February 22, 1963, she took the time to write me a nice note complimenting me on my schoolwork. It meant so much to me that I've kept it in an old scrapbook for three decades. She carefully pointed out my best personal attributes, and gave me a lot of encouragement and support. I know that her kind words and good teaching helped guide me toward the life I now enjoy. She deserved to hear my appreciation. When I called Madalen Rentz after 30 years, I delighted a charming 84-year-old woman who is still full of zest and enthusiasm. I feel grateful to have her back on my conveyor belt.

Who has contributed significantly to *your* success? Which of your teachers did an especially good job of guiding you through a difficult subject? What mentors took the time to counsel you? Who helped build your self-esteem by taking the time to notice what you were good at and praising you for it?

Call the people who have helped you get where you are today. Send them notes of appreciation. Call them out of the blue. Renew relationships that have faltered. Be as conscientious with your personal relationships as you are with those in your business life.

Treat your customers like important people, and treat your important people like customers. Turn *all* your relationships upside down.

Thank you for reading my book, and for putting these ideas to work.

Index

AAA (American Automobile Association), 58–61

Accounts receivable (*see* Collections strategy)

Acquisition costs, of obtaining customers, 1, 16, 193

Active listening, 37–38

Advertising:
by catalogue mailers, 76, 172–174
in lead generation, 172–174
(*See also* Publicity, negative word-of-mouth)

AEI Music Network, Inc., 91–95

Aggressive listening, 87–95

Air courier services, 85, 96, 151–153

Airborne Express, 85, 151–153

Airline industry, 45–46

American Automobile Association (AAA), 58–61

American Express, 5, 61–62, 152

American Network, 188

Ameritech Publishing, 23–25

Apple Computer, 160–163

AT&T, 188, 190

Attorneys, marketing by, 185–186

ATTUNE, 154–156

Auto Locator, 17–18

Automotive industry, 17–18, 54–55, 156–159

Avon Cosmetics, 96–97

Banking industry, 87–91, 105–108, 142–143, 149–150, 176

Bartholomew, John, 87–91

Benchmarking studies, 113

Blown-in postcards, 173

Body language, 36–37

Book distribution, 29–30, 109

Brochures, fax, 189–190

Brock, Richard, 129–132

Brock Control Systems, 128–133

Cable television, 64–66

CareerTrack, 111–112

Catalogue mailers, 76, 172–174

Celestial Seasonings tea, 138–140

Churn rate, 2

Clinipad Corporation, 116–120

Collections strategy, 51–74
and lifetime value of customer, 54–58
listening as, 57–58, 64–66
negative labels in, 51–54
positive partnering with customer as, 67–70
positive reinforcement as, 62–64
reselling as, 58–62
"thank-you" calls as, 63–64
tips for, 72–74

Communication:
body language in, 36–37
building bridges in, 40–41
creating rapport in, 38–39
empathy in, 39–40
one-way, 110
ongoing, 108–116
two-way, 110–112
(*See also* Listening)

Competition, monitoring, 84–85

Complaints:
agreement with customers in resolving, 44–45
and anger of customers, 36, 38
and apologies, 41, 46
avoiding customers', 77–79
building bridges with, 40–41
and customer loyalty, 14

Complaints (*Cont.*):
  encouraging, 13–15
  follow-up on, 45–46
  game plan for handling, 36–46
  importance of, 11–13
  listening to, 36–40, 77–79
  meetings in resolving, 19
  missing, 86–87
  and negative word-of-mouth publicity,
    9–10, 13–18, 198
  positive outcomes from, 16–18
  as research tool, 18–19
  strategies for handling, 18–35
  tips for handling, 46–49
  United States Office of Consumer
    Affairs research on, 11–15, 79
  unresolved, 16
  (*See also* Listening; Silence, of cus-
    tomers)
Computer industry, 5, 133–136, 152,
  154–156, 160–163
Consultative selling, 195–199
Courier industry, 85, 96, 151–153
Credit industry, 5, 54–55, 61–62, 152
Cross-selling, 105–108, 142–143, 149–150
Cruise lines, 77–79
Customer-contact program (*see*
  Relationship marketing)
Customer loyalty:
  and customer complaints, 14
  and relationships with new customers,
    103–108, 170
  (*See also* Silence, of customers)
Customer service:
  employee empowerment in, 42–44
  importance of, 2, 128–136
  and new customers, 104
  as profit center, 3
Customers:
  churn rate of, 2
  coercion of, 52–54
  collecting from (*see* Collections strategy)
  complaints of (*see* Complaints)
  cost of acquiring, 1, 16, 193
  expectations of, 159–163
  follow-up with (*see* Follow-up)
  frequency of contact with, 136–140
  inactive, 79–82
  isolation from, and middlemen, 116–120
  lifetime value of, 54–58

Customers (*Cont.*):
  listening to (*see* Listening)
  needs of, analyzing, 150–156, 159–165
  negative labeling of, 51–54, 194–195
  neglect of, 75–76
  new (*see* New customers)
  obtaining feedback from, 4, 85–87, 108–120
    (*See also* Complaints; Listening)
  one-way communication with, 110
  ongoing communications with, 108–116
  and relationship marketing (*see*
    Relationship marketing)
  silence of (*see* Silence, of customers)
  two-way communication with, 110–112

Decision making, employee empower-
  ment in, 42–44
Dombrowski, Jim, 80–82
Drucker, Peter, 169

Embassy Suites, 30–35
Empathy, in listening, 39–40
Exception reporting, 95–97
Ex-customers, as prospects, 2, 4–6
Expectations, of customers, 159–163

Fax-on-demand, 189–190
Federal Express, 96
Feedback, from customers, 4, 85–87,
  108–120
  (*See also* Complaints; Listening; Silence,
    of customers)
Financial services (*see* Banking industry;
  Credit industry; Insurance industry)
First impressions, 19, 184–187
Focus groups, 113–114
Follow-up:
  on customer complaints, 45–46
  first impressions in, 184–187
  in problem solving, 190–191
  timing of, 183–187
Food and beverage products, 138–140
Ford Motor Credit, 54–55
French, John, 157–159

Gardner, Greg, 114

Getting the Love You Want (Hendrix), 39
Goals, organizational, 2–3
Goodman, John, 15
Graphic Controls, 80–82
Group W Cable, 64–66
GTE, 113–114

H-E-A-T formula, 34, 35
Haddad, Anita, 20–23
Halo effect, 126–127
Hart, Matthew, 18–19
Hendrix, Harville, 39
Hopkins, Tom, 25–29
Hospitality industry, 18–19, 30–35, 77–79
How to Get the Most Out of Trade Shows
  (Miller), 175–176

IBM, 5, 133–136, 152
Inactive customers, 79–82
Incremental pricing, 141–142
Ingram, 29–30
Insurance industry, 83–84, 143–145, 149,
  174–175
Intuit, Inc., 154

Jukes, Terence, 96

Kraemer, Greg, 23–25

Labeling, negative, 51–54, 194–195
Lead generation, 170–176
  cost of fulfilling leads, 170–171
  qualifying customers in, 174–179
  reasons for, 171–172
  role of media and advertising agencies
    in, 172–174
  tips for, 179–181
  from unqualified prospects, 179
Lexus, 157–159
Listening:
  active, 37–38
  aggressive, 87–95
  and body language, 36–37
  building bridges with, 40–41
  as collections strategy, 57–58, 64–66

Listening (*Cont.*):
  in creating rapport, 38–39
  in customer needs analysis, 150–156
  empathy in, 39–40
  importance of, 76–79, 82–87, 110–112,
    115–116, 197
  mirroring in, 39–40
  (*See also* Communication; Complaints)
Loyalty (*see* Customer loyalty)

Maloney, Tom, 59–61
Market research (*see* Research)
Market By Calling Customers (MBCC),
  115–116, 143
MCI, 188–189
Medical supplies industry, 20–23, 116–120
MedSurg Industries, 20–23
Megatrends (Naisbitt), 189
Mergers and acquisitions:
  and communication with customers, 109
  and customer loyalty, 105–108
Meyerson, Dan, 85–86
Miller, Steve, 175–176
Mirroring, 39–40
Misco, 95–96
Multiple-choice questions, 196
Music industry, 91–95

Naisbitt, John, 189
Needs analysis:
  expectations of customers and, 159–163
  in new product development, 150–159
  tips for, 163–165
Negative word-of-mouth publicity, 9–10,
  13–18, 198
Neglect, of customers, 75–76
Neutron Industries, 190–191
New customers:
  and lead generation, 170–181
  qualifying, 174–179
  relationships with, 103–108, 170
  selling to, 193–200
  (*See also* Customers)
New Pig Corporation, 3–4
New product development, 85–86
  needs analysis in, 150–159
Newsletters, marketing, 110
Notes, personal, 185

Office supplies industry, 80–82, 95–96
Open-ended questions, 196–197
Opportunity cost, of customer silence, 83

Performark, 129, 183
Personalization, in selling, 197, 198
Peters, Tom, 115
Phone Power (Walther), 36, 197
Positive reinforcement, as collections
    strategy, 62–64
*Power Talking: 50 Ways to Say What You
    Mean and Get What You Want*
    (Walther), 37, 194
Price Costco, 83
Pricing, incremental, 141–142
Principal Financial Group, 83–84
Problem solving, timing of, 190–191
Processes, improving, 84
Product improvements, 83–84
Professional Photographers Association
    (PPA), 160–163
Profitability, of existing versus potential
    customers, 2–3
Prospecting (*see* Sales prospecting)
Publicity, negative word-of-mouth, 9–10,
    13–18, 198
Publishing industry, 23–25, 85–86, 109,
    172–174

Questions:
    in consultative selling, 196–197
    types of, 196
Quill Office Supplies, 95–96

Rapport, creating, 38–39
Real estate industry, 137
Recommending, in selling, 198–199
Referrals:
    asking clients for, 143–145
    of customers, to other suppliers,
        178–179
Relationship marketing, 108–116
    benchmarking studies in, 113
    continuity in, 128–140
    cross-selling in, 105–108, 142–143, 149–150
    and direct contact with customers,
        114–120

Relationship marketing (*Cont.*):
    focus groups in, 113–114
    frequency of contact in, 136–140
    and halo effect, 126–127
    increasing volume in, 140–142
    newsletters in, 110
    personal contact in, 110–112
    referrals in, 143–145
    selling versus, 194–199
    tip of the day in, 127–128
    tips for, 120–123, 146–148
    (*See also* Communication; Complaints;
        Listening; Silence, of customers)
Research:
    benchmarking studies, 113
    complaints in, 18–19
    and continuity of contact, 133–136
    on customer needs, 150–156
    focus group, 113–114
    internal versus external, 114–116,
        154–156
    surveys, 77–79
Reselling:
    as collections strategy, 58–62
    of inactive customers, 5, 79–82, 125–128
Response cards:
    preparing, 172–174
    sleuthing with, 184
Results, Ltd., 25–29
Retailing, 56–57

Sahady, Michael, 21–22
Sales prospecting, 169–181
    among ex-customers, 2, 4–6
    costs of, 193
    lead generation in, 170–181
    qualifying customers in, 174–179
    for relationships, 170
    tips for, 179–181
Selling, 193–200
    consultative, 195–199
    cross-selling, 105–108, 142–143, 149–150
    lead generation in (*see* Lead generation)
    meaning of, 194
    personalization in, 197, 198
    prospecting in (*see* Sales prospecting)
    relationship marketing versus, 194–199
    reselling, 58–62, 79–82
    tips for, 179–181

Seminar industry, 25–29, 111–112, 141–142
Siegel, Mo, 138–140
Silence, of customers:
    costs of, 82–87
    and exception reporting, 95–97
    and neglect of relationships, 75–76
    tips for handling, 97–99
    unintended, 79–82
    (*See also* Listening)
Smith, Greg, 111–112
Software industry, 128–133, 154–156
Sprint, 188, 189
Suggestions, customer, 83–84
Surveys, 77–79

Taylor, T, 138–140
Technical Assistance Research Programs
    (TARP), 11–15, 79
Telecommunications industry, 5–6, 67–70,
    86–87, 104, 113–114, 125–127, 187–189,
    190
TeleMark Financial Group, 87–91
Telemarketing:
    for customer feedback, 85–87, 109
    to resell customers, 5, 79–82, 125–128
Thackoorie, Phillip, 17–18
"Thank-you" calls, 63–64
Thorndike Press, 109
Time-Life Libraries, 85–86
Tip of the day, 127–128
Toyota, 156–159

Trade shows, qualifying leads in,
    175–176
Transactional analysis, 36
Tweedy, Scott, 67–70

United Airlines, 45–46
U. S. Bank, 176
United States Office of Consumer Affairs,
    11–15, 79
US WEST Cellular, 5–6, 67–70, 86–87, 104,
    125–127

Vella, Nino, 4
Video industry, 85–86
Voice mail, 190
Volume, benefits of increasing, 140–142

Washington Mutual Savings Bank,
    105–108
Westin, 18–19
Weyerhaeuser, 175
Wintermann, Charlotte, 91–95
Wisconsin Restaurant Association, 76

Yes/No questions, 196

Zero-dollar accounts, 80–82

About the Author

George R. Walther is a professional speaker and president of Speaking From Experience, Inc., based near Seattle, Washington. His previous business books, *Phone Power* and *Power Talking*, have sold more than 195,000 copies in the United States, and they have been translated into several languages. Mr. Walther holds both the highest award for platform excellence (CPAE) and the Certified Speaking Professional (CSP) designation from the National Speakers Association. Fewer than 50 other speakers worldwide have been so honored. His presentations are in great demand throughout North America, Europe, and the Pacific Rim.

AN INVITATION FROM THE AUTHOR

I'd love to hear from you, whether you want to let me know about your own upside-down marketing success stories, request my availability for a speaking engagement, or find out more about audio and video programs based on this book.

I invite you to contact me in one of these four easy ways:

1. *Call me from your fax machine.* My automatic fax reply system is the fastest, easiest way to get information and my latest helpful "Tip for the Week." The prompts will give you several choices, and you can receive an immediate fax reply. Call 24 hours: 1-206-235-6360 *from your fax machine.*

2. *Send or fax me a copy of this page.* I'll quickly get you what you need.

3. *Reach me on-line from your computer.* My personal CompuServe mailbox address is: 73742,506.

4. *Call me anytime.* If I'm traveling to a speaking engagement or working on my next book, I'll serve you via voice mail 24 hours daily. At any time, call 1-206-255-2900.

George R. Walther
Speaking From Experience, Inc.
6947 Coal Creek Parkway, Suite 100
Renton, WA 98059
Fax: 1-206-235-6360; Phone: 1-206-255-2900

George, please:

- ☐ Contact me about your availability to speak at my company or professional association.
- ☐ Send me information about audio and video programs based on *Upside-Down Marketing*.
- ☐ Send me information about your other published materials, including the books *Phone Power* and *Power Talking*.

Name _____ Title _____

Company _____

Address _____

City _____ State _____ Zip _____

Fax No. _____ Phone No. _____